CHRISTIE'S

REVIEW OF THE YEAR
1997

JOHN FAED, R.S.A. (1820-1902)
Portrait of George Washington taking the Salute at Trenton
oil on canvas
56 x 41½ in. (142 x 105.5 cm.)
New York, 31 January 1997, $662,500 (£404,125)

CHRISTIE'S

REVIEW OF THE YEAR
1997

Edited by
Terence Rodrigues

Assisted by
Sylvie Ijsselstein

CHRISTIE'S

A CIP catalogue record for this book is available from the
British Library.

ISBN 0-903432-49-8

Printed by White Brothers Ltd., London

front cover:
PABLO PICASSO (1881-1973)
Le rêve
signed and dated
oil on canvas ·
51⅛ x 38⅛ in. (129.8 x 97.2 cm.)
Painted in Boisegeloup, 24 January 1932
Sold from the Collection of Victor and Sally Ganz
New York, 10 November 1997, $48,402,500 (£28,640,533)
The highest price paid for a work of art at auction in 1997
and the second highest price for the artist at auction

back cover:
An early Ming underglaze-copper-red Vase *(Yuhuchunping)*
Hongwu (1368-1398)
12¾ in. (32.5 cm.) high
Hong Kong, 5 November 1997, HK$22,000,020 (£1,760,000)
A world record auction price for a piece of underglaze-decorated
Chinese porcelain

end-papers:
Anonymous
Edo period, early 17th century
Tigers and Leopards among Bamboo
one of a pair of six-panel screens, ink, colour and gold leaf on paper
60¾ x 140¼ in. (154.3 x 356.2 cm.)
New York, 24 November 1997, $112,500 (£66,375)

frontispiece:
JOHN FAED, R.S.A. (1820-1902)
Portrait of George Washington taking the Salute at Trenton
oil on canvas
56 x 41½ in. (142 x 105.5 cm.)
New York, 31 January 1997, $662,500 (£404,125)

All prices include the buyer's premium. The currency equivalents
given throughout the book are based on the rate of exchange prevailing
at the time of the sale.

CONTENTS

CONTENTS

FOREWORD

THE 1997 *Review* shows, once again, what an exciting year it has been at Christie's with higher sales than any other auction house. Sales totalled over £1.2 billion.

The year's high point was undoubtedly the sale of the Victor and Sally Ganz Collection, which, at over $200 million, was the largest single-owner sale ever.

Christie's will also be remembered for another great event, marred by subsequent tragedy, the sale of Dresses of Diana, Princess of Wales. The feeling of loss felt throughout the world was shared by those at Christie's who knew Diana and who will never forget her.

To open 1997 Christie's held a fascinating exhibition of works of art bought for the nation with the help of the National Art Collections Fund, *Treasures for Everyone* (see page 251). Generously sponsored by Glaxo Wellcome plc, the exhibition included masterpieces by artists as varied as Poussin and Baselitz. It was attended by over 16,000 visitors.

The year saw a growth in the whole scope of Christie's worldwide operations. A new office was opened in Los Angeles at 360 North Camden Drive, and work started on our new premises in New York at No. 10 Rockefeller Plaza, which will open in early 1999. We also signed a lease for new premises in Paris at 9 avenue Matignon, where sales will be held as soon as French law permits – hopefully also at the beginning of 1999.

Hubert de Givenchy, the internationally renowned couturier, became President of Christie's France in succession to Nicholas Clive-Worms, whom we have to thank for his contribution; The Earl of Halifax became Deputy Chairman of Christie, Manson & Woods; Marcia Hobbs, Chairman of Christie's Los Angeles and John Groen, Chairman of Christie's Holland.

Christie's selling year began with the sale of Old Master Pictures in New York in which a world record price was established for a picture by El Greco: the hauntingly beautiful *Christ on the Cross*, which made $3.6 million.

London was memorable for the sale of the 10th century bronze figure of a deer once from the caliphal palace at Cordoba, which fetched £3.6 million – a record for Islamic art.

Spring belonged to Impressionist painting from the Collection of John and Frances Lehman Loeb. This collection had a special place in my affections. The sale totalled $92 million, with the portrait of *Madame Cézanne* making $23 million. What is more, the two greatest pictures from the collection, the stunning 1901 Picasso *Arlequin* and the equally beautiful Van Gogh *Oleanders* had already been donated to the Metropolitan Museum of Art, New York.

The Loeb sale was followed by a particularly successful auction of Impressionist pictures which emphasized the strong market for paintings by Auguste Renoir. An equally strong Contemporary sale took place the following week.

In the summer, Christie's London focused on furniture from the collection of the Marquess of Zetland. The pair of gilt armchairs designed by Robert Adam and made by Thomas Chippendale reached £1.7 million, a record for any piece of Chippendale furniture, and an important contribution towards the sale's outstanding total of over £9.5 million.

Christie's' outstanding second half started in London with three extraordinary sales. First, great clarets, *Grands Crus*, saw every lot selling, with very high prices for Mouton Rothschild, Cheval Blanc, Pétrus and Château Latour. Strong Asian buying contributed to a sale total of over £7 million.

Christie's rooms were then transformed into a maharaja's palace for a sale of Indian jewellery, with a spinel bead and diamond necklace making £881,500 in a sale totalling £4 million.

The following day, Christie's fifth German sale saw Gustav Klimt's *Schloss Kammer am Attersee II* fetch £14.5 million, the highest price ever obtained for a German work of art and the highest price for a picture sold in London since 1990. This sale showed conclusively that the London art market is not in decline, and it was a boost to the morale of both Christie's and the whole art market.

Our December Impressionist sale showed again that works of art can be sold in London as successfully as anywhere. I hope our legislators and European partners will take note of this before throwing up further barriers to trade which could cause irreparable harm to London as a commercial art centre.

Christie's Los Angeles had a great baptism with the auction of the *Paloger Collection of Muhammad Ali Memorabilia*. Ali's robe for 'the rumble in the jungle', that great fight with George Foreman, made $156,500, with other records being set for gloves, trunks, shoes and boxing documents: the Foreman fight boxing shoes, at $59,700, easily outsold Nureyev's ballet slippers, which sold at Christie's in 1995 for $18,619.

Memories of great fights turned to memories of great auctions when, on 10 November, at Christie's Park Avenue premises, Christopher Burge ascended the rostrum. That historic evening did for 20th century painting what the Goldschmidt sale had, in 1958, done for Impressionism. It was a landmark sale and reflected enormous credit on Victor and Sally Ganz as collectors and on all those involved in the preparation of the sale and its execution.

An observer of the Loeb and Ganz sales would have been struck, forcibly, both by their quality and by how dissimilar these two collections were – one composed almost entirely of 19th century paintings, the other of works executed in this century. Although the collectors' lives overlapped, their taste did not. At the time that both these sales were being organized, Christie's was implementing a re-structuring of its 19th/20th century departments and contemporary sales to reflect the tastes and buying habits of those, on the one side, principally interested in 19th century paintings and, on the other side, 20th century works of art. This reorganization has also embraced the contemporary department, and the birth of a new approach to contemporary art at auction which will take us into the next millennium.

In a brief summary it is impossible to mention every office and every department but I would like to note that our international jewellery team produced a steady stream of notable results. A jadeite necklace, sold in Hong Kong on 10 November, fetched $5.8 million, despite the turmoil of the Asian economies.

Like the larger rooms in Park Avenue and King Street, Christie's South Kensington and Christie's East had exciting sales, and record prices were achieved in Australia and Singapore.

Once again I would like to thank my colleagues and all our clients, both dealers and private collectors, for making it such a memorable year for Christie's.

LORD HINDLIP
CHAIRMAN, CHRISTIE'S INTERNATIONAL

SALES TO THE NATION

1997 ended on a high note with the sale to the National Gallery of Stubbs's masterpiece *Whistlejacket* (see p. 10). Other notable private treaty sales have been those of a marble group of *A Nymph and Cupid* by John Gibson (1790-1866) to the National Museum and Art Gallery, Cardiff and of a group of six pictures by L.S. Lowry to the Salford Art Gallery.

Acceptances in lieu of tax included an important Queen Anne year-long long-case clock by Quare, allocated to the Collection of the Worshipful Company of Clockmakers, for display in the Clock Room in the Guildhall Library; a fine group of pictures including two Monets, a Bonnard and a Modigliani, which passed in accordance with the owner's wishes, to the Fitzwilliam Museum, Cambridge; and the attractive *Still Life with an upturned Roemer* of 1638 by Willem Claesz. Heda, which went, as the owner wished, to the Castle Museum in Norwich.

As a lawyer, the author of this article was particularly gratified by the successful offer, subject to a wish that it be displayed at the House of Lords, where it had long been on loan, of Romney's fine portrait of Lord Chancellor Thurlow (1731-1806).

GEORGE ROMNEY (1734-1802)
The Rt.Hon. Edward, Lord Thurlow
oil on canvas
82¼ x 58 in. (208.9 x 147.3 cm.)

that he was 'an old sailor'. This story would seem to provide some testimonial to Romney's powers of flattery as a portraitist! As to Thurlow's disposition and foul temper, Eldon recounts an altercation between the Lord Chancellor and his servant known as 'Busy'. To his master's enraged: 'I wish you were with the Devil, Busy', the man is reported as replying: 'I wish indeed, my Lord, I was. I think I should be in a better place than I am in, when living with your Lordship'. Busy's employment appears to have survived this exchange, perhaps an indication that despite his master's evident ruthlessness, there was a softer side to his character, also borne out by his interest in the gentler sphere of the arts – he counted Samuel Johnson and the poets Crabbe and Cowper among his circle.

In his Annual Report this year, the Director of the Tate Gallery, Mr Nicholas Serota, underlined the importance of the acceptance-in-lieu arrangement to the Nation's heritage. He observed: 'The system by which the British Government accepts works of art in lieu of inheritance tax is of vital importance, as it is a security both for collectors and gallery visitors.

Thurlow is depicted in his judicial finery, very much a 'pillar of the establishment'. Although Thurlow is not well remembered as a lawyer, he is reputed to have dispensed patronage in a judicious manner, one of his most notable appointments being that of Lloyd Kenyon (1732-1802) as Lord Chief Justice. The Romney portrait was probably given by Thurlow to Kenyon in whose family it passed by descent. Thurlow's easy relationship with Kenyon, and the young Eldon (1751-1838), later himself Lord Chancellor, is well observed in the latter's famous *Anecdote Book*. If the evidence of the *Anecdote Book* is any guide, Eldon, one of the greatest lawyers ever to sit on the Woolsack, took a jaundiced view of Thurlow's abilities as a lawyer, his personal appearance and disposition. In regard to his appearance, Eldon records that, at the time Thurlow was Lord Chancellor, he was stopped on his way home at night by the press gang and detained by them for some time in the belief

Collectors know that if by their foresight the things they have bought become very valuable, then future inheritance tax may be discharged in a way that directly benefits British national and regional collections as an advantage for their heirs. The gallery visitors in turn know that there exists a means of ensuring that the best things from British collections will be preserved in Britain'. There would be many bare walls and empty display cases in museums in this country if the scheme – which has existed in one form or another since 1953 – had not been available to offer our museums, the public generally, collectors and their heirs, the opportunities Mr. Serota refers to in his report. Christie's join him in hoping that the benefits of the scheme will become even better known and its use more widespread.

EDWARD MANISTY
DIRECTOR OF THE HERITAGE AND TAXATION DEPARTMENT,
CHRISTIE'S LONDON

A STUBBS MASTERPIECE FOR THE NATIONAL GALLERY, LONDON

JUST before Christmas the south side of the National Gallery was lit up by the image of a huge horse. It was George Stubbs's magnificent portrait of *Whistlejacket*, a masterpiece just acquired by the nation for a gross price of £15.75 million. Christie's was privileged to have acted for the sellers, the Trustees of a Fitzwilliam Family Settlement, whose beneficiaries are heirs of the 2nd Marquess of Rockingham, for whom the picture was painted.

Whistlejacket is a big picture. Its exceptional power comes not just from its size but also from its convincing realism (as Taylor wrote, Stubbs 'knew the structure and function of every muscle and bone in *Whistlejacket's* body') and from the horse's superb position in its own space and its rare lack of background.

Little is known of the artists who influenced Stubbs. Except for a short apprenticeship to Hamlet Winstanley, a landscape painter who worked almost exclusively for Lord Derby at Knowsley, he appears to have been self-taught, but this writer has always wondered whether he was aware of the great Velázquez portraits without backgrounds. Stubbs and Velázquez were both excellent landscape painters but *Whistlejacket*, like Velázquez's *Infanta Don Carlos*, stands on its own, a complete work of art in need of no anecdotal background.

What Rockingham and Stubbs originally had in mind when they planned this picture is unclear: family tradition has it that Rockingham intended a monumental equestrian portrait of his sovereign, King George III, mounted on *Whistlejacket*, but his resignation as Lord of the Bedchamber and his (temporary) loss of the Lieutenancy of the North and East Ridings of Yorkshire probably altered his intentions. The likely date of the painting – 1762 – which coincides with Rockingham's period of opposition both to the King and the Government strengthens this theory.

Whistlejacket was one of two life-size portraits of Rockingham's stallions. *Scrub*, now back in Yorkshire in the possession of the Earl of Halifax, was the other. They must have been intended to hang together, at Wentworth Woodhouse, Lord Rockingham's palatial Yorkshire house; that they never did was due to another change of heart on Rockingham's behalf. The portrait of Scrub was sold on almost immediately while the horse itself stayed at Wentworth until given, in retirement, to its jockey John Singleton, who by an extraordinary coincidence lived and died at Givendale, now part of Lord Halifax's estate.

Whistlejacket, whatever the reason for the commission is, without doubt, one of the finest images ever produced by a British artist. Not only is it among the greatest British pictures, it is also one of the most moving portrayals of an animal ever executed.

George Stubbs, A.R.A., was the 'court painter' to a group of aristocrats who governed Britain during that short period of time when British architects, artists and craftsmen rivalled the best in the world. He was the contemporary of Reynolds and Gainsborough, Adam, Chippendale and Wedgwood, his special friend and collaborator. The interests of these artists' patrons lay in politics and sport, in racing and hunting with hounds. How ironic it is that the negotiation for the sale of *Whistlejacket* should have taken place at the same time as the bill to outlaw hunting was introduced in the House of Commons. Whatever the outcome, one thing is for certain: the opponents of hunting who claim such affection for animals will never leave a legacy like those sportsmen: Rockingham, Grosvenor, Grafton, Richmond and Yarborough, who gave us *Whistlejacket; Mambrino; Mares and Foals; The Duke's Horses at Exercise* and *Ringwood*!

The acquisition of *Whistlejacket* by the National Gallery is a source of great satisfaction to Lady Juliet Tadgell, Lord Rockingham's direct descendant, and her Trustees. Its purchase was made possible by a generous grant from the Heritage Lottery Fund, and the picture is already proving to be one of the most popular in the Gallery. This demonstrates once again the importance of Lottery funding and, although the sums of money made available for the various good causes by the Lottery strike some commentators as enormous, it must always be remembered that set against the wider background of the international art market and the huge resources available to overseas museums, they are not. Those who would like to divert it to other causes – however worthy – should visit the National Gallery before deciding that the money could be better spent elsewhere.

LORD HINDLIP
CHAIRMAN, CHRISTIE'S INTERNATIONAL

GEORGE STUBBS (1724-1806)
Whistlejacket
oil on canvas
115 x 97 in. (292 x 246.4 cm.)
Painted in 1762

A DAVID MASTERPIECE
FOR THE LOUVRE

NEVER reproduced, often quoted, always coveted, a masterpiece by one of France's most famous artists has just entered the Louvre. The last work by Jacques-Louis David (1748-1825) is also one of his most ambitious achievements.

The portrait of Juliette de Villeneuve (1802-1840) remained in the hands of the family of the sitter from the time it was painted in 1824 until Christie's negotiated the sale to the French nation. Juliette de Villeneuve was the daughter of Honorine Clary, a member of the famous Marseilles family closely related to the Bonapartes. David was an ardent supporter of Napoleon, who appointed him his official painter. One of Honorine's sisters married Napoleon's brother, and became Queen of Naples and then of Spain; her other sister married General Bernadotte, later King of Sweden and Norway. After the fall of Napoleon, the Clarys, like many dignitaries of the former French Empire, were scattered around Europe. Juliette de Villeneuve's family moved to Brussels. There, in her aunt Julie's salon, she met the painter David, also in exile. After the final defeat of Napoleon at Waterloo in June 1815, Paris became a dangerous place for his supporters. David thought of fleeing to England or Switzerland, but a number of his pupils were Belgian, notably François-Joseph Navez and Joseph-Denis Odevaere, who invited him to Brussels. David handed his teaching studio over to his faithful pupil Gros and left Paris in January 1816, never to return. In Brussels, David received a warm welcome and settled down happily. He built up a considerable portrait practice, painting a whole series of former revolutionaries and supporters of Napoleon, who were fellow exiles.

In 1821 David painted the double portrait of Juliette de Villeneuve's first cousins Zénaïde and Charlotte Bonaparte (now in the J. Paul Getty Museum, Malibu). It is interesting to note that David was paid 4,000 francs for this painting, while he received 6,000 francs for the portrait of Juliette de Villeneuve.

This full-length portrait (which is almost two metres high) represents Mademoiselle de Villeneuve wearing an elegant black velvet dress which contrasts with her somewhat plain features. In the grand manner of his rare full-length portraits, such as the portrait of Monsieur et Madame de Lavoisier (Metropolitan Museum, New York) or Napoleon's portrait (National Gallery of Art, Washington), the artist took great care with the details of the décor. The blue silk upholstered chair, on which one can read the signature 'David, Bruxelles 1824', the important contemporary Ehrard harpsichord, the superb harp, the music stand and the two shawls all evoke the elegant and refined life of the 'Napoléonides' in exile. In particular, the splendid, nankeen-coloured hat, hanging prominently in the foreground, is a *tour de force*. It recalls the sophisticated Directoire green hat which graces Madame Sériziat in the famous portrait (now in the Louvre), painted about 30 years earlier, in 1795. The simplicity of the composition and the very warm tones are characteristic of David's Brussels period, which, until this purchase, was not represented in the Louvre.

David's last nine years, his period in Brussels, have been relatively neglected by art historians, though David himself felt that the pictures he painted there were among his best. It is hoped that the acquisition of this portrait will help redress the balance and lead to a better understanding of David's work during this period.

Christie's was privileged to have been entrusted with the sale of this masterpiece to the French nation. The painting has now joined the other masterpieces by David in the Louvre's collection, among them the celebrated portrait of Madame Récamier and the enormous *Coronation of Napoleon*. It bears witness to the extraordinary talent of one of the greatest French painters who, even at the age of 76, was able to produce a work of consummate artistry.

BERTRAND DU VIGNAUD
DEPUTY CHAIRMAN, CHRISTIE'S FRANCE

JACQUES-LOUIS DAVID (1748-1825)
Mademoiselle Juliette de Villeneuve
oil on canvas
78 x 48½ in. (198 x 123 cm.)
Painted in 1824

A GOYA MASTERPIECE
FOR THE PRADO

DOÑA Manuela Isidra Téllez Girón y Alonso Pimentel, Duquesa de Abrantes (1794 1838) was the third and youngest daughter of don Pedro de Alcántara Téllez Girón y Pacheco, Marques de Peñafiel, 9th Duque de Osuna (1755-1807) and his wife, doña María Josefa de la Soledad Alonso Pimentel y Borja (1752-1834).

In 1813 Doña Manuela married the 8th Duque de Abrantes, don Angel María de Carvajal. Three years later, aged twenty-two, she sat for this portrait by Goya. According to the account books of the Osuna family, this particular portrait was a gift from the Duquesa de Osuna and this same account records that on 30 April 1816 the artist received for his work the sum of 4,000 reales de vellon.

The Duquesa de Abrantes was brought up in the highly artistic and musical ambiance of the Osuna family. Goya was the most favoured painter of this refined court. His first commission for the family was a pair of full-length portraits of the Duque and Duquesa, which were executed in 1785. These were closely followed by a commission for a set of decorative pictures depicting genre scenes, which were painted for the Duquesa's private salon in the Osunas' country house 'El Capricho' at la Almeda near Madrid. Commissioned in 1786 and delivered by 22 April 1787, these six canvases, together with the great series of tapestry cartoons commissioned for the Dining Room of the Pardo Palace, mark Goya's coming of age as a master of decorative genre scenes. The sequence of Osuna commissions form the artist continues with other family portraits, such as the great family group of 1788 (Prado Museum, Madrid). By 1799, the Osuna family had built up a collection of about thirty pictures by the artist. In 1805, the family commissioned a portrait of their second daughter, the Marquesa de Santa Cruz, which was sold by Christie's in 1986 to the Spanish Government and is now in the Prado Museum.

It has therefore been a special privilege for Christie's to negotiate the sale of the portrait of the third daughter of this illustrious family, painted by the pre-eminent Spanish portraitist of the time. Both daughters inherited their mother's passion for music, as indicated by the presence of a musical reference in each of their portraits. The Marquesa de Santa Cruz is depicted full-length, in a recumbent pose, holding a lyre-guitar and wearing a wreath of vine leaves. Her younger sister, the Duquesa de Abrantes, who was apparently known for her beautiful voice, was depicted eleven years later in this magnificent three-quarter-length portrait with flowers in her hair and holding a sheet of music in her hand, a reference to the muse Euterpe. Both girls were raised in a household where music and theatre were a part of daily life. The Duquesa de Osuna was described by the great English traveller and diarist Lady Holland as the most distinguished lady in Madrid, for both her accomplishment and her good taste. The Duquesa had been brought up by her grandfather, the Duque de Huesca, a man known for his refinement and love of music. The Duquesa de Osuna invited Boccherini to play at her private concerts and to write the music for some of the plays which were staged at the Osunas' palaces. Her library and collection of musical instruments were much praised and admired. It is no wonder that she should choose to have her daughter depicted as Euterpe. The artist had previously depicted the Duque de Alba, full-length, resting his arm on a pianoforte while studying a sheet of music by Haydn (Prado Museum, Madrid).

It is interesting to compare the portraits of the two sisters and to see how the artist's style has evolved. The brushwork in the portrait of the Duquesa de Abrantes is much freer and looser and clearly looks forward to the great work of Goya's Bordeaux period. In this portrait, the artist is in full control of his art, in terms of both colour and composition. The *pentimenti* in the music sheet clearly show the artist's concern with the balance of the composition and the harmony of the painting. The portrait of the Duquesa de Abrantes is clearly a *tour de force* of painting as well as a true-to-life depiction of a very important sitter.

JUAN VAREZ
ASSISTANT VICE PRESIDENT, CHRISTIE'S NEW YORK

FRANCISCO GOYA Y LUCIENTES (1746-1828)
Doña Manuela Isidra Téllez Girón y Alonso Pimentel, Duquesa de Abrantes
oil on canvas
36¼ x 27½ in. (92 x 70 cm.)
Painted in 1816

THE COLLECTION OF VICTOR AND SALLY GANZ

IN one of the greatest auctions ever of modern art, the Collection of Victor and Sally Ganz was sold at Christie's on 10 November 1997 for $206.5 million, the highest total for a single-owner sale in history. The collection was an extraordinary assemblage of masterpieces, including seventeen works by Picasso, eleven by Johns, seven by Rauschenberg, seven by Stella, and pieces by Hesse, Smithson and others.

The works by Picasso formed the most important part of the collection. Together the eleven paintings and one drawing by Picasso made $164.3 million, and the five prints earned an additional $379,750. At the very heart of the collection was Picasso's 1932 masterpiece, *Le rêve*. This portrait of Picasso's mistress, Marie-Thérèse Walter, was the very first work Victor and Sally Ganz ever purchased. Painted with undulating lines and rich pure pigments of great intensity, the picture had long ago achieved world renown and critical acclaim, described by major Picasso scholars as representing one of the pinnacles of Picasso's *oeuvre* and as 'the Mona Lisa of the 20th century'. It sold for $48.4 million, the second highest price ever for a work by Picasso at auction.

Another highlight of the collection was the group of four paintings from the *Femmes d'Alger* series. Picasso intended this series, painted in 1953 and 1954, as a dual tribute to Delacroix and Matisse. It was the first extended series that he made after Old Master paintings – two works by Delacroix, bearing the same title. The Ganzes owned four of the fifteen canvases in the group and hung them in the so-called 'Red Room' in their apartment. *Version H*, the earliest of the works offered in the auction, sold for $7.2 million; *Version K*, the first of the monochromatic pictures from the series in the auction, $7.3 million; *Version M*, also in grisaille but larger and more cubist than *K*, $11 million. *Version O*, the final and most famous canvas in the series, is notable for its balance of colour and line, for its bold mixture of references to works of the past, including *Las Meninas* and *Les demoiselles d'Avignon*, and for the portrait of Jacqueline Roche, Picasso's new love, on the left side of the picture. *Version O* sold for $31.9 million, the highest price ever for a post-war work by Picasso.

Femme assise dans un fauteuil (Eva), Picasso's portrait of his mistress Eva Gouel, from 1913, is one of the greatest masterpieces of Cubism; its mixture of representational and abstract modes and its evocation of both sexual attraction and physical repulsion retain extraordinary power. This beautiful picture reached $24.8 million, the highest price ever paid for a Cubist-period Picasso. Painted in 1942, *Nu couché* is the second largest picture that Picasso made in occupied Paris and it constitutes a brilliant

meditation both on the theme of the nude and on the aesthetic power of Cubism. It realized $14.5 million, a record price for a Picasso from the 1940s. Other war-period pictures in the collection were the 1939 *Chat à l'oiseau*, which sold for $8.3 million; the 1940 *Nature morte au boudin* – the first of the wartime still lifes – which fetched $1.4 million; and *Le marin*, a moving self-portrait painted in 1943, which sold for $8.8 million.

The Ganz collection was also distinguished for its holdings of contemporary American art, especially works by Johns, Rauschenberg, Stella and Hesse. Johns's paintings of numbers and alphabets are among his most original and influential works. The 1959 *White Numbers*, a classic example of Johns's early style, sold for $7.9 million. Another work of great sophistication and subtlety is the 1974 *Corpse and Mirror*, one of Johns's greatest cross-hatch paintings, a diptych, the left side in oil, the right side in encaustic over collage, which sold for $8.4 million. The colourful and highly self-referential *Decoy* of 1971 sold for $4.4 million; and *Souvenir 2*, Johns's great self-portrait from 1964, sold for $2.1 million. Together the four paintings by Johns made $22.8 million.

Rauschenberg's 1955 *Red Interior*, a beautiful and nostalgic work that boldly unites elements of painting and collage, sold for $6.4 million.

The sculptures of Eva Hesse were much admired by the Ganzes, who bought works at her first show and quickly became her most important patrons, eventually owning sixteen pieces by the artist. There were three sculptures in the auction. The first was *Unfinished, Untitled or Not Yet*, one of her works in three dimensions. A deceptively simple work – nine string bags filled with clear polyethylene, paper and sand – it is nonetheless powerfully anthropomorphic, the sacks suggestive of breasts or scrota. A masterpiece of contemporary American sculpture, it sold for $2.2 million, a record price for the artist. The other sculptures by Hesse in the sale were *Vinculum I* 1969, which sold for $1.2 million, and *Ennead* (1966), which fetched $827,500. The Ganzes were fascinated by Frank Stella's works. The most important of these, his early Black painting, *Turkish Mambo* (1959-60), a large and powerful picture, sold for $4 million.

Victor and Sally Ganz were among the greatest American collectors of modern art. Their passion and discrimination were inspiring and illuminating for all who met them, and the extraordinary success of the sale of the collection is testimony to their taste and vision.

FRANCK GIRAUD
HEAD OF 19TH AND 20TH CENTURY PICTURES,
CHRISTIE'S NEW YORK

In the bedroom, left to right:
JASPER JOHNS (b.1930), *White Numbers* (1959), $7,922,500 (£4,674,275) and
JASPER JOHNS (b.1930), *Corpse and Mirror* (1974), $8,362,500 (£4,933,875)

In the dining room, left to right:
EVA HESSE (1936-1970), *Unfinished, Untitled, or Not Yet* (1966), $2,202,500 (£1,299,475);
FRANK STELLA (b.1935), *Turkish Mambo* (1959-60), $3,962,500 (£2,337,875); and
EVA HESSE (1936-1970), *Vinculum I* (1969), $1,212,500 (£715,375)

PABLO PICASSO (1881-1973)
Le rêve
signed and dated
oil on canvas
51⅛ x 38⅛ in. (129.8 x 97.2 cm.)
Painted in Boisgeloup, 24 January 1932
New York, 10 November 1997, $48,402,500 (£28,557,475)

PABLO PICASSO (1881-1973)
Femme assise dans un fauteuil (Eva)
signed, inscribed and dated
oil on canvas
59 x 39⅛ in. (149.8 x 99.3cm.)
Painted in 1913
New York, 10 November 1997, $24,752,500 (£14,603,975)

PABLO PICASSO (1881-1973)
Les femmes d'Alger (Version "O")
signed and dated
oil on canvas
44⅞ x 57⅝ in. (114 x 146.4cm.)
Painted in 1955
New York, 10 November 1997, $31,902,500 (£18,822,475)

ROBERT RAUSCHENBERG (b.1925)
Red Interior
combine painting
56¼ x 61½ in. (142.8 x 156.3 cm.)
Executed in 1954-55
New York, 10 November 1997, $6,382,500 (£3,765,675)

A UNIQUE SALE OF DRESSES

WHEN Diana, Princess of Wales, at the suggestion of her son Prince William, decided to auction a selection of 79 evening dresses in aid of charity, Christie's was honoured to be asked by the Princess to conduct a not-for-profit auction.

The sale, which took place on 22 June in New York, attracted worldwide attention and, more importantly, realized $3.3 million (£2 million). The two benefiting charities, AIDS Crisis Trust and the Royal Marsden Hospital Cancer Research Fund, had been loyally supported by the Princess for a number of years.

During the eight months' preparation of the sale and its catalogue, immense secrecy had to be observed by Christie's. A small team set to work, with the active help of the Princess, on the final selection of the dresses to be sold and on the photography for the catalogue. A secret studio location was chosen, and the dresses left Kensington Palace in a series of anonymous cars which changed day by day in order that the press would not become suspicious.

The code name 'Dresses', adopted initially for the sale, eventually became its formal title, and, as the months went by and preparations progressed, a special catalogue was designed. For the first time in the long history of Christie's catalogues, it was prepared in three editions. First was a limited large-format edition of 250, which was signed and numbered by the Princess. These sold out virtually immediately. A second large tier hardback catalogue was limited to an edition of 5,000, a few of which remain for sale from Christie's. A third softback tier was unlimited. By the end of 1997, Christie's had sold more than 24,000 softback copies, the profits from which also went to the charities, making this the most successful auction catalogue in Christie's history. Two receptions, one at Christie's in King Street and one at Christie's Park Avenue, were attended by the Princess, and these raised further revenue for related American charities. A series of new portraits of the Princess, commissioned by Christie's at her request and taken by Mario Testino, a leading photographer, to publicize the sale raised even further revenue in international syndication fees, kindly donated to charities by Mr. Testino.

The no-reserve, no-estimate sale attracted an extraordinary level of international attention and, on the evening of the auction, Christie's two auction rooms at Park Avenue were full, in addition to which, 50 telephone lines were open to bidders from all over the world. There were more than fifty television crews and over two hundred journalists covering the sale.

Taken by Lord Hindlip, Christie's Chairman and one of its principal auctioneers, the auction got off to a flying start with the first dress selling for $82,000 (£52,340). The highest price of the evening ($222,500, £137,000) was paid for a navy blue velvet Edwardian-inspired dinner dress by London designer Victor Edelstein, who had created the dress for the Princess to attend a state dinner at the White House with President and Mrs. Reagan. After dinner, the Princess had danced with John Travolta. Clients included many private buyers, museums and magazines and newspapers which ran competitions for their readers after the sale.

All of us at Christie's were proud and honoured to have been entrusted by the Princess with this sale, and we are delighted that the results will help, as the Princess had wished, so many AIDS sufferers and to further the cause of cancer research.

MEREDITH ETHERINGTON-SMITH
GROUP CREATIVE MARKETING DIRECTOR

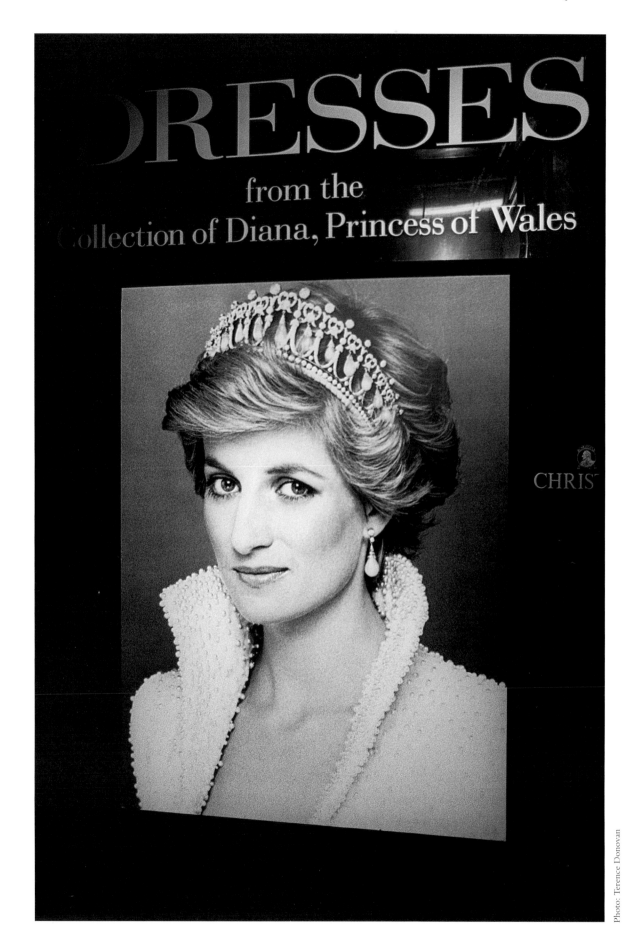

DRESSES
from the
Collection of Diana, Princess of Wales

CHRIST

Photo: Terence Donovan

HOUSE SALES

THE number of country house sales conducted in the United Kingdom in the past few years has reflected the state of the property market, which has enjoyed a steady increase in value owing to a relative shortage of sellers and a surfeit of buyers. It is a long time since there was a major sale of the entire contents of an English country house such as Elveden in 1984 or Godmersham Park in 1990. This is due to a variety of factors including a strong farming economy, vastly improved management and a variety of commercial opportunities open to the owners of large country houses. Additionally, our strong economy has halted the flow of sales such as we saw in the 1970s and early 1980s, helped also by increased awareness of heritage issues, with grants for maintenance funds and advantageous tax opportunities for well planned handovers to the next generation of owners.

Kasteel van Rumbeke

when he took a lease on this former monastery in the town of Roeselare, which he painstakingly restored and filled with works of art ranging from Old Master paintings to European furniture and sculpture. His passionate interest in pottery was reflected in the 600 lots of varied European manufacture, including Dutch Delftwares, Belgian provincial pottery and a varied group of highly decorative French faïence, which generated worldwide interest.

In June 1997, Christie's South Kensington conducted a sale in a marquee at 85 Old Brompton Road of works of art from English country houses for four clients who wished to arrange attic disposals which individually did not warrant a sale on the premises. Christie's was able to bring together the four houses and create a highly successful event by pooling the properties in one sale in central London. The sale total was £720,000 with 96% of the property finding buyers.

Horsenden Manor in Buckinghamshire was the sole entire contents sale on the premises in the United Kingdom in 1997. As the owners' ten children had grown up and left the family home, the owners decided to retire to a smaller property. The sale was extremely well attended by a public starved of such events. Prices achieved were consistently above estimate, and the top price paid was £37,800 for a neoclassical Russian table.

Conversely, sales of castle and country houses on the Continent have increased. Our most recent sale was at Kasteel van Rumbeke in May 1997, comprising the stock-in trade and private collection of the Belgian dealer Eric Loncke and his family. The event attracted large crowds of Belgians fascinated by a carefully restored 16th century castle in the south of the country. Prices at or above estimate were sustained throughout the four days of the sale, resulting in a total of £1.3 million.

Eric Loncke's interest in art history stemmed from boyhood (he bought his first painting at the age of ten) and was manifested

Sales from primary sources still continue to attract the greatest interest from dealers and collectors, who are willing to pay more for the opportunity to buy property with a distinguished provenance; this alone will ensure that the sale on the premises will continue to be the best method of disposing of works of art from one source.

1998 will see the first major sale in England for a number of years, at Hackwood Park in Hampshire, formerly the home of the late Lord Camrose. We also look forward to other house sales in the United Kingdom (starting with Boughton Monchelsea in Kent), in Germany and in Switzerland, and an expanding demand from clients throughout Europe for our expertise in the disposal of entire contents of houses.

DERMOT CHICHESTER
CHAIRMAN, CHRISTIE'S SOUTH KENSINGTON
AND CHRISTIE'S SCOTLAND

JOOS VAN CLEEVE (1485-1540)
Saint Jerome in his Study
inscribed, oil on panel
23⅞ x 18⅜ in. (60.7 x 46.7 cm.)
Sold from the Estate of the 2nd Viscount Camrose
by Order of the Executors
London, 3 Decmber 1997, £210,500 ($353,640)

PICTURES, DRAWINGS, WATERCOLOURS & PRINTS

LUCA CARLEVARIJS (1663-1730)
The Molo and the Piazzetta, Venice, looking West towards the Marciana Library (one of a pair)
signed with initials
oil on canvas
29⅞ x 39¾ in. (76 x 101 cm.)
London, 3 December 1997, £1,651,500 ($2,774,520)

Carlevarijs was the unrivalled master of Venetian view paintings until the mid-1720s, when progressive paralysis put an end to his career – and by which time his successor had already appeared in the form of the young Canaletto.

The pair of paintings of *The Molo* (one illustrated above) are late works, dating to the 1720s, and show to what extent Carlevarijs' achievements prefigure those of Canaletto; moreover, the pairing of the two views of the Molo was one which the younger artist was particularly to favour.

Carlavarijs' novel interest in capturing both the buildings and the bustling life of Venice is shown by the attention given to the figures. A surviving group of 49 oil studies of figures, themselves worked up from drawings, is in the Victoria and Albert Museum. These were used by the artist throughout his career, and a number of figures in this picture are taken from them.

There can be little doubt that this picture formed part of the splendid collection built up by William Bateman (c.1695-1744), the son of a notably rich Lord Mayor of London, in the course of his Grand Tour in 1718.

GIOVANNI ANTONIO CANAL,
IL CANALETTO (1697-1768)
The Grand Canal, Venice, looking South-East from
San Stae to the Fabbriche Nuove di Rialto
oil on canvas
18½ x 30⅝ in. (47 x 78 cm.)
London, 4 July 1997, £2,311,500 ($3,906,435)

Canaletto was at the peak of his career in the 1730s: he executed the famous series of 24 canvases which remain intact at Woburn Abbey; the series of 21 oils dispersed by the Harvey Trustees in 1957; and one of his greatest masterpieces, the *Riva degli Schiavoni, looking West from San Biagio*, commissioned by Marshal Schulenburg (now in Sir John Soane's Museum, London). The present picture was painted around 1738 and shows a stretch of the Grand Canal very rarely depicted in art. The scene is dominated by Sant' Eustachio, known as San Stae, built by Domenico Rossi in 1709-10, surmounted by Antonio Corradini's statues of the Redeemer, Faith and Hope. The tallest building beyond is the great baroque palazzo, the Ca' Pesaro, designed by Baldassare Longhena (1652).

Joseph Smith, the British Consul in Venice, was Canaletto's most active publicist and patron. His most successful marketing tool was the *Prospectus Magni Canalis Venetiarum*, an album of prints by Visentini, after Canaletto. The first edition was published in 1735 and showed 14 paintings by Canaletto. The second edition, published in 1742, contained 24 additional plates: the painting chosen to represent the Grand Canal at San Stae was not that in the Harvey series but the present work.

GASPAR VAN WITTEL, called
GASPARE VANVITELLI (1652/3-1736)
The Port of the Ripa Grande, Rome
signed and dated 1690
oil on canvas
20¼ x 39¾ in. (51.5 x 101 cm.)
London, 4 July 1997, £617,500 ($1,043,575)

Gaspar van Wittel was born in Holland and received his early training there, but he had moved to Rome by 1675. He worked as a draughtsman on a scheme for regulating the Tiber, and this probably gave him the idea of making very accurate topographical drawings which could be worked up into view paintings. Indeed, he is known above all as a view painter.

Almost all the buildings in this picture were destroyed to make way for the Collegio di San Michele and subsequently, in the 19th century, for the construction of the Lungotevere. On the right, at the foot of the Aventine Hill, is the Via Marmorata, used for transporting marble from the quarries at Carrara and also leading to the ancient salt works.

MARCO RICCI (1676-1730)
A wooded Landscape with Gentlemen in a Carriage on a Road
oil on canvas
31¾ x 44 in. (80.8 x 112 cm.)
New York, 31 January 1997, $343,500 (£213,354)

Painter, printmaker and stage designer, Marco Ricci, like his distinguished uncle Sebastiano, was born in Belluno and travelled extensively outside Italy. He made two visits to England, working in partnership with his uncle, the collaboration continuing after they returned to Venice in 1716. There he produced stage designs for Venetian theatres and undertook commissions for Consul Smith, known above all as Canaletto's patron and publicist, who owned 42 of Marco's paintings and 150 of his drawings.

Marco's most original contribution is in landscape. Many of his works are in gouache on kidskin: 32 are in the Royal Collection at Windsor Castle. The present work dates, like the Windsor Castle pictures, to the late 1730s: its elegant composition, superb lighting and colour, and delicacy of touch make it a masterpiece of Marco's mature period.

JAN DAVIDSZ. DE HEEM (1606-1683/4)
A Pie on a pewter Plate, a partly peeled Lemon and a silver Spoon
on a pewter Plate on a partly draped Table in an Interior
signed and dated 1649, oil on canvas
29¾ x 48⅝ in. (75.5 x 123 cm.)
London, 3 December 1997, £1,651,500 ($2,774,520)

Considered one of the greatest still life painters of the 17th century, de Heem trained in his native Utrecht, worked first in Leiden, then moved in 1636 to Antwerp, where he spent most of his active life. He was influenced initially by Balthasar van der Ast, Claesz. and Heda, but is best known for the larger, more exuberant works he produced in Antwerp.

The present still life of 1649 is a work of dazzling virtuosity and shows de Heem at the height of his powers: he gives free rein to his love of rich colour and lighting effects, precious objects and fruits of the earth in abundance. Notable are reflections such as those of the grapes in the glass, of a painting on an easel in the central boss of the silver-gilt cup and of elements of the still life in the cartouche of the silver ewer. Beyond can be made out a candlestick and books and – tantalizingly imprecise - perhaps the artist himself seated before an easel.

JUAN DE ZURBARÁN (1620-1649)
Apples in a wicker Basket with Pomegranates on a silver Plate and
Flowers in a glass Vase on a stone Ledge
oil on canvas
32 x 43 in.(81.3 x 109.2 cm.)
New York, 31 January 1997, $2,862,500 (£1,777,950)

It was relatively recently that art historians discovered the identity of Juan de Zurbarán, whose work had previously been confused with that of his illustrious father, Francisco. Juan was probably one of the first Seville painters to specialize in still life painting. His career spanned scarcely a decade and was brought to an untimely end: he died of bubonic plague at the age of 29.

Only three signed works by Juan are known today – all still lifes dated between 1639 and 1643 - but several others have been securely attributed to him. The present picture, never before published or exhibited, can be ranked amongst his finest productions. Unlike his father's cerebral still lifes, Juan's paintings are characterized by dramatic tenebrism and an earthy, sensuous quality, which, though innately Spanish in feel, probably also reflects the impact of recent Neapolitan still lifes collected by Spanish aristocrats abroad.

The composition of this work has a monumentality and simple grandeur typical of the artist's work. Strong light combined with dark shadows impart a real sense of plasticity to the foreground objects. Passages such as the reflected light on the flange of the silver plate and the reflection and highlights in the glass vase show the young artist's unerring observation of accidental detail. The work is a *tour de force*, which confirms Juan's position as one of the great masters of Spanish still life painting.

ANNE VALLAYER-COSTER (1744-1818)
Flowers in a celadon porcelain Vase and a Bust of Flora
on a Louis XVI Desk
signed and dated 1774, oil on canvas
60⅝ x 51⅛ in. (154 x 130 cm.)
New York, 31 January 1997, $706,500 (£438,820)

Women painters played a prominent rôle in the artistic life of France in the 18th century. Anne Vallayer-Coster was elected to the Académie in 1770, at the age of 26. Most women academicians, lacking the opportunity to study from the nude model, tended to concentrate on portraits and still lifes. Anne Vallayer-Coster exhibited at the Salon from 1771 to 1817. Her work received great critical acclaim; indeed one contemporary commentator, referring to the present work, accorded her what he doubtless perceived to be the ultimate accolade – that her work was painted as well as a male artist.

Having been made *chef du cabinet de peinture* to Marie-Antoinette, Vallayer-Coster fled to the provinces during the Revolution, returning to Paris in 1796.

Her work shows the influence of Dutch painters, perhaps through the intermediary of Largillière, but has an unmistakable delicate, elegant French feel, which makes her – after Chardin and Oudry – one of the most charming still life painters of 18th century France.

DOMÉNIKOS THEOTOKÓPOULOS, EL GRECO (1541-1614)
Christ on the Cross
signed (in cursive Greek)
oil on unlined canvas reinforced with jute
17 x 11 in. (43 x 28 cm.)
New York, 31 January 1997, $3,605,000 (£2,239,130)

Though usually regarded as a Spanish painter, El Greco was born in Crete and had a very formative sojourn in Italy before he settled in Toledo. Precise dates are not known, but he is documented as being in Venice in the late 1560s and moving in about 1570 to Rome, where he was introduced by Giulio Clovio, the Croatian-born miniaturist, to the entourage of Cardinal Alessandro Farnese. He made mainly small-scale paintings in Rome, and indeed it was as a miniaturist that he gained admission to the Academy of St Luke. *Christ on the Cross* belongs to this crucial period in El Greco's development, providing a synthesis of his past and an adumbration of his future. Clues to his Cretan origins are to be found in the Greek lettering of his signature, in the fact that Christ's feet are attached to the cross with two nails rather than one, and in the spare composition of the work. As in the other small devotional works that El Greco produced in Italy – and unlike the later works that he produced in Spain – Christ is shown dead. The handling of the paint suggests the influence of Titian and Tintoretto, and the figure of Christ powerfully evokes Michelangelo, whose drawings and sculpture El Greco greatly admired. However, the sweeping curves of the atmospheric landscape, the unnaturalistically mauve clouds, the dramatic diagonals of the sky – all herald the emergence of a new and highly original artistic personality. Moreover, we already sense here the passionate intensity of mood which was to become the hallmark of El Greco's art.

TWO GOYA MINIATURES REDISCOVERED

IN May 1824, the 78-year old Goya wrote, in a letter to the Spanish King Fernando VII, that he wished to leave Spain in order to go to France to 'take the mineral waters at Plombières to diminish the illness and attacks which troubled him at his advanced age'. After visits to doctors in Paris, Goya settled in Bordeaux where he was to remain until his death four years later.

From there in December 1825 he wrote to his friend Joaquín Maria Ferrer:

> 'Last winter I painted on ivory and I have a collection of nearly forty exercises ('ensayos'), but they are original miniatures which I have never seen the like of before because the whole is made up of points and things which look more like Velázquez's brushwork than that of Mengs. I have neither eyesight, pulse, pen nor ink. I lack everything and the only thing I have in excess is will-power'.

Of the 'nearly forty' miniatures to which Goya refers, the whereabouts of only fourteen were known until the rediscovery of *Judith and Holofernes*, sold at Christie's New York in January 1997, and the subsequent reappearance of another miniature from the series, *Two Orientals*, sold in London in December 1997.

With this series of *ensayos*, Goya created a wholly new approach to miniature painting, replacing the meticulous and painstaking technique previously employed with a method which was far more spontaneous. The artist Antonio Brugada's first-hand account of Goya's new techniques, described in Laurent Matheron's 1857 biography of Goya, relates in great detail his method of painting these miniatures:

> 'He blackened the ivory plaque and let fall on it a drop of water which removed part of the black ground as it spread out, tracing random light areas.

Goya took advantage of these traces and always turned them into something original and un-expected. The little works were still in the vein of the *caprichos*…the dear man…wiped off many of them in order to economise on the ivory.'

Goya thus worked his images from dark to light, using a kind of *grafitti* technique, whereby he scraped off some of the black, allowing the translucency of the white ivory to show through. He would then articulate this with bold yet simple brushstrokes to form the contours of the figures - this is particularly remarkable in the outlines and folds of the draperies of the *Two Orientals*. Another favourite trick of the artist was to apply small, often quite transparent washes of blue or red to highlight certain features. Thus, in the *Judith and Holofernes*, flecks of red are applied with horrific effect to depict the blood streaming from the neck of Judith's victim; in the *Two Orientals*, a lighter red brings out the full character of the protagonists' faces.

The subject matter of many of the miniatures is clearly related to the artist's drawings and lithographs of the same years and also to the 'Black' paintings, the group of fourteen canvases which Goya painted between 1820 and 1823 for his newly acquired country house near Madrid, the 'Quinta del Sordo'. No one theme, however, unites the series of miniatures. What they do all have in common is the depiction of a single moment in time, spontaneously and vigorously expressed by a great artist as he neared the end of his extraordinary life.

PAUL RAISON
SPECIALIST, OLD MASTER PICTURE DEPARTMENT,
CHRISTIE'S LONDON

FRANCISCO GOYA Y LUCIENTES (1746-1828)
Judith and Holofernes (actual size)
carbon black and watercolour on ivory
3⁵⁄₁₆ x 3⁵⁄₁₆ in. (9 x 8.5 cm.)
New York, 31 January 1997, $937,500 (£582,298)

FRANCISCO GOYA Y LUCIENTES (1746-1828)
Two Orientals (actual size)
carbon black and watercolour on ivory
3⅜ x 3⅛ in. (8.5 x 8 cm.)
London, 3 December 1997, £639,500 ($1,074,360)

PIETER DE HOOCH (1629-1684)
A Gentleman reading a Letter to his Wife (?) in an Interior
signed, oil on canvas
31 x 27½ in. (77.9 x 69.9 cm.)
London, 4 July 1997, £716,500 ($1,210,885)

Generally counted among the painters of the School of Delft, de Hooch nevertheless had a very productive stay in Amsterdam, where he moved in the early 1660s and where he died in 1684. This picture can be dated to *circa* 1670-74 and shows the sustained brilliance of de Hooch's art at about the middle of his activity in Amsterdam. His interest in three-dimensional effects, his ability to render the texture of surfaces and to express the quiet poetry of often simple domestic circumstances was to inspire even Vermeer. The reading of a letter was a popular theme in painting of this period, though the precise relationship between the two characters in this picture and the import of the letter remain a mystery.

WILLEM VAN MIERIS I (1662-1747)
An Owl on a Perch (actual size)
signed and dated 1686
oil on copper
5⅞ x 4¾ in. (14.6 x 12 cm.)
London, 3 December 1997, £166,500 ($279,720)

Frans van Mieris I (1635-1681) was the most distinguished member of a family of artists who worked in Leiden. He had two sons, who both became painters, Jan and Willem.

Like many Dutch 17th century paintings, this picture probably served to convey a proverb. The owl, though traditionally a symbol of wisdom, here seems to bear a different significance. Though it sits calmly and proudly on its perch, the owl is in fact tethered as a decoy bird and is probably about to be mobbed by the hawks in the background.

AERT VAN DER NEER (1603/4-1677)
A Winter Landscape with an elegant Couple, Skaters and Kolf Players
signed, oil on panel
18 x 27 in. (46.2 x 70.2 cm.)
London, 4 July 1997, £2,311,500 ($3,906,435)
A record auction price for the artist

Aert van der Neer's reputation rests on his moonlit scenes and his winter landscapes with skaters, of which this picture is a splendid example. Here he displays his mastery of light effects and subtle modulation of colour. He was clearly influenced by Hendrick Avercamp (1585-1634), though the rendering of the figures probably owes more to Jan van Goyen (1596-1656). The costume of the couple in the foreground would suggest that the picture dates from *circa* 1650-60.

FRANS JANSZ. POST (1612-1680)
Indians hunting in a Brazilian Landscape
signed and dated
oil on panel
21 x 17¼ in. (53.3 x 43.7 cm.)
Amsterdam, 7 May 1997, Nlg. 1,268,520 (£393,241)

Frans Post arrived in Recife in Brazil in 1637, one of a group of artists and scientists who accompanied Prince Johan Maurits van Nassau-Siegen, the first Dutch Governor-General of Brazil. Post's brilliant depictions of the exotic flora and fauna of Brazil found an enthusiastic public. He is recorded as having painted at least eighteen pictures during his stay in Brazil, but only seven of these have so far been traced. After his return to Haarlem, he painted about 150 Brazilian views, based on sketches that he had made in South America. Illness brought a premature end to his career in about 1669.

GIOVANNI ANTONIO CANAL, IL CANALETTO (1697-1768)
The Riva degli Schiavoni, seen from the Market at the Molo at the foot of the Column of Saint Theodore, the Doge's Palace on the left
black chalk, pen and brown ink, grey wash, perspectival indications in black chalk
13¾ x 9⅜ in. (35.1 x 23.9 cm.)
London, 1 July 1997, £243,500 ($404,210)

Sold along with two other drawings by Canaletto, this sheet belonged to the distinguished 18th century English collector John Barnard. Barnard's collection consisted of drawings by both earlier masters and contemporary artists. Some of Barnard's contemporary drawings were commissioned directly from artists, such as Zuccarelli, and it is possible that the collector commissioned this large and finished composition from Canaletto while the latter was in England between 1746 and 1755.

GIOVANNI ANTONIO CANAL, IL CANALETTO (1697-1768)
View of the Venetian Lagoon with the Torre di Malghera
black chalk, pen and brown ink
5⅝ x 12⅞ in. (14.5 x 32.8 cm.)
London, 1 July 1997, £69,700 ($115,702)

This is the only known drawing by Canaletto to have been used by Guardi as the chief source for one of his paintings (now in the National Gallery London). It is likely that Guardi had access to the drawing through the good offices of Consul Smith, who was a patron of both artists. Guardi also used a painting of the Molo by Canaletto and a set of twelve prints from the Solennita Dogali as sources for his early views. The Torre di Malghera depicted in this drawing was built near Mestre in the 15th century, but was destroyed in 1842.

This spontaneous and lively drawing was executed by Giovanni Domenico while touring with his father, Giovanni Battista, in the Veneto in the late 1750s. During the tour they decorated the Villa Valmarana, near Vicenza, and the chapel of the Purità at Udine.

GIOVANNI DOMENICO TIEPOLO (1727-1804)
A Lock Gate and Bridge over a River
black chalk, pen and brown ink, brown wash
5 x 8⅜ in. (12.7 x 21.3 cm.)
New York, 30 January 1997, $40,250 (£24,552)

TADDEO ZUCCARO (1529-1566)
Saint Paul
brush and red ink, red wash, heightened with white
15¼ x 9¼ in. (38.8 x 24 cm.)
London, 1 July 1997, £54,300 ($90,138)

GIOVANNI FRANCESCO BARBIERI, IL GUERCINO (1591-1666)
Hercules slaying the Hydra
pen and brown ink, brown wash on green-blue paper,
watermark encircled device
12½ x 8⅜ in. (32 x 21.3 cm.)
London, 1 July 1997, £100,500 ($166,830)

This striking and previously unrecorded drawing was part of Zuccaro's compositional study for the figure of Saint Paul in the frescoes of the *Blinding of Elymas* and the *Raising of Eutychus* in the Frangipani Chapel in the church of San Marcello al Corso, Rome. It was not used by Taddeo in any of his finished works, but the artist's younger brother, Federico, employed it for the figure of Christ in the *Raising of Lazarus* in the Grimani Chapel in the church of San Francesco della Vigna, Venice.

The fresco decoration in *chiaroscuro* of the façade of the Palazzo Tanari in Bologna, for which this drawing is a study, was one of the earliest important commissions awarded to Guercino. The artist was twenty-seven at the time. This is the largest of the three drawings connected with the fresco.

GIULIO CESARE PROCACCINI (1574-1625)
A seated Figure and a Putto seen 'di sotto in su',
and a subsidiary study of the same figure:
black and white chalk on blue-grey paper
8⅝ x 11¾ in. (21.9 x 30.1 cm.)
London, 1 July 1997, £65,300 ($108,398)

This design is a study for one of the prophets painted by Procaccini on a ceiling compartment of the chapel of Saints Nazarius and Celsus in Santa Maria presso San Celso in Milan, between 1604 and 1607. The composition is divided horizontally into two parts, representing alternative studies for the prophet. Procaccini finally used the lower composition for the fresco.

FRANÇOIS BOUCHER (1703-1770)
A young Girl lifting her Apron: 'La belle cuisinière'
red and white chalk
14¼ x 7½ in. (36.2 x 19.2 cm.)
New York, 30 January 1997, $151,000 (£92,110)

This drawing was a preparatory study for *La belle cuisinière*, dated to before 1735 and now in the Musée Cognacq-Jay, Paris. It was re-used later for the print *Des radis, des Raves*, part of the series of the *Cris de Paris*, published in 1737. The image of the young girl carrying what appears in the painting to be eggs in her apron has its origin in Dutch paintings and is traditionally construed as a symbol of endangered virginity. Greuze was later to paint a very similar subject, now in the Metropolitan Museum of Art, New York.

PHILIPS KONINCK (1619-1688)
An extensive Landscape with Farm Buildings and a Windmill
signed and dated 'p-ko 1671'
black chalk, pen and brown ink, brown wash, watercolour, pen and brown ink framing lines
4⅝ x 9½ in. (11.9 x 24 cm.)
London, 1 July 1997, £166,500 ($276,390)

above:
Sold from the estate of the late Lore and Rudolf Heinemann, this splendid composition is one of a handful of landscape drawings executed by Koninck, one of Rembrandt's best pupils. Although Koninck painted various subjects, his fame now rests on his landscapes, which are usually broad panoramas.

right:
Adam Elsheimer excelled in small-scale works, as exemplified by this intimate bodycolour. The rather enigmatic subject, a seated, partly draped, girl with a sad and intense expression, may represent Bathsheba, the future wife of King David, or it could be an academic exercise executed for its own sake. This is one of only six bodycolours known to have been executed by the artist.

ADAM ELSHEIMER (1578-1620)
Bathsheba
bodycolour on brown prepared paper
3 x 2⅞ in. (7.5 x 7.2 cm.)
London, 1 July 1997, £111,500 ($185,090)

REMBRANDT HARMENSZ. VAN RIJN (1606-1669)
Thomas Haaringh ('Old Haaringh')
drypoint and touches of engraving, *circa* 1655
second (final) state
P. 7⅝ x 5⅝ in. (19.4 x 14.4 cm.)
Prints by Rembrandt from the Collection of Walter J. Johnson
New York, 13 May 1997, $145,500 (£90,210)

Thomas Haaringh held the position of *concierge* at the City Hall of Amsterdam. Part of his responsibility was supervising bankruptcy sales within the *Desolate Bodelkamer* (a court which handled bankruptcy proceedings), including that of Rembrandt himself in 1656.

The portrait is worked almost exclusively in drypoint, a fugitive medium, which accounts for the rarity of impressions.

REMBRANDT HARMENSZ. VAN RIJN (1606-1669)
Abraham entertaining the Angels
etched copper plate
signed and dated in reverse, only state
6 x 5 in. (16.2 x 13.3 cm.)
Executed in 1656
London, 26 June 1997, £210,500 ($349,430)

The copper plate of *Abraham entertaining the Angels* was discovered at Christie's on the back of an oil painting attributed to the Circle of Pieter Gysels (1620-1691). Whereas the majority of Rembrandt's plates were re-worked by later publishers and print dealers, *Abraham entertaining the Angels* has never been retouched or rebitten and therefore directly reveals Rembrandt's hand. All existing impressions seem datable to 1656, the year the plate was etched – and the year that Rembrandt was declared bankrupt. Rembrandt may have had to dispose of the plate because of insolvency problems, but how the plate came into the hands of the Flemish painter, Pieter Gysels, remains unknown.

AFTER SIR JOSHUA REYNOLDS (1723-1792)
A collection of mezzotints and engravings, mounted in fifteen elaborate albums
large albums: 31 x 25 in. (81 x 64 cm.); small albums: 22 x 19 in. (58 x 49 cm.)
Sold by Order of the Executors and the Trustees of the Residue Funds of the 6th Marquess of Bute
London, 26 June 1997, £177,500 ($294,650)

The collection of prints after Sir Joshua Reynolds is one part of the magnificent Bute Collection of portraits after Reynolds, Romney and Gainsborough which were all successfully sold at Christie's. The earliest records of print collecting in the Bute family date from the mid-18th century when the 3rd Earl of Bute (1713-1792) formed a major collection which was sold on his death in 1792. His successor John, 4th Earl and 1st Marquess of Bute (1744-1814), began collecting portrait prints in the 1770s. The collection of mezzotints, however, was significantly expanded by John, 4th Marquess of Bute (1881-1947).

The collection represents the greatest period of English portraiture in mezzotint, inspired by the revival of English portrait painting in the latter half of the 18th century, led by Reynolds, Romney and Gainsborough. Reynolds, first President of the Royal Academy, established a tradition of portraiture 'in the Grand Manner'. His vast output of portraits includes almost every gentleman and lady of note in the latter part of the 18th century. The creative force and freedom of the handling of paint finds its match in the boldness of execution of the very finest mezzotints in this collection, which transcend their status as interpretive works to become masterpieces in their own right.

SIR PETER LELY (1618-1680)
Portrait of Miss Wharton
oil on canvas
50½ x 40½ in. (128.2 x 102.8 cm.)
London, 11 July 1997, £166,500 ($281,385)

This previously unrecorded portrait is a particularly fine example of Lely's portraiture in the early 1660s. The artist had already established a reputation as the pre-eminent portrait painter in England, which was reflected in his appointment as Principal Painter to King Charles II in October 1661.

JONATHAN RICHARDSON, SEN. (c. 1665-1745)
Double Portrait of Edward Rolt and his sister Constantia
oil on canvas
76 x 58¾ in. (193.1 x 149.2 cm.)
London, 14 November 1997, £133,500 ($225,882)

The sitters were the children of Sir Thomas Rolt of Sacombe Park, Hertfordshire, and the great-grandchildren of Sir Oliver Cromwell of Hinchingbrooke, the Lord Protector's uncle. Richardson, a pupil of John Riley, was the most accomplished native portrait painter of his generation and was to become the most influential English connoisseur of Old Master drawings in his time. This double portrait probably dates from the latter half of the 1690s.

Seymour was one of the leading sporting painters of the first half of the 18th century. His earliest recorded picture dates from 1721 and shows that at the age of 19 he was already an artist of considerable talent. The pack depicted is believed to have been a private one, which later developed into the well-known pack, the Tidworth Hounds. One of the most interesting aspects of this picture is the existence of extensive *pentimenti*, which demonstrate how the artist developed the composition.

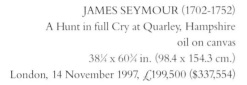

JAMES SEYMOUR (1702-1752)
A Hunt in full Cry at Quarley, Hampshire
oil on canvas
38¼ x 60¾ in. (98.4 x 154.3 cm.)
London, 14 November 1997, £199,500 ($337,554)

This picture, painted *circa* 1754-1755, when the artist was still in his twenties, is a characteristic composition of his Suffolk period. Gainsborough had developed a personal and yet strongly rococo landscape idiom based on an elaborate repertoire of rustic motifs. In this landscape, many of his favourite motifs from this period appear together: the plough team, the windmill, the church half-hidden by trees, the two donkeys and the lopped tree-trunk. His primary concern was to convey the atmosphere and character of the Suffolk landscape, rather than to strive for topographical accuracy.

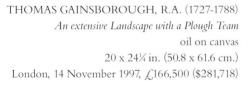

THOMAS GAINSBOROUGH, R.A. (1727-1788)
An extensive Landscape with a Plough Team
oil on canvas
20 x 24¼ in. (50.8 x 61.6 cm.)
London, 14 November 1997, £166,500 ($281,718)

GEORGE ROMNEY (1734-1802)
Portrait of Mrs. Henry Maxwell
oil on canvas
94 x 58¼ in. (238.8 x 148 cm.)
Property from the Collection of Lord and Lady White of Hull
sold by the White Trust and Lady White of Hull
London, 11 July 1997, £177,500 ($299,975)

The sitter, the second surviving daughter of Edward Brydges of Wootton Court, Kent, married Henry Maxwell of Eushot House, Crondall, Hertfordshire, in 1780. This picture epitomizes the stylish qualities that ensured the artist a steady supply of commissions from his fashionable clientèle, despite the competition from both Sir Joshua Reynolds and Thomas Gainsborough.

GEORGE ROMNEY (1734-1802)
Master Pelham: Portrait of John Cresset-Pelham
oil on canvas
52¼ x 58½ in. (132.7 x 148.6 cm.)
Sold from the Mildmay Collection
London, 14 November 1997, £529,500 ($895,914)
A record auction price for the artist

The sitter was the son of Henry Pelham (later Cresset-Pelham) of Crowhurst Place, Sussex, and Cound Hall, Shropshire. John was Member of Parliament for Lewes from 1796 to 1802, for Shropshire from 1822 to 1832, and for Shrewsbury from 1835 to 1837. In his memoirs, the artist's son, the Rev. John Romney, alluded to this picture, describing the brace of partridge as 'so perfect that one might almost be tempted to go and take them up'. Datable to the mid 1780s, *Master Pelham* is one of Romney's most successful later works .

JOHN CONSTABLE: DRAUGHTSMAN

CONSTABLE has long been considered one of the great innovators in the history of landscape painting; he is now regarded equally as a draughtsman. It is a comparatively rare event to see as many as ten of his drawings coming under the hammer in one sale and rarer still to have five 'lost' drawings. These five, in Christie's sale in November, were all from an album sold in 1946 by Charles Bostock. Among collectors of Constable's graphic work Bostock must rank with his two great contemporaries, J. P. Heseltine and Dr. H. A. C. Gregory, for his album contained no less than thirty-six sheets, ranging from an early study of an oak (*circa* 1799) to one of the artist's last sketches from nature, the *Dowles Brook* (1835). So far, of the original 36, only fourteen of the drawings have been located.

Three of the five Bostock drawings are pencil studies. The first, a deftly executed work from the sketchbook used in 1817 and 1820, is of a baroque, gazebo-like feature at the end of a wall (since 1946, entitled *At East Bergholt*). The second, dated 2 December 1816, of the shore at Osmington Mills, was drawn towards the end of Constable's six-week stay in Dorset on his honeymoon with his friends, the Fishers. This sheet is of considerable interest because there are three painted versions of the subject. For paintings executed in the studio, Constable nearly always referred to earlier oil or pencil sketches made on the spot. It was unusual, however, for just one drawing to be the source, as in this case. The scene, sketched with great simplicity, is of the beach, with crab-pots and a small flotilla of boats. The third pencil sketch is an impressive, strongly worked tonal drawing of the woods near Arundel from the sketchbooks of 1834 or 1835.

Both of the remaining Bostock drawings are in pen and ink: a study of an uprooted plant inscribed 'Butter Burr/Jany. 2d. 1826' and a sketch of deer beneath oaks in Englefield Park, dated 25 August 1832. Depictions of country houses are not uncommon in Constable's oeuvre. He painted an oil of Englefield Park

JOHN CONSTABLE, R.A. (1776-1837)
Jaques and the wounded Stag
pen and brown ink, brown wash
5⅝ x 4⅛ in. (14.2 x 10.6 cm.)
London, 11 November 1997, £43,300 ($73,480)

(exhibited in 1833) but encountered difficulties with the owner. The cattle and sheep were objected to and had to be replaced by a herd of deer; the 'specky and spotty appearance' of Constable's touch was considered unattractive; his perspective was criticized and, finally, there was even some haggling over the agreed price – 100 guineas.

The other Constable items in the sale in November were two studies for *Jaques and the wounded Stag*; two pen and ink sketches of Swanevelt etchings which Constable wanted, with a letter to the dealer W. W. B. Tiffin; a pencil drawing, probably executed in 1829 when he was staying with Fisher at Salisbury; and two Lake District watercolours (*recto* and *verso*). These last, a classic view of Borrowdale from the road which wound its way into the valley from Derwentwater and a misty hill-top scene, were executed during Constable's memorable tour of 1806, a year when his output greatly exceeded that of any other twelve-month period in his working life.

Although both *Jaques* studies depict the same scene, they are very different and otherwise unrelated. The subject is taken from Shakespeare's *As You Like It*. The earlier is a preliminary pencil composition of 1828 for a watercolour which Constable eventually exhibited in 1832. The second, here illustrated, was one of nearly twenty that Constable made in 1835 for an engraving to illustrate *The Seven Ages of Shakepeare*, a publishing venture planned by the bibliographer, John Martin. A number of similar 'blottessques' from the later years have survived, but there is no series to compare with these wild pen and ink studies, which for us, in our post-Jackson Pollock years, have such an immediate appeal.

IAN FLEMING-WILLIAMS, O.B.E.
AUTHOR OF *CONSTABLE AND HIS DRAWINGS*, LONDON, 1990,
AND JOINT CURATOR OF THE EXHIBITION *CONSTABLE*
AT THE TATE GALLERY, LONDON (SEPTEMBER 1991)

This magnificent watercolour is one of Lear's greatest Venetian views. Executed in preparation for an oil painting commissioned by Lady Waldegrave, the watercolour is inscribed with the exact time and date of execution ('3pm 13 Novbr. 1865') and, despite its comparatively finished state, is annotated with the artist's colour notes.

EDWARD LEAR (1812-1888)
The Grand Canal, with Santa Maria della Salute,
Venice
pencil, pen and ink and watercolour
13¾ x 19¾ in. (34.9 x 50.1 cm.)
London, 8 April 1997, £73,000 ($118,552)

This drawing has been dated to about 1780. By the 1770s Gainsborough had completely abandoned the use of pencil in his drawings in favour of chalk. His picturesque landscapes were often drawn in the studio from models made up of stones, twigs and other objects.

THOMAS GAINSBOROUGH, R.A.
(1727-1788)
Cattle watering below a Church
black and white chalk, on blue paper
11 x 13¾ in. (28 x 35 cm.)
London, 8 April 1997, £29,900 ($48,558)

JOSEPH MALLORD WILLIAM TURNER, R.A. (1775-1851)
The Lake of Thun, Switzerland
watercolour with scratching out
10⅞ x 15⅜ in. (27.7 x 39 cm.)
London, 8 July 1997, £254,500 ($428,578)

Based on sketches in the *Lake Thun Sketchbook* made on Turner's first visit to the Continent in 1802, this important watercolour was executed for plate 15 of Turner's *Liber Studiorum*, published in 1808. Ruskin considered that Turner's early Swiss watercolours brought a new dimension to the artist's depiction of lake and mountain scenery beyond that developed in Wales, the Lake District and Scotland. Although Niesen and Stockhorn are recognizable, the watercolour is in fact a *capriccio* of various views of Lake Thun from his sketchbook. Bought by the artist's greatest patron Walter Fawkes, the watercolour was sold at Christie's in 1979 in the celebrated sale of the Newall Collection.

The Lake of Thun and *Gosport, the Entrance to Gosport Harbour* (illustrated overleaf) are two of seven major watercolours by Turner which the British Drawings and Watercolours department sold in 1997. These watercolours offer a view of the breadth and power of Turner's work and the individual genius he brought to the landscape watercolour.

The other watercolours were *A Scene in the Val d'Aosta* £139,00 ($234,076); *The Valley of the Washburne* £133,500 ($216,804); *A mountainous Landscape* £133,500 ($216,804); *Cassiobury* £84,000 ($141,456); and *Aberdulais Mill* £67,500 ($113,670).

JOSEPH MALLORD WILLIAM TURNER, R.A. (1775-1851)
Gosport, the Entrance to Portsmouth Harbour
watercolour, heightened with gum arabic and with scratching out
11½ x 17 in. (29.2 x 43.2 cm.)
London, 11 November 1997, £155,500 ($263,883)

Painted *circa* 1829 and published as plate 39 of Turner and Charles Heath's *Picturesque Views in England and Wales*, this watercolour is based on sketches in the *London Bridge and Portsmouth Sketchbook* and the *Gosport Sketchbook*. The watercolour was previously owned by John Ruskin, who wrote in the appraisal for the Fine Arts Society exhibition in 1878: 'A delightful piece of fast sailing…delicious in no explicable manner. It was the second drawing of his I ever possessed and would be among the last I should willingly part with.' Turner captures the excitement of the moment as a brig and a cutter narrowly avoid collision in the choppy waters of the harbour. His use of scratching out brilliantly conveys movement and the turbulence of the water.

Thomas Daniell and his nephew William (1769-1837) were amongst the leading European artists to visit India in the late 18th century and played a pre-eminent rôle in recording and documenting the country during their seven-year tour between 1786 and 1793. In the range of their subjects and the sheer number of works they produced, they remain unrivalled. This magnificent oil was painted on an expedition into the Himalayan foothills in 1789 and features an impressive banyan tree, used to house a Hindu shrine.

THOMAS DANIELL, R.A. (1749-1840)
A Banyan Tree at a Shiva Shrine, Hardwar, Uttar Pradesh
oil on canvas
37 x 53½ in. (94 x 134.6 cm.)
A world record auction price for the artist
London, 10 June 1997, £139,000 ($226,987)

Edwin Lord Weeks was the most famous American Orientalist painter in the expatriate community of academic artists in Paris in the late 19th century. He ventured into India on three lengthy expeditions and painted *in situ*, despite the rigours of travel and climate. This painting is an excellent example of Weeks' working method. The background of the picture was initially executed *in situ*, probably in 1895, with the elephants and foreground figures added later, in the studio. The largest city in Rajasthan after Jaipur, Jodhpur stands at the edge of the Thar Desert. It is a splendid city, founded in 1459, famous for its superb city walls, formidable fort and the labyrinth of narrow streets in the old quarter.

EDWIN LORD WEEKS (1849-1903)
A Street in Jodhpur, India
signed, oil on canvas
19¾ x 24½ in. (50.2 x 61.3 cm.)
London, 10 June 1997, £54,300 ($88,672)

THE ALMA-TADEMA PIANOFORTE

A pianoforte and pair of stools,
designed by Sir Lawrence Alma-Tadema, O.M., R.A.,
action by Steinway, New York, No. 54538,
Model D Grand, completed 6 October 1884,
executed by Johnstone, Norman and Co., London,
with painted panel by Sir Edward John Poynter, P.R.A.
London, 7 November 1997, £716,500 ($1,208,019)
A world record auction price for a piano

THE embellishment of this magnificent Steinway piano is considered by many to have been the greatest decorative arts commission of the 19th century. Henry Gurdon Marquand, a New York financier and Director of the Metropolitan Museum of Art, granted Sir Lawrence Alma-Tadema a limitless budget to decorate the Music Salon of his Madison Avenue mansion 'after the Antique'. Not only were the resulting paintings and furniture a triumph of craftsmanship – the piano case was executed by Johnstone, Norman & Co., 'Artistic Furniture Manufacturers' to Queen Victoria - but they also celebrated artistic excellence in the emblems they carried. Executed in ebony, sandalwood, boxwood, ivory, coral and mother of pearl, the lid of the piano bears the Greek names of Apollo and the Nine Muses in ribbon-tied wreaths. The sides of the case are adorned with laurel-wreathed medallions in which Delphic tripods are crowned with laurel, reminiscent of the prizes awarded for artistic excellence in ancient Greece. A golden libation patera, or medal, cast with a lyre and inscribed with the Greek word 'excellence' also crowns one of the supports.

Under the lid is inscribed a roll of honour of celebrated artists who have performed on the instrument. They include Victor Herbert, Sir Arthur Sullivan, Walter Damrosch and Richard Rogers. The painted panel above the keyboard is by Sir Edward John Poynter: a maiden twirls a *thyrsus*, emblem of Bacchus, god of wine and festivity, while her companions dance in a circle reminiscent of Poussin's *Dance to the Music of Time*. Poynter was so impressed by the piano that he wrote: 'I have no hesitation in saying that it is the most beautiful piece of work, both for the design and the workmanship that I ever saw. In fact, I do not believe that anything has ever been done to equal it'.

The piano was bought by the Sterling and Francine Clark Institute of Williamstown, Massachusetts, where it will continue to be played.

PETER BROWN
SPECIALIST, BRITISH DRAWINGS AND WATERCOLOURS
DEPARTMENT, CHRISTIE'S LONDON

JOHN RODDAM SPENCER STANHOPE (1829-1908)
Love and the Maiden
signed and dated
tempera with gold paint and gold leaf on canvas
54¼ x 79¾ in. (138 x 202.5 cm.)
London, 6 June 1997, £727,500 ($1,185,825)
A record auction price for the artist

Love and the Maiden is Spencer Stanhope's masterpiece. Utterly characteristic in style and sentiment, it was painted on an exceptionally ambitious scale when he was at the height of his powers. It was included in the first exhibition at the Grosvenor Gallery in 1877, an event of unique significance in late Victorian art. Executed in tempera, the picture is a testament to its creator's passion for the art of the *quattrocento* and owns an obvious debt to Botticelli's *Primavera* and *Birth of Venus*, both in the Uffizi, Florence. A grandson of the agricultural reformer Thomas Coke, Earl of Leicester, Stanhope had settled in Florence for health reasons in the early 1870s. His house, the Villa Nuti at Bellosguardo, became a centre for the local English community and visitors from England.

When it was exhibited at the Grosvenor Gallery, the picture aroused the same feelings of bewilderment and outrage that greeted the paintings of Stanhope's friend and mentor Edward Burne-Jones, which were hung nearby. However, Oscar Wilde found 'extreme loveliness in [the] figure of Love' and thought 'the whole picture…full of grace'.

SIR EDWARD COLEY BURNE-JONES, BT., A.R.A. (1833-1898)
Music
signed and dated, oil on canvas
27⅛ x 17¾ in. (68.9 x 45.1cm.)
London, 14 March 1997, £496,500 ($789,435)

Music, when it appeared at Christie's this year, was an important rediscovery. Though well documented and included in Burne-Jones's memorial exhibition of 1898-9, it had not been seen on the London art market since 1921 and had remained, unknown to scholars, in an American private collection since 1950. Started in 1875 and completed the following year, the picture is the earlier of two versions, which have been much confused. Burne-Jones sold it to a client (possibly a dealer) called Benjamin, and by 1898 it belonged to Robert Henry Benson. A financier whose name lives on in that of the banking house Kleinwort Benson, formed by merger in 1961, Benson owned a number of paintings by Burne-Jones and was also a passionate collector of Italian Old Masters. He was influenced both by his father-in-law, Robert Holford of Dorchester House, and by William Graham, who, as well as being Burne-Jones's greatest patron, was devoted to the works of the early Italian school.

In view of this background it is not surprising that the second version of *Music* was acquired by John Graham, William Graham's uncle, probably on the advice of his nephew, or that the composition is intensely Italianate. The pictures were painted within a few years of Burne-Jones's last two visits to Italy (1871 and 1873), at a time when his work was particularly influenced by Botticelli, Mantegna, Michelangelo and others. There is an echo of the Sibyls on the Sistine ceiling in the pose of the seated figure, and the background derives from sketches of Italian landscape which Burne-Jones had made in 1871.

HENRY MEYNELL RHEAM (1859-1920)
The Sleeping Beauty
signed and dated
pencil and watercolour, heightened with white
37¼ x 55½ in. (94.6 x 141 cm.)
London, 7 November 1997, £109,300 ($184,280)
A record auction price for the artist

Rheam's interpretation of the fairy tale by Charles Perrault (1628-1703), later recast by the brothers Grimm and by Tennyson in his poem *The Day Dream*, is one of his most striking compositions. Burne-Jones's famous *Briar Rose* series, similarly inspired by the tale, had been exhibited at Agnew's in 1890 and published in photogravure, and it is possible that Rheam had these compositions in mind. A cousin of Henry Scott Tuke, Rheam settled first in Polperro in Cornwall and then in Newlyn, moving there initially to support the cricket team of local artists in their annual match against St. Ives. However, in his meticulous use of watercolour and preference for literary subjects, he remained an atypical member of the Newlyn community, which, with the remarkable exception of T. C. Gotch, was almost entirely concerned with the realistic depiction of local life.

In 1887, after an extended visit to Egypt, Logsdail settled in Primrose Hill and began the series of London views for which he is now best remembered. In his memoirs he noted: 'I had always thought that London, of all places in the world, ought to be painted, but it appeared too formidable, too unassailable…I do not wonder that so few have even dared to touch it. I did take courage to try and leave a few records of it, only after a very few years to acknowledge myself beaten'.

The present picture is the first of these records, all of which attempted to capture the bustle, noise and smog of contemporary London. They were not immediately popular with a public used to anecdote and idealism: the critic Claude Philips, for instance, deplored their unvarnished account of 'the hideous prose of modern life in a great city'. This painting, however, has consistently been highly prized by collectors for its technical virtuosity and its brilliant evocation of a Victorian city.

WILLIAM LOGSDAIL (1859-1944)
St. Paul's and Ludgate Hill
signed, oil on canvas
28⅞ x 19⅞ in. (73.3 x 55 cm.)
London, 14 March 1997, £115,900 ($184,281)

Scarborough, like so many of Grimshaw's works, represents a contrast, in terms of both its subject and the depiction of light. The old life of the fishing port is juxtaposed with the new life of the town, while moonlight vies with the glare of gas lamps.

JOHN ATKINSON GRIMSHAW
(1836-1893)
Scarborough
signed and dated, oil on panel
11¼ x 17¼ in. (28.5 x 44 cm.)
London, 6 June 1997,
£117,000 ($190,710)

THE COLLECTION OF
THE LATE LORE AND RUDOLF HEINEMANN

FLORENTINE SCHOOL, *circa* 1475
Portrait of a Youth
tempera on panel
15 x 10½ in. (38 x 26.7 cm.)
London, 4 July 1997, £172,000 ($290,680)

DISTINGUISHED art dealer, connoisseur and collector, Dr. Rudolf Heinemann (1901-1975), was born in Munich but moved to the United States in the late 1930s.

He played an important role in building up the collections of Baron Thyssen at the Villa Favorita in Lugano (Switzerland) and of major museums in the United States. With his wife Lore, likewise an exile from Germany, he built up a splendid art collection himself. Lore survived her husband by more than twenty years and maintained enthusiastic involvement with the great museums of her adopted country.

Following her death in September 1996, several museums received benefactions of remarkable generosity. The Metropolitan Museum, New York, received pictures by Giovanni di Paolo, Taddeo Gaddi, Uccello, Poussin and Guardi and an exquisite watercolour by Adriaen van Ostade. The Pierpont Morgan Library, New York, received a matchless collection of Tiepolo drawings. The National Gallery of Art, Washington, received an outstanding oil sketch by Rubens, drawings by Piazzetta and Cariani's *Three Musicians*, recognized as the masterpiece of this 16th century Venetian painter.

The Pierpont Morgan Library and the National Gallery of Art were the principal beneficiaries, moreover, of the series of sales of property from the Heinemann Collection which Christie's conducted in London and New York in the course of 1997 and which raised in total $13.5 million.

Cézanne's shimmering *L'Estaque vu à travers les arbres*, dated 1878-9, was sold for $5.5 million. An elegant pair of *capricci* by Guardi fetched £166,500. A charming late 15th century Florentine *Portrait of a Youth* sold for £172,000. The highlight of the Old Master drawings was the spare, airy panorama by Philips de Koninck (see p. 45). The Heinemanns had a special admiration for Ingres and owned a group of drawings chosen to reflect many facets of his draughtsmanship, outstanding among which was the *Portrait of Général Louis-Étienne Dulong de Rosnay*, which realized $1.6 million (see p. 68). Corot's *La jeune Grecque drapée* sold for $937,500. The sales also included other pictures, silver, porcelain, carpets, furniture and jewellery; particularly notable were a pair of George II armchairs, which raised $211,500, and a sapphire and diamond parure, which realized $145,500.

NOËL ANNESLEY
DEPUTY CHAIRMAN, CHRISTIE'S INTERNATIONAL

PAUL CÉZANNE (1839-1906)
L'Estaque vu à travers les arbres
oil on canvas
17½ x 21 in. (44.3 x 53.1 cm.)
Painted in 1878-79
Sold for the benefit of the Pierpont Morgan Library, New York and
the National Gallery of Art, Washington
New York, 14 May 1997, $5,502,500 (£3,356,525)

TWO PARIS PAINTINGS
BY JAMES TISSOT

THREE of the four paintings by Tissot sold at Christie's during 1997 were painted while the artist was working in Paris. *La cheminée* and *Dans la serre* formed part of the John and Frances L. Loeb Collection, sold in May, and can be dated to the late 1860s, when the artist was establishing his reputation while sharing a studio with Edgar Degas. *La cheminée* is the first of a series of pictures depicting an errant woman, the setting here being the artist's own home on the avenue l'Impératrice. The identity of the sitter remains a mystery and yet she was clearly a favourite model of the artist. In *A la rivière*, she stares at the viewer, a daisy hanging from her mouth, and in *Jeune femme en bateau* her direct gaze leaves no doubt as to the picture's meaning. Such pictures show the dramatic new direction that the artist had taken, away from the Faustian themes earlier in the decade which display the influence of the Belgian artist Baron Leys. While the com-position of this work draws on the work of another popular Belgian, Alfred Stevens, Tissot's own personal style was now fully developed and would give him public and personal recognition.

Tissot became interested in realism and the depiction of every-day life through the influence of Degas and Manet. Degas wrote to Tissot to try to convince him to exhibit in the first Impressionist show of 1874: 'Look here, my dear Tissot, no hesitations, no escape. You positively must exhibit at the Boulevard. It will do you good…and us too.' Tissot declined the offer, fearing that to associate with the renegade group could

JAMES JACQUES JOSEPH TISSOT (1836-1902)
L'escalier nord du Louvre
oil on canvas
35⅜ x 19⅜ in. (89.9 x 49.3 cm.)
Painted *circa* 1879
New York, 22 October 1997, $387,500 (£240,250)

damage his burgeoning career. However, the Franco-Prussian War, and the Commune which followed, forced the artist to leave the Salon behind and further his career across the Channel.

The artist moved to London in 1876. The focus of his paintings changed almost exclusively to his mistress, Kathleen Newton, resulting in the artist's most intimate compositions. *L'escalier nord du Louvre* was probably conceived during a trip to Paris in 1879, taken while the couple were still living together in St. John's Wood. Two other works from the in-complete series *L'étrangère*, entitled *L'esthétique* (Museo de Arte de Ponce, Puerto Rico) and *La voyageuse* (Koninklijk Museum voor Schone Kunsten, Antwerp), were painted between 1883 and 1885, after Tissot had returned to Paris. Typically, the focus of all these works is Kathleen. In *L'escalier nord du Louvre*, her indifference to her surroundings, in contrast to his connoisseur friends who study either their books or the architectural details above them, provides an amusing aspect to the work.

In 1882, following the death of Kathleen, Tissot returned to Paris. After a vision he experienced in 1885, he underwent a religious conversion and thereafter devoted himself to religious subjects, far removed from the scenes of fashionable life which had fascinated him earlier.

NICHOLAS MACLEAN
HEAD OF THE 19TH CENTURY PICTURE DEPARTMENT,
CHRISTIE'S NEW YORK

JAMES JACQUES JOSEPH TISSOT (1836-1902)
La cheminée
oil on canvas
20⅛ x 13½ in. (51 x 34.2 cm.)
Painted *circa* 1869
New York, 22 May 1997, $1,872,500 (£1,142,225)

JEAN-AUGUSTE-DOMINIQUE INGRES (1780-1867)
Général Louis-Étienne Dulong de Rosnay
black lead on paper
17¾ x 13½ in. (45.0 x 34.7 cm.)
Executed in 1818
Property from the Collection of the late Lore and Rudolf Heinemann
sold for the benefit of the Pierpont Morgan Library, New York and the National Gallery of Art, Washington
New York, 22 May 1997, $1,652,500 (£1,008,025)
A record auction price for a drawing by the artist

This drawing represents one of Napoleon I's generals, one of the heroes of the *Grande Armée*. Ingres drew this veteran against a view of Rome, a city which Napoleon had attempted to conquer and in which Ingres had spent many years as a young artist building a reputation as a history painter. The attention to detail within the drawing achieves a psychological sense of balance between the decorum of an official portrait and the humane depiction of a veteran still imbued with the dreams and disillusionment of the fall of the Empire. The portrait descended through the sitter's family until 1959, when it was purchased by Lore and Rudolf Heinemann.

WILLIAM ADOLPHE BOUGUEREAU (1825-1905)
L'éveil du coeur (The Heart's Awakening)
oil on canvas
64 x 43½ in. (162.5 x 109.8 cm.)
Painted in 1892
New York, 22 May 1997, $1,410,500 (£860,405)
A record auction price for the artist

L'éveil du coeur is representative of the important part of Bouguereau's *oeuvre* which the artist referred to as *tableaux de fantaisie*. These paintings describe the artist's reponse to the classical poems dedicated to Eros and Psyche. These mythological figures seem to have been the perfect subject for Bouguereau's art of beautiful forms and harmonious colours. His *tableaux de fantasie* exhibit, however, a characteristic restraint and decorum; they are rarely narrative but are, rather, emotive and evocative, like the poetry from which the artist drew his inspiration.

JEAN-LÉON GÉRÔME AND THE ORIENTALISTS

IN *fin de siècle* Paris, Jean-Léon Gérôme was one of the artists who dominated the Salon, while Renoir, Van Gogh and Monet were struggling for survival and recognition. In a hundred years tastes have changed, and the Impressionist and Post Impressionist painters are now all household names. It is therefore exciting that since the 1970s the work of Gérôme has been re-appraised and, moreover, re-evaluated in the salerooms.

Although Gérôme had first built his reputation as a painter of mythological subjects, his journeys to Turkey and Egypt provided the main inspiration for his *oeuvre*. Following in the foot-steps of Delacroix, Chassériau and Decamps – the first generation of Orientalist painters – Gérôme was drawn to the Middle East in search of the exotic. Enamoured of the Orient after a short stay in Constantinople in 1855, he spent most of the late 1850s and 1860s travelling in Egypt and Asia Minor.

Of the fourteen works by the artist sold at Christie's in 1997, eleven had Orientalist themes. Among these was *Veiled Circassian Lady*, which sold in February in New York for $580,000 (£348,000). The portrait is in the same format as the series of three paintings of patrician Turkish women which Gérôme painted after returning to Paris from Constantinople in 1875. The model's pose is similar to that of the Turkish ladies, but her wonderfully structured face, seen through the back veil, is captured with even greater delicacy and sensitivity.

Gérôme's unmatched gift for sensuousness is powerfully witnessed by two of his canvases sold at Christie's in 1997: *Les baigneuses*, which sold for £271,000 ($430,890), and *La poursuite*, exhibited in the 1900 Salon, which achieved £100,500 ($153,500) in March.

The highest price of the year for a work by the artist – $1,597,500 (£958,500) – was paid for the monumental *Napoleon and his General Staff in Egypt*, sold in February at Christie's New York.

1997 also saw an exceptional price for a work by the Orientalist Alberto Pasini, whose exquisite paintings recently gained inter-

JEAN-LÉON GÉRÔME (1824-1904)
Veiled Circassian Lady
oil on canvas
17 x 13 in. (43 x 33 cm.)
Painted *circa* 1875
New York, 11 February 1997,
$580,000 (£353,800)

national recognition thanks to the exhibition *Alberto Pasini, da Parma a Costantinopoli via Parigi* in Parma in 1996. In June at Christie's London Pasini's *Un angolo del giardino dell'harem* (1877) realized £430,500 ($701,715), a world record price for the artist.

From 1867 to 1869 Pasini was in Constantinople, where he painted a group of four pictures of *odalisques* in gardens in Pera, off the coast of the Golden Horn. Pasini was mesmerized by Turkish women and their rich costumes, which formed the most unexpected harmonies of colours against the azure background of the Bosphorus, and was inspired to paint the *harem* series, of which *Un angolo* is the most sumptuous.

Another Italian artist was captivated by the exotic atmosphere of the Bosphorus: Fausto Zonaro was court painter to Sultan Abdul Hamid II from 1896 to 1909. In his *Sulla riva di Dolmabahçe a Costantinopoli*, which sold for the record price of £161,000 ($262,430) in London in June, elegant Turkish and European ladies promenade indolently along the Bosphorus.

The second half of the 19th century saw artists from England, Italy, Spain, Holland, Belgium, Scandinavia and Austria travelling to North Africa, Egypt, the Holy Land, Syria and Turkey.

In 1997, Christie's retraced the story of this adventurous 'Grand Tour', presenting at auction the works by the best Orientalist artists. Along with Gérôme, Pasini and Zonaro, particularly appreciated were the Danish painter Martinus Rørbye, whose *A Turkish Notary drawing up a Marriage Contract* sold for £254,500 ($430,105), the Austrian Rudolph Ernst (*Le bain turc*, £103,800 ($169,194)), and the French Léon-François Comerre, whose *Haifa*, portraying a splendid *odalisque* in a luxurious garden, sold for £227,000 ($360,930), a world record price for the artist.

WENDY GOLDSMITH
DIRECTOR OF THE IMPRESSIONIST AND
19TH CENTURY PICTURE DEPARTMENT, CHRISTIE'S LONDON

ALBERTO PASINI (1826-1899)
Un angolo del giardino dell'harem
signed and dated
oil on canvas
29⅛ x 25 in. (76 x 63.6 cm.)
Painted in 1877
London, 13 June 1997, £430,500 ($701,715)
A record auction price for the artist

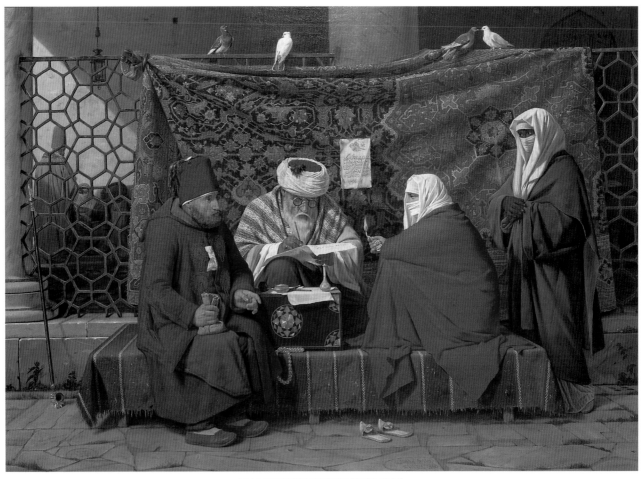

MARTINUS RØRBYE (1805-1848)
A Turkish Notary drawing up a Marriage Contract in front of the Kiliç Ali Pasha Mosque, Tophane, Constantinople
signed and dated
oil on canvas
37½ x 51⅛ in. (95 x 130 cm.)
Painted in Rome, 1837
London, 21 November 1997, £254,500 ($429,087)
A world record auction price for the artist

Rørbye was the pupil of the acknowledged 'father' of the Golden Age of Danish Painting, Christoffer Wilhelm Eckersberg (1783-1853), the first Danish artist to have painted *en plein air* in Rome. Like many of his contemporaries, Rørbye searched outside his homeland for inspiration, spurred no doubt by the work of his master and by his desire to record foreign and exotic cultures. In 1834 he began an extensive tour of Europe which took him to Paris, Rome, Greece and Turkey, and returned to Copenhagen in 1837.

The present work, conceived in Constantinople in 1835-36 (the Islamic date '1251' is inscribed on the purse held by the figure to the far left of the picture) is a superb example of Rørbye's close observation of other cultures. He left Constantinople in December 1836, returning to Rome to complete the picture. There, on 21 March 1837, he recorded his increasing frustration in rendering the final, painstaking details of his work: 'My mood was no better today than it was yesterday, when the draperies in my painting brought me almost to despair'. Rørbye's fascination with Turkish costume is visible here in the precision with which he painted the notary's shawl.

A watercolour version of the same subject, executed in Rome in 1836, is in the Kobberstiksamling, Statens Museum für Kunst, Copenhagen.

JEAN-LÉON GÉRÔME (1824-1904)
Napoleon and his General Staff in Egypt
oil on panel
23 x 34¾ in. (58.4 x 88.2 cm.)
Painted by 1867
New York, 11 February 1997, $1,597,500 (£974,475)

Napoleon and his General Staff in Egypt depicts the general and his army retreating along the arid plains of Egypt after a disastrous defeat by the British at Saint Jean d'Acre – a defeat which cost the French four thousand men, a third of Napoleon's army. Gérôme's rendering of the scene is masterful in every way, from the complex composition to the convincingly realistic depiction of the great sand clouds stirred up by the troops, successfully conveying the deep discomfort of the passage through the desert. This major work by Gérôme was rediscovered after almost seventy years in obscurity. An oil sketch is in the Hermitage Museum, St. Petersburg.

ADOLPH FRIEDRICH ERDMANN VON MENZEL (1815-1905)
Maurer an einem Hausbau
signed and dated
watercolour and bodycolour heightened with gum arabic
15¾ x 10¼ in. (40 x 26 cm.)
Executed in Berlin, 1875
London, 9 October 1997, £166,500 ($269,730)
A record auction price for the artist

PETRUS VAN SCHENDEL (1806-1870)
A vegetable Market by Candlelight
signed
oil on panel
39½ x 30⅜ in. (100.3 x 77.2 cm.)
London, 21 November 1997, £188,500 ($317,811)
A record auction price for the artist

Menzel's parents moved to Berlin from Breslau in 1830, part of the massive influx which transformed the city in the 19th century. A minor regional centre with an estimated population of 200,000 at the end of the Napoleonic era, Berlin grew to well over two million inhabitants by the time of Menzel's death in 1905.

Against a backdrop of such expansion, the recurrence of the building site in Menzel's *oeuvre* comes as no surprise. It was unquestionably the building boom at this time in Germany, known as the *Gründerjahre* (founder's years), that led Menzel to make such a large number of critical and documentary drawings. Finished works, however, are relatively rare.

Maurer an einem Hausbau, is related to ten studies of workers in the 1874-75 sketchbook, now in the Berlin Kupferstichkabinett. A fascinating character study of the six workers, *Maurer an einem Hausbau* is set against the still green expanse of trees in the middle background and is eloquent of the conflict between industrialization and nature.

Petrus van Schendel trained in Antwerp, under Mathieu Ignace Van Brée (1773-1839). He stayed on in Antwerp until 1828, moving to Amsterdam for four years and then Rotterdam for six years and then The Hague for seven years. In 1845 he settled permanently in Brussels. He was elected to the Rijksakademie in Amsterdam and was a member of the Rotterdam society, Arti Sacrum.

Influenced by 17th century Dutch painting, Schendel specialized in genre scenes and interiors lit by moonlight or candlelight in the tradition of Gerrit Dou. Indeed in France he was nicknamed 'Monsieur Chandelle'.

Mesdag was born in Groningen into a family of grain merchants and bankers. He seemed destined for a career in banking but an inheritance enabled him to devote himself entirely to art. His cousin, Laurens Alma-Tadema, introduced him to the landscape painter Willem Roelofs in Antwerp, with whom he studied for a time. *His Brisants de la mer du Nord* earned him a gold medal at the 1870 Paris Salon, immediately establishing his reputation.

Mesdag was a central figure in the artistic circles of The Hague and became chairman and later honorary chairman of the Pulchri Studio Art Society. Between 1887 and 1894, he painted a series of large atmospheric landscapes depicting sunsets or summer evenings. As Mesdag gave the title *Coucher de soleil* to many of his works, it has become difficult to identify his pictures with certainty. The present picture may well be identical, however, with *Coucher de soleil* inv. no. 23745 in the sales lists of Goupil & Cie., The Hague. Mesdag not only purchased works for his own collection at Goupil's but also sold the bulk of his own work through the gallery.

HENDRIK WILLEM MESDAG (1831-1915)
Coucher de soleil
signed and dated
oil on canvas
39⅜ x 48¾ in. (100 x 124 cm.)
Painted in 1893
Amsterdam, 29 April 1997, Nlg. 542,0004 (£172,943)

The composition of this painting is unusual in that Munnings has depicted the horses moving from right to left (most European paintings read from left to right). The inclusion of the single distant grey horse gives proportion and depth to the landscape and balance to the composition. Munnings wrote of this picture that he was particularly pleased as he was able successfully to 'harness colour and movement in perfect harmony.'

SIR ALFRED MUNNINGS, P.R.A. (1878-1959)
Steeplechasing: Going down to the Start
oil on canvas
24½ x 33 in. (62.2 x 83.8 cm.)
Painted *circa* 1936
New York, 3 December 1997, $497,500 (£303,353)

THOMAS COLE (1801-1848)
View of Boston
oil on canvas
34 x 47⅛ in. (86.3 x 119.7 cm.)
New York, 5 June 1997, $1,102,500 (£676,172)

Thomas Cole, founder of the Hudson River School of American landscape painting, painted the *View of Boston* between 1837 and 1839 and delivered the canvas in late 1839 to Joshua Bates (1788-1864), an American expatriate resident in London, who had commissioned it in 1830. The painting connected Cole's native country (he was born in Bolton-le-Moor, England) to his adoptive one through the Massachusetts-born patron, who was a formidable financial and quasi-diplomatic interlocutor between Britain and the United States for many years. The scene that Cole painted for Bates is still recognizable today, though significantly altered. Still visible are Charles Bulfinch's magnificent domed State House, Peter Banner's single-spired Park Street Church and parts of the elegant residential neighbourhood of Beacon Hill. *View of Boston* stands as a singularly inspiring landscape that speaks of the promise and blessed prospects of the young Republic.

GEORGE HENRY HALL (1825-1913)
Bric-à-Brac Still Life
signed and dated
oil on canvas
48 x 36 in. (121.9 x 91.9 cm.)
New York, 5 June 1997, $167,500 (£102,729)

During his lifetime, Hall was among the most influential American still life painters. Elected to the National Academy of Design in 1868, he also kept a studio in the prestigious Tenth Street Studio Building – home of such figures as Winslow Homer and William Merritt Chase. *Bric-à-Brac Still Life* represents the pinnacle of Hall's still life *oeuvre* with its intricate textures, exotic subject matter and brilliant use of colour.

WINSLOW HOMER (1836-1910)
Home, Sweet Home
signed
oil on canvas
21½ x 16½ in. (54.6 x 41.9 cm.)
New York, 5 June 1997, $2,642,500 (£1,620,668)
A record auction price for the artist

The market for 19th century American art is strong, especially for works of exceptional historical importance and artistic merit, such as Winslow Homer's *Home, Sweet Home*, which sold at Christie's, New York for $2.6 million. It was the finest Civil War painting by the artist remaining in private hands. It was bought by the National Gallery of Art, Washington. An important addition to the museum's impressive holding of works by America's most beloved artist, the painting explores heartfelt sentiment as two Union soldiers listen to the song of a nearby military band, which probably stirs thoughts of their loved ones at home – a scene both universal and timeless in its poignancy.

Watercolours by the American realist painter Thomas Eakins are among the rarest and most sought-after works of late 19th century American art. *Mending the Net*, a view of shad fishermen along the Delaware River, is the most important work on paper by Eakins to appear at auction since 1990, when Christie's New York sold Eakins' masterful watercolour *John Biglin in a Single Scull* (now in the collection of Paul Mellon, Upperville, Virginia), a work executed nine years earlier in 1873, which sold for $3.5 million, a world record auction price for the artist.

THOMAS COWPERTHWAITE EAKINS
(1844-1916)
Mending the Net
signed and dated
watercolour on paper
11⅛ x 16¾ in. (28.7 x 42.5 cm.)
New York, 5 June 1997, $1,542,500 (£946,028)

Whether depicting a weather-beaten fence post, an empty cornfield after the harvest or the wrinkled face of an old man, Andrew Wyeth's paintings bear witness to the passage of time. A study of the vernacular architecture and aged farm implements of rural Pennsylvania, *Marsh Hawk* is among the artist's most sensitive interpretations of this theme. The artist wrote of *Marsh Hawk* as follows: 'The hay wagons were given to me by the Harveys, who lived nearby. I found their colors wonderful and their craftsmanship beautiful. I was taken by the shape of the carts and the way the wheels were built. They dated back to around 1850-60. Their wheels and hubs were magnificently constructed. Some of my best drawings are details of them. To think that these very wagons rolled over those rugged hills of Chadds Ford! The title comes from the marsh hawk sitting on the stump in the left distance. Late afternoon light is streaking across. The wagons were all swept away in a flood down the river to Wilmington. Nothing lasts. Shouldn't.'

ANDREW WYETH (b.1917)
Marsh Hawk
signed
tempera on masonite
30½ x 45 in. (77.3 x 114.4 cm.)
New York, 5 June 1997, $1,432,500 (£878,564)

WILLARD LEROY METCALF (1858-1925)
Fish Wharves, Gloucester
signed and dated
oil on canvas
29¼ x 23¼ in. (74.3 x 59 cm.)
New York, 5 June 1997, $552,500 (£338,853)

Willard Leroy Metcalf's *Fish Wharves, Gloucester* epitomizes American Impressionism. Painted in 1896 at the fashionable summer resort of Gloucester, Massachusetts, the canvas is filled with the brilliant light and colour which characterize this artistic movement. With its strong diagonals and complex composition, *Fish Wharves, Gloucester* illustrates the artist's fascination with design and provides a unique perspective of this celebrated seaside town. Metcalf painted the work to repudiate earlier criticism of his lack of artistic innovation.

MARY STEVENSON CASSATT (1844-1926)
Marie-Thérèse Gaillard
signed
pastel on paper
20¼ x 21¼ in. (51 x 54 cm.)
New York, 5 June 1997, $1,542,500 (946,028)

Among Mary Cassatt's most celebrated works are her images of children, a subject she explored particularly during the 1880s and 1890s. *Marie-Thérèse Gaillard*, a portrait of 1894, is a tender and intimate image which displays all the hallmarks of Cassatt's finest pastels from this period. The sitter was the daughter of Dr. Théodore Gaillard, an early friend and patron of Cassatt and other Impressionist painters, who acquired paintings by Renoir, Sisley and Degas, among others. Over the years Cassatt became a friend of the Gaillard family and a frequent guest in their home. Until its sale at Christie's New York in 1997 for $1,542,500, the pastel had remained in the family of the sitter.

THE JOHN AND FRANCES L. LOEB COLLECTION

THE sale of the John and Frances L. Loeb Collection was one of the greatest events in modern auction history. At the single-owner evening sale on 12 May 1997, twenty nine lots sold for a total of $92.8 million, the third highest total ever for a single-owner sale. This extraordinary result reflected the supreme quality of the collection, which included masterpieces by nearly every Impressionist and Post-Impressionist painter – Cézanne, Gauguin, Lautrec, Manet, Renoir, Seurat – as well as great works by other 19th and 20th century artists, such as Delacroix, Tissot, Dalí and Moore.

The three paintings by Cézanne constituted what was perhaps the strongest part of the collection. Cézanne's portrait of his wife, *Madame Cézanne au fauteuil jaune*, of 1888-90, sold for $23.1 million, the second highest price ever at auction for the artist. It is one of four closely related canvases, all depicting Madame Cézanne seated with her hands in her lap, and wearing a red house dress with a shawl collar (the other three versions are in the Art Institute of Chicago, the Metropolitan Museum of Art, New York, and the Museo de Arte, Sao Paulo). Like the other versions, the Loeb painting is a work of the very highest quality. The cool palette, prismatic brushwork and psychological ambivalence of the sitter in this picture are fully characteristic of Cézanne. His paintings of Madame Cézanne occupy an important place in the development of the modern portrait. Indeed, they were a key source of inspiration both for Matisse's *Portrait de Madame Matisse* (1913, Hermitage Museum, St. Petersburg) and Picasso's *Femme assise dans un fauteuil* (1913, formerly Ganz collection; sold at Christie's New York on 10 November 1997 for $24.8 million).

Another star of the sale was Cézanne's *Les toits de l'Estaque*, which sold for $12.7 million. Painted in 1883-85, it was one of the last of Cézanne's views of the Bay of Marseilles still in private hands. Along with the paintings of Mont Saint-Victoire, these pictures rank among Cézanne's most important contributions to landscape painting. The third work by Cézanne in the Loeb collection was *L'Oncle Dominique*, which sold for $2.9 million. Painted *circa* 1866, this bold early work is rendered with extremely thick and viscous impasto, applied in unusually large brushstrokes. It is one of ten portraits Cézanne made of his uncle.

Portrait de Manet par lui-même, en buste is one of only two self-portraits Manet painted. He shows himself as both *boulevardier* and artist: although holding palette and brushes in his hands, he wears an elegantly tailored jacket of pale saffron, and his tie is fixed with a pearl stick-pin. The ideal of the gentleman-artist is an ancient one, exemplified by Velázquez, one of Manet's favourite artists.

Indubitably, Manet intended to invoke this tradition here – his pose even explicitly recalls that of Velázquez in *Las meninas*. The Loeb painting is of extraordinary sensual beauty – the brushwork loose and lush, the application of the blacks, whites and yellows especially stunning. The *chiaroscuro* on the face is masterly: the light illuminates the eyes, while much of the face is cast in shadow; this combination, borrowed from Rembrandt, produces a strong impression of melancholy and reflection. The picture is at once an *hommage* to the grand tradition of Old Master painting and the product of an unmistakably modern sensibility. *Portrait de Manet par lui-même, en buste* is among the greatest self-portraits of the 19th century. It sold for $18.7 million.

Toulouse-Lautrec's *Danseuse assise aux bas roses* (1890) sold for $14.5 million, the highest price ever paid for a work by the artist. In this magnificent character study, a solitary dancer is seated on a couch or a bed; leaning forward just enough to emphasize the cleavage of her breasts, she folds her hands between her legs in a gesture of apparent repose. Rendered in pastel and *peinture à l'essence*, a combination of media characteristic of the artist, the painting is a work of extraordinary delicacy and power. Particularly delightful are the overlapping, diaphanous veils of her tutu, which form a kind of billowy cloud around the dancer. This makes a striking contrast with the thicker application of pigment on her arms, legs and face and the sketchy rendering of the background.

The Loeb collection contained other superb works of Impressionist and Post Impressionist painting. Seurat's jewel-like *Femmes au bord de l'eau*, one of the preparatory studies for *La Grande Jatte*, sold for $1.5 million. Renoir's 1887 *Baigneuse debout*, derived from his figure studies for the monumental *Les grandes baigneuses* (Philadelphia Museum of Art) went for $4.3 million. Monet's *Iris mauves* is a large and mesmerizingly beautiful example of the artist's late style; it sold for $3.9 million. The Loeb collection was also extremely strong in other 19th and 20th century artists. Especially noteworthy were the two works by Tissot: *La cheminée* (see pp. 66-67), a *tour-de-force* of delicate realism, showing Tissot at the peak of his talents, soared to $1.9 million, and his portrait of a fetching young model, *Dans la serre*, sold for $486,500.

In its thematic diversity and formal complexity, the Loeb Collection is testimony to the breadth and richness of 19th century and modern painting.

FRANCK GIRAUD
HEAD OF 19TH AND 20TH CENTURY PICTURES DEPARTMENT,
CHRISTIE'S NEW YORK

PAUL CÉZANNE (1839-1906)
Madame Cézanne au fauteuil jaune
oil on canvas
31⅝ x 25⅜ in. (80.4 x 64.4 cm.)
Painted in 1888-1889
New York, 12 May 1997, $23,102,500 (£13,861,500)

PAUL CÉZANNE (1839-1906)
Les toits de l'Estaque
oil on canvas
23¾ x 28¾ in. (60.2 x 73 cm.)
Painted in 1883-1885
New York, 12 May 1997, $12,652,500 (£7,591,500)

EDOUARD MANET (1832-1883)
Portrait de Manet par lui-même, en buste (Manet à la palette)
oil on canvas
33⅜ x 28 in. (85.3 x 71 cm.)
Painted *circa* 1878
New York, 12 May 1997, $18,702,500 (£11,221,500)

HENRI DE TOULOUSE-LAUTREC (1864-1901)
Danseuse assise aux bas roses
peinture à l'essence and pastel on board
signed
22⅜ x 18¼ in. (56.8 x 46.4 cm.)
Painted in 1890
New York, 12 May 1997, $14,522,500 (£8,713,500)

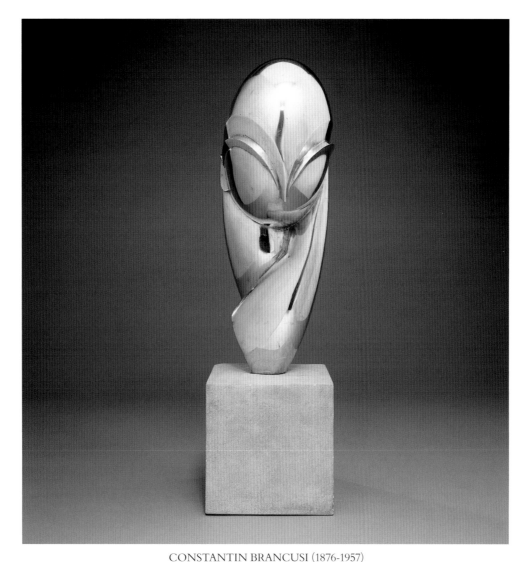

CONSTANTIN BRANCUSI (1876-1957)
Mademoiselle Pogany II
signed
polished bronze
17¼ in. (43.8 cm.) high
Executed in 1920-1925
New York, 14 May 1997, $7,042,500 (£4,225,500)

Mademoiselle Pogany II is the second of three portraits which Brancusi executed between 1912 and 1931 of Margit Pogany, a Hungarian art student whom he met in Paris in 1910. In its formal purity, radical simplicity and physical radiance, *Mademoiselle Pogany II* embodies the most important characteristics of Brancusi's art and is at the centre of his achievement as a sculptor; as Henri-Pierre Roché stated in a letter to the American collector John Quinn, dated 1 February 1920: '[This] extraordinary female head shows a breakthrough in Brancusi's evolution'.

The present cast of *Mademoiselle Pogany II* originally belonged to the painter and photographer Edward Steichen, who probably acquired it during his stay in Paris in the late 1920s. Steichen photographed Brancusi in his studio on several occasions and initiated an exhibition of the sculptor's work at Alfred Stieglitz's gallery in New York in 1914. It was Steichen, along with Marcel Duchamp, who famously filed the protest in 1927 against the classification of Brancusi's works by U.S. Customs as 'miscellaneous' rather than as works of art. This *Mademoiselle Pogany* has never been exhibited publicly and was unknown to experts until its appearance at Christie's.

MONET: FROM IMPRESSIONISM
TO ABSTRACTION

CLAUDE MONET (1840-1926)
Sur les planches de Trouville
signed and dated, oil on canvas, 19¾ x 27½ in. (50 x 70 cm.)
Painted in 1870
London, 9 December 1997, £4,181,500 ($6,882,749)

THIS year saw the sale of three major oils by Monet at Christie's. Few disputed that these were amongst the finest Monets of their type to come on the market for many years. Unusually there was not a *Nymphéas* among them; instead, the subjects were Trouville, Argenteuil and Waterloo Bridge. The first of them was painted when Monet was only thirty years old, the last when he was sixty-three: the three pictures thus chart several of the most eventful years of the artist's life.

The first, *Sur les planches de Trouville*, was one of the auction discoveries of the decade. Painted in 1870, the picture had been bought by the vendor's family in 1884. Its appearance at auction marked the first time that the picture had been seen in public for over one hundred years. The painting is one of only a handful of oils that Monet painted in Trouville on this visit. The late 1860s were difficult years for Monet: in 1869 his paintings were rejected

by the Salon committee, he was finding it increasingly hard to sell his work and he was coming under growing pressure from his creditors. Boudin persuaded Monet that he should join him in Trouville, where the former had met with great success selling his beach scenes to the wealthy Parisians who visited the resort each summer. His long summer in Trouville with Boudin was to mark a major turning point in Monet's career.

Sur les planches de Trouville is an extraordinarily brave painting. It is almost the work of an angry young man, out to prove a point to the Salon committee members who had so recently spurned his work. It is often argued that great painting is born of adversity, and these Trouville pictures seem to validate this view. The painting is a *tour de force* of light effects, dramatic colour contrasts, paint textures and dynamic brushwork. Its artistic immediacy amounts to the painter's equivalent of a poet's stream of consciousness.

CLAUDE MONET (1840-1926)
La Seine à Argenteuil
signed and dated
oil on canvas
23½ x 31⅜ in. (59.8 x 79.8 cm.)
Painted in Argenteuil, 1875
Sold from the Property of San Francisco Museum of Modern Art
to benefit its Helen Crocker Russell Art Purchase Fund
New York, 14 May 1997, $8,362,500 (£5,017,500)

La Seine à Argenteuil, painted some five years later, is far more restrained but no less dramatic. Monet's paint surface has become much drier, his brushwork more feathered and his touch much lighter. Exhibited at the second *Exposition des Artistes Indépendants*, *La Seine à Argenteuil* is the archetypal *plein air* Impressionist picture. Unsurprisingly, these Argenteuil pictures proved immensely popular,

and, for the first time in Monet's career, he enjoyed significant commercial success. Between 1871 and 1873 Monet's diaries reveal that he earned 37,000 francs, a considerable sum given that the average salary of a lawyer or doctor in Paris was then around 9,000 francs a year. The dark days of 1869 were now well and truly behind him.

CLAUDE MONET (1840-1926)
Waterloo Bridge, soleil voilé
signed and dated, oil on canvas, 25⅝ x 39⅝ in. (65.1 x 100.7 cm.)
Painted in London, 1903
Sold from the Gabrielle Oppenheim-Errera Estate
New York, 11 November 1997, $8,252,500 (£4,868,975)

By 1903 Monet was at the peak of his powers and four years into his largest and most ambitious project to date: his views of the River Thames in changing weather conditions. Whereas in the 1870s Monet provoked a reaction by a form of visual assault on the viewer, whom he would seduce with colour, brushwork and dazzling light effects, now Monet sought the same response by understatement. The colours are subdued almost to the point of being monochromatic. His public had never seen anything like it. Octave Mirbeau called the series 'a miracle' and continued: 'It's almost a paradox that one can, with impasto on canvas, create an impalpable matter, imprison the sun…to make shoot forth from this Empyrean atmosphere, such splendid fairy lands of light. And yet, it's not a miracle, it's not a paradox: it's the logical outcome of the art of M. Claude Monet' (quoted in G. Seiberling,

exh. cat., *Monet in London*, High Museum of Art, Atlanta, 1989, p. 83).

With financial pressures far behind him, Monet was no longer concerned with pandering to his public. Instead, the lessons learned from his extremely commercial *plein air* paintings of the 1870s were now being applied to a high art which verged on pure abstraction. It is fascinating to see how, out of pure impressionism, he was able to develop an intellectualized, analytical form of painting where tone and texture in themselves justify the subject.

JUSSI PYLKKÄNEN
DIRECTOR OF THE IMPRESSIONIST AND
19TH CENTURY DEPARTMENT, CHRISTIE'S LONDON

GEORGES BRAQUE (1882-1963)
Le port de l'Estaque, l'Embarcadère
oil on canvas
23¾ x 28¾ in. (60.5 x 73 cm.)
Painted in 1906
London, 9 December 1997, £1,596,500 ($2,627,839)

Previously owned by Wilhelm Uhde, the famous German art historian and dealer, *Le port de l'Estaque, l'Embarcadère* is one of the masterpieces of Braque's Fauve period. Although frequently illustrated and cited, this major work had not been seen in public since the celebrated exhibition of Fauvism and German Expressionism held in Paris and Munich in 1966, where it was illustrated as the frontispiece to the catalogue. In October 1906 Braque moved from Antwerp to l'Estaque in the south of France, where he stayed until February the following year. He returned to Paris in the spring of 1907 in order to exhibit at the Salon des Indépendants, where he showed six l'Estaque pictures including the present work, which is the larger version of the picture with the same title in the Musée National d'Art Moderne, Paris.

BERTHE MORISOT (1841-1895)
Après le déjeuner
signed
oil on canvas
3¾ x 39⅜ in. (80.7 x 100 cm.)
Painted in 1881
New York, 14 May 1997, $3,577,500 (£2,146,500)

Between 1881 and 1884, Morisot and her family spent their summers at a country house in Bougival, a resort on the Seine not far from Versailles, where Monet, Renoir and Pissarro had all painted before the Franco-Prussian War. *Après le déjeuner* is an exemplary work from a series of outdoor portraits which Morisot executed at Bougival, depicting her family, friends and neighbours in the lush grounds surrounding her home. With their complex treatment of colour and space, the Bougival pictures mark a turning point in Morisot's artistic development.

Twelve of the pictures which Morisot painted during the summer of 1881, *Après le déjeuner* among them, were included in the seventh Impressionist exhibition in Paris in March 1882. Durand-Ruel was particularly impressed by Morisot's contributions to the exhibition: he purchased a painting of Morisot's daughter Julie playing in the garden at Bougival and took *Après le déjeuner* and an additional garden scene on consignment. *Après le déjeuner* later passed to the celebrated New York collectors of Impressionist and Modern art, Albert and Mary Lasker.

PIERRE-AUGUSTE RENOIR (1841-1919)
Jeune femme se baignant
signed and dated
oil on canvas
32 x 25¾ in. (81.2 x 65.4 cm.)
Painted in 1888
New York, 14 May 1997, $12,432,500 (£7,459,500)

The 1880s was one of the most productive and fertile decades of Renoir's career, and the present painting exemplifies his best work of this period. The pose of the woman derives from that of the *Venus de' Medici*, the *Capitoline Venus* and *Venus Anadyomene*, famous Antique sculptures. The present work also derives from Renoir's studies for *Les grandes baigneuses*, in the Philadelphia Museum of Art, a monumental canvas which the artist hoped would be recognized as a masterpiece to rival great interpretations from the past of the subject of the female nude.

The warmth and luminosity of the present picture, its open, active brushwork, and its variegated, polychrome background are typical of Renoir's most attractive paintings of this period.

SCHLOSS KAMMER AM ATTERSEE II:
IN SEARCH OF MODERNISM

GUSTAV Klimt is recognized as one of the most significant landscape painters of his time: 'He saw in landscape the means of entering a mood, a sort of creative stimulus like a 'jewel', a 'firework', he saw the landscape's structure and the unfolding of elemental biological life forces, but the secret of his art as a landscape painter lies in the manner in which these different ways of seeing are layered and interlaced…The landscape was for him a place of contemplation, a source of joy' (S. Partsch, *Klimt, Life and Work*, London, 1989, p. 282).

Although Klimt did not turn his attention to landscape painting until relatively late in his career, landscapes represent some 25% of his oeuvre. His first known landscapes date from 1898 and were painted in St. Agatha, a village near Goisern in Upper Austria. With the exception of three others painted in the South Tyrol, the remainder were all painted on the Attersee. Situated not far from Salzburg, the Attersee is one of the area's quietest and most picturesque lakes, nestling in the foothills of the Alps, a place to which, during the summer months, Klimt would escape from the bustle and heat of Vienna.

The early landscapes of the late 1890s find Klimt employing a vertical format and a style demonstrating two clear influences: the mysterious quality of the work of the Belgian symbolist, Fernand Khnopff (1858-1921), and the cut perspectives of the great Japanese printmakers. From 1900 onwards Klimt's landscapes are, without exception, square in format. Sylistically these later landscapes transcend symbolism, adopting a neo-pointillist technique that the artist was to make entirely his own. 'The majority have an extremely high horizon line or lack one altogether, so that their subjects, whether flower beds, woods or meadows, seem to unfurl before the eye from top to bottom of the canvas more like tapestries or rugs than paintings' (F. Whitford, *Klimt*, London, 1990, p. 184).

Klimt generally painted these landscapes *en plein air*. It is known from contemporary accounts that he would roam the countryside near the Attersee carrying a small ivory tablet in which was cut a small rectangular hole through which he would view the landscape to ascertain whether a particular section might lend itself to painting. This framing technique allowed him to paint out-of-doors directly onto canvas without the need for preliminary sketches, just as his Impressionist predecessors had done. Like them, he would often hide his easel in the bushes in order to take up painting at the same place the next day. However, whilst his method may have owed much to the Impressionists, his primary artistic concern was to investigate and challenge the fundamental laws of perspective beyond the mere treatment of the subject-matter.

Schloss Kammer am Attersee II comes from a celebrated series of five paintings which Klimt executed of the Schloss Kammer during the summers of 1908 to 1912. Of the five views, the present composition is the only one seen from the garden. Three works show the house from the lake, *Schloss Kammer am Attersee I, III* and *IV*, whilst the fifth, *Allee im Park von Schloss Kammer*, depicts a perspective of the avenue of trees leading up to the house. All but the present are owned or on loan to major European museums.

There are several reasons why these Attersee landscapes are considered so important. Firstly, they were executed by an artist whose technique is absolutely faultless; secondly, they show Klimt's extraordinary understanding and development of the colourist principles of both Impressionism and Pointillism; thirdly, and perhaps most importantly, Klimt's obsession with the natural geometry of his landscapes shows him coming as close as any 19th century painter to the purist geometrical and planar experiments of Kandinsky and Mondrian.

THOMAS SEYDOUX
SPECIALIST IN THE IMPRESSIONIST AND 19TH CENTURY
PICTURE DEPARTMENT AT CHRISTIE'S LONDON

GUSTAV KLIMT (1862-1918)
Schloss Kammer am Attersee II
signed
oil on canvas
43¼ x 43¼ in. (110 x 110 cm.)
Painted in the summer of 1909
London, 9 October 1997, £14,521,000 ($23,524,830)
A record auction price for the artist and the highest price paid at auction in Europe for a modern picture this decade

THE NATURAL HEIRS OF FAUVISM
GERMAN AND AUSTRIAN ART

HAD it not been for the First World War, there is no doubt that German art would have had a stronger impact on the development of 20th century art. Most art historians recognize the importance of *Der Blauer Reiter* and *Die Brücke*, and quite rightly so, but rarely discuss what influence the great artists of these movements could have had if there had been a Europe without war and they had been able to work alongside the great avant-garde painters of France such as Picasso, Braque and Matisse. As it was, Marc was killed by a grenade near Verdun in 1916, Macke fell at Perthe-les-Hurles in the autumn of 1914, Kirchner became seriously ill and retired to Switzerland in 1916, and Pechstein left for the tropical island of Palau in the South Seas in 1914.

For those who survived the war, such as Schmidt-Rottluff, Nolde, Kirchner and Pechstein, the outrageously daring spirit of Expressionism had been lost forever. What did survive however, was a very precious body of work, executed between 1909 and 1915, which is remarkable for its quality and inventiveness. The Germans were the natural heirs of the colourist experiments of van Gogh and the Fauves and between these years they added raw colour, explosive brushwork, irreverent perspectives and extreme colour combinations to the vocabulary of 20th century painting.

It comes as no surprise, therefore, that it is these pivotal works which have become amongst the most sought-after paintings on the international art market. Thanks to the special sales of German and Austrian Art held at Christie's in London each October, several major international collectors have felt able to release their best pictures onto the market. This year's sale of German and Austrian Art was unquestionably the most exciting yet. Collectors were drawn to London from all over the world, and the tension in the saleroom was so great that the room exploded into applause at the end of the auction.

We were particularly proud to be given the opportunity to handle the sale of ten major paintings from the collection of

KARL SCHMIDT-ROTTLUFF (1884-1976)
Dangaster Park
signed and dated
oil on canvas
30 x 33¼ in. (76.2 x 84.5 cm.)
Painted in Dangast in 1910
London, 9 October 1997, £925,500 ($1,499,310)

Hans Ravenborg which had been bought over three decades: each was a classic example of its type with its own fascinating history. The highlight of the group was August Macke's *Paar am Gartentisch*, which is one of the most lyrical Expressionist oils to have appeared on the market for many years. It was painted in July 1914, only two months before Macke died, and shows the artist at his mature best, painting with a rare combination of control and freedom. The fact that at the age of only twenty-seven Macke was able to exhibit such extraordinary sensitivity to colour and composition, perfectly illustrates what he might have achieved had he survived the war and been able to share his artistic vision with his French contemporaries.

In contrast to the radiant beauty and lyricism of the Macke, Karl Schmidt-Rottluff's superb *Dangaster Park* of 1910 illustrates the power of the very best early German Expressionist paintings. More explosive than a Collioure period Matisse or Derain, this oil perfectly demonstrates how the Germans infused their colourist oils with passion. It was bought by the present owner's father-in-law in 1922 and research revealed that it had been exhibited at the avant-garde Galerie Commeter in Hamburg shortly after it was executed. In the true spirit of the Expressionist movement, it also came with a frame hand-carved and painted by the artist. Fierce competition saw it almost double its pre-sale estimate. One of the most satisfying elements of the sale for the experts at Christie's was the knowledge that they had helped to locate a major Expressionist picture which had long been considered lost.

The search for major Expressionist pictures continues as we prepare for our next German and Austrian Art sale in October 1998, and doubtless we will have further discoveries and excitements to recount next year.

JUSSI PYLKKÄNEN
DIRECTOR IN CHARGE OF THE GERMAN AND AUSTRIAN ART SALES

AUGUST MACKE (1887-1914)
Paar am Gartentisch
signed and dated
oil on canvas
21⅜ x 18⅜ in. (54.3 x 46.6 cm.)
Painted in Bonn in July 1914
London, 9 October 1997, £2,091,500 ($3,388,230)
A record auction price for the artist

WASSILY KANDINSKY (1866-1944)
Dünaberg
signed and dated
oil on board
13 x 17¾ in. (33 x 45 cm.)
Painted in 1909
London, 23 June 1997, £1,651,500 ($2,729,929)

Kandinsky's artistic evolution from 1908 to 1910 can be most easily followed in the treatment of a single motif: the church of Murnau. *Dünaberg*, painted in Murnau in 1909, is one of the artist's most powerful depictions of the beloved theme. Kandinsky had first discovered the small town south of Munich in June 1908 and returned soon afterwards with Gabriele Münter for a longer stay. Intensely inspired by the visual environment, the rolling hills by the Staffelsee and the Wetterstein Alps, he painted landscapes which were crucial in his development towards abstraction. The works of 1909 are the most poetic of this series; the volumes of the objects are reduced to a minimum, while the colours 'glow like illuminated windows at night…The hill near the church has no more body and weight than the conglomeration of white clouds…At some points nothing is to be seen but a tapestry of colour tones' (W. Grohmann, *Wassily Kandinsky: Life and Work*, London, 1959, p. 60).

FERDINAND HODLER (1853-1918)
Thunersee mit Grundspiegelung
signed
oil on canvas
31⅞ x 39⅜ in. (81 x 100 cm.)
Painted in 1904
Zurich, 14 April 1997, SFr. 3,334,900 (£1,417,333)

From July to August 1904 Hodler was in Leissigen, on Lake Thun. Deeply inspired by the breathtaking beauty of the surroundings, he devised a new approach to landscape painting: his research resulted in superb depictions of the mountain ranges reflected in the perfect circle of the lake. This series achieved its climax with two most celebrated versions of Lake Thun: the present painting and another, originally in Hans Mettler's collection, of St. Gallen, sold by Christie's London in 1979 for the record price of SFr 1,200,000. Paul Klee was mesmerized by the colours of Hodler's Thun landscapes; he told his wife, Lily Stumpf: '…Ich habe kaum je solche prachtvollen Dinge gesehen (I have never seen anything so magnificent).'

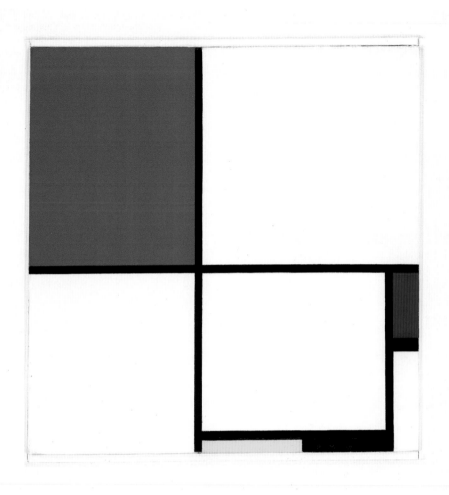

PIET MONDRIAN (1872-1944)
Composition No. III (Composition with Red, Blue, Yellow and Black)
signed and dated
oil on canvas in artist's original frame
19¾ x 19¾ in. (50.3 x 50.3 cm.)
Painted in 1929
New York, 14 May 1997, $4,182,500 (£2,509,500)

The late 1920s are recognized as one of the high points of Mondrian's career. At that time, he attained a level of purity and balance in his painting that has inspired many critics to speak of his style as 'classical'. Mondrian himself has given the best description of the combination of balance and dynamism in the paintings of this period: 'This equilibrium is clearly not that of an old gentleman sitting in an armchair or of two equal sacks of potatoes on the scales. On the contrary, equilibrium through equivalence excludes similarity and symmetry, just as it excludes repose in the sense of immobility.'
In 1930 Mondrian gave *Composition No. III* to his close friend Michel Seuphor, who later wrote one of the major studies on the artist. Seuphor, a critic, aesthete and writer, had met Mondrian in April 1923 and soon after began to assist the artist in editing and translating his theoretical texts; in 1926 Mondrian designed the sets for Seuphor's avant-garde play *L'éphemère est l'éternel*, and in 1928 Mondrian and Seuphor collaborated on a *tableau-poème* entitled *Textuel*. *Composition No. III* was purchased in 1975 by an important European collector and was part of a group of eight paintings and sculptures which Christie's sold on his family's behalf in May 1997.

RENÉ MAGRITTE (1898-1967)
La belle société
signed
oil on canvas
31⅞ x 25½ in. (81 x 64.8 cm)
Painted in 1965-66
London, 23 June 1997, £936,500 ($1,548,034)

Recently exhibited at the major Magritte exhibition at the Montreal Musée des Beaux Arts, *La belle société* is a combination of two images realized by Magritte in gouache, both in 1965: *La belle promenade*, where the figure is made of sky, and *L'homme et la forêt*, where the human silhouette is composed of tree foliage. The painting is also a unique synthesis of Magritte's most important icons: the bowler-hatted man – an image which the artist first used in 1926 in *Les rêveries du promeneur solitaire* and which soon came to be equated with himself – and the human body as a frame within which to depict a landscape. In Magritte's pictorial *corpus*, the human body is always represented without a face. In an interview with Jean Neyens in 1965 Magritte explained: 'Each thing we see hides another: we always want to see what is being hidden by what we see. There is an interest in what is being hidden and what the visible does not show us. This interest can take the form of a fairly intense feeling, a kind of contest I could say between the hidden visible and apparent visible. The Chaplinesque bowler-hatted man constitutes Magritte's most original contribution to Surrealism.

CONTEMPORARY ART

1997 proved to be an outstanding year for the sale of contemporary art at Christie's, reflecting the growing international strength of the market and reaffirming our position as the auction leaders in this field. We were privileged to offer in New York a number of pre-eminent works spanning Abstract Expressionism to Pop Art and Minimalism, while London achieved an aggregate total of £21 million. This is the highest annual total for contemporary art ever achieved at Christie's in London and surpasses the totals realized at the height of the boom market in 1989 and 1990.

With the continuing growth of the market, many private collectors have been encouraged to offer fresh and important works for sale, and this has resulted in fierce competitive bidding and a number of remarkable prices. The New York sale in May saw some classic examples of Pop Art achieving record prices. Andy Warhol's *Big Torn Campbell's Soup Can* sold for $3.5 million, far exceeding expectation and achieving the fourth highest price for Warhol ever. Roy Lichtenstein's *BLANG* sold for $2.9 million, and Wayne Thiebaud's *Bakery Counter* nearly tripled its estimate when it sold for $1.7 million and set a new record for the artist. The November sale was dominated by Abstract Expressionism with classic works by Franz Kline and Mark Rothko selling well and two important pictures by Willem de Kooning, *Two standing Women* and *Woman (Blue Eyes)*, rising well above their estimates and selling for $4.2 million and $2 million respectively.

One of the major trends of the year was an increasing internationalism in the bidding. While there has been consistent interest from Asian and European collectors in the New York sales, American collectors bought many of the top items in the London auctions. In addition, European artists traditionally sold in London, such as Pierre Soulages, Lucio Fontana, Jean Dubuffet and Yves Klein, attracted an increasing number of buyers from Asia and the Americas. Jean Dubuffet's atmospheric *Paris-Montparnasse*

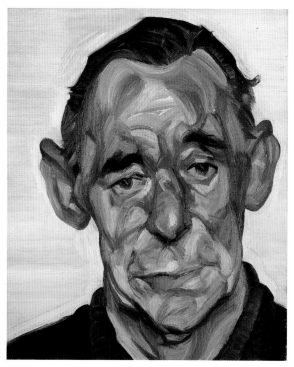

LUCIAN FREUD (b.1922)
John Deakin
oil on canvas
11 x 9 in. (30.2 x 24.8 cm.)
Painted in 1963-1964
London, 25 June 1997, £892,500 ($1,486,905)
A world record auction price for the artist

sold to an American private collector for £1.8 million ($3 million).

The highlights of London's highest grossing year were a number of exceptional works which reached world record prices, the most notable being Lucian Freud's *Portrait of John Deakin* of 1963 to 1964. This powerful portrait of the photographer, who was a close friend of both the artist and Francis Bacon in the bohemian community of 1950s Soho, sold for nearly three times its high estimate at £892,500. In the same sale a record was set for a work by Emil Schumacher when his *Peinture* realized £161,000 ($268,226). Sigmar Polke's humorous *Untitled* of 1985, sold for £386,500 ($643,909), also a record price for the artist. This last result reflects a huge surge of interest in Polke's work throughout the year that has been evident in sales on both sides of the Atlantic, and reaffirmed Polke's status amongst collectors as one of the most sought-after living artists.

Indeed, the success of Polke and Schumacher in particular reflects the current strength of German art as a whole. Augmented by another record-breaking German sale at Christie's in the autumn, German art continues to sell well to a world-wide audience. Works by Gerhard Richter consistently achieved high prices throughout 1997 – his enormous *Wolken (Fenster)* sold in New York in November for $552,500, while in London his *Abstraktes Bild* of 1986 sold well over the estimate at £287,500 ($475,525).

The overall buoyancy of the contemporary art market in 1997 has drawn many new collectors to the field and we are confident that this pronounced interest will continue. With our newly structured and re-defined departments for 20th century and contemporary art, our international team of specialists are convinced that Christie's will play a dramatic and innovative role in the sale of 20th century art in 1998.

BRETT GORVY
DIRECTOR OF 20TH CENTURY ART, CHRISTIE'S LONDON

WILLEM DE KOONING (1904-1997)
Two standing Women
signed
oil, enamel and charcoal on composition board
30 x 27 in. (76.2 x 68.6 cm.)
Painted in 1949
New York, 18 November 1997, $4,182,500 (£2,467,675)

Willem de Kooning's paintings of women are among the most famous and enduring images of 20th century art. Alone of all the celebrated Abstract Expressionists, de Kooning shocked the art world and his fellow artists in the 1940s by returning to the human figure in his work. In *Two standing Women*, de Kooning powerfully combines his earlier abstract painting of the 1940s with a ferocious sexually-charged rendering of the figure. Widely considered to be his greatest achievement, de Kooning's paintings of women from the late 1940s and early 1950s are, as Irving Sandler has written, in their 'restlessness, claustrophobia, density, rawness, violence and ambiguity…like a walk down a Manhattan street'.

JEAN DUBUFFET (1901-1985)
Paris-Montparnasse
signed and dated
oil on canvas
65 x 86¾ in. (165 x 220.5 cm.)
Painted in 1961
London, 25 June 1997, £1,827,500 ($3,033,650)

Paris-Montparnasse is one of the largest and most representative of Dubuffet's most highly acclaimed series of works, the *Paris Circus*. This painting in particular is a panoramic extravaganza which joyously evokes the hurly-burly of the city to which Dubuffet returned in 1961 after a break of nearly six years in the French countryside. *Paris-Montparnasse* encapsulates the jazzy bustle and frenetic pulse of the city's street life through Dubuffet's use of overpainting and a shimmering line that radiates with vitality. The figures and the street vehicles are jumbled together in a series of fantastic and sometimes impossible relationships that all explode with life while the painting as a whole is enveloped in an electric blue-grey mist that clearly situates the scene in a northern European city. The energy of the painted surface is so intense that one can almost hear the tooting of the traffic and smell the petrol fumes of this Montparnasse boulevard.

WAYNE THIEBAUD (b.1920)
Bakery Counter
signed and dated
oil on canvas
54⅞ x 71⅞ in. (139.4 x 182.6 cm.)
Painted in 1962
New York, 7 May 1997, $1,707,500 (£1,144,025)

A symbol of the taste for wholesome living in America in the 1950s and 1960s, *Bakery Counter* is one of the largest works from the artist's most acclaimed period. It is a highly balanced and coordinated composition. The thick impasto has the texture of icing sugar and the sugary pastel colouring actively takes on the physical appearance of the items it portrays. Thiebaud's subjects from this period are all nostalgic, harking back to his childhood, when he would regularly walk past the candy and bakery counters and window displays on the Long Beach boardwalk near his home.

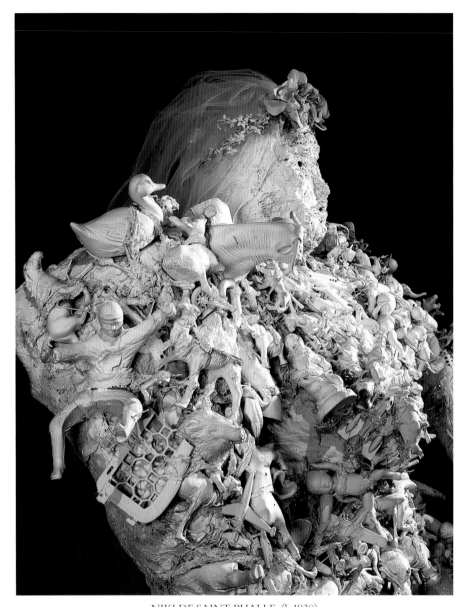

NIKI DE SAINT-PHALLE (b.1930)
La mariée [detail]
assemblage
71⅝ x 70⅛ x 39⅜ in. (182 x 178 x 100 cm.)
Executed in 1963
London, 25 June 1997, £128,000 ($212,480)

La mariée is the most important work by Niki de Saint-Phalle ever to appear on the auction market. Its haunting and macabre presence is a deliberate and provocative contrast to the traditional notion of the blushing virgin bride and reflects the artist's own ideas of womanhood and the position of women in 1960s society. *La mariée* is both an expression of the pain and guilt that de Saint-Phalle felt in rejecting the conventional rôle of mother and home-maker in her own life, as well as a dramatic assertion of her own sense of independence and power in her rôle as an artist. This enormous work is at once a rebellion against the sacred notion of motherhood within marriage and a celebration and dramatization of the primordial power of the feminine in the manner of ancient Mother-Goddess figures. Using toys and other plastic objects that appealed to her because of their uselessness, de Saint-Phalle merges these two seemingly contrasting themes into a unique and powerful image of woman.

ANDY WARHOL (1928-1987)
Big Torn Campbell's Soup Can (Pepper Pot)
signed and dated
acrylic and graphite on canvas
72 x 54 in. (182.9 x 137.2 cm.)
Painted in 1962
New York, 7 May 1997, $3,522,500 (£2,360,075)

More than any other image created by the artist, the Campbell's Soup Can has become the symbol of Warhol's art and indeed of the whole aesthetic of the 1960s Pop Art movement. Turning this instantly recognizable leading American product into an icon of the modern consumerist era was a single act that was not only responsible for projecting Warhol to international stardom, but also set the agenda for much of the rest of the artist's *oeuvre*. Of the numerous images that Warhol created of the soup can in 1962, the most dramatic are the group of four *Big Torn Campbell's Soup Cans*, of which this is one.

GERHARD RICHTER (b.1932)
Wolken (Fenster)
signed and dated
four panels – oil on canvas
78¾ x 157½ in. (200 x 400 cm.) overall
Painted in 1970
New York, 18 November 1997
$552,500 (£325,975)

The largest of Richter's cloud paintings, *Wolken (Fenster)* – 'Clouds (Window)' – is a powerful and imposing work that deliberately looks back to the 19th century northern Romantic tradition of painting, while at the same time ironically commenting upon it. Like Caspar David Friedrich in particular, Richter takes as his subject the sublime in Nature. The grandiose spread of the skyscape is punctuated by a subtle but radiant light which, like so much of Friedrich's work, suggests the presence of the divine. The polyptych format, usually associated with altarpieces, also lends a quasi-religious resonance to the work. Richter, however, secularizes the painting by giving it the subtitle *Fenster* and by framing each panel with a white surround.

Since 1969 almost all of Baselitz's paintings have depicted an upside-down image, challenging the viewer to see the format and painterly aspects of the work and not just the contents. 'The hierarchy which has located the sky at the top and the earth at the bottom is only a convention,' he has said. 'We have got used to it but we don't have to believe in it'. *Akt und Stilleben* marks an important decision in the artist's career, the one he made in 1977 to work in a diptych form based on compositions of abstract images of nudes and still lifes. Through the free and gestural application of the paint Baselitz deliberately breaks down the borders between the two separate images creating an overall rhythm and syntax that gives the work an unexpected harmonious unity.

GEORG BASELITZ (b.1938)
Akt und Stilleben (Nude and Still Life)
signed, titled and dated
oil on plywood
98⅜ x 134 in. (250.5 x 340.4 cm.) overall
Painted in April 1978
London, 11 December 1997, £180,560 ($297,924)

SIGMAR POLKE (b.1941)
Untitled
signed
mixed media on printed fabrics
71 x 59 in. (180 x 150 cm.)
Executed in 1985
London, 25 June 1997, £386,500 ($641,590)

Polke has been described as the artist who has made a style out of not having a style. In this highly accomplished work a combination of various styles and techniques wittily reflects the artist's concern with the way we perceive reality. Painted on industrially produced patterned fabrics instead of canvas, this work incorporates layer upon layer of visual puns that reflect and poke fun at many modern debates over painterly style. The painting incorporates his trademark – 'Polke-dots' – and is humorously signed 'S. Polek', on a wooden batten affixed to the stretcher – a direct reference to the most famous of the Abstract Expressionist painters.

JEAN-MICHEL BASQUIAT (1960-1988)
Untitled
signed and dated
coloured oilsticks and masking tape on paper
60 x 40 in. (152.4 x 101.6 cm.)
Executed in 1982
New York, 19 November 1997, $255,500 (£150,745)
A record auction price for a work on paper by the artist

This vibrant drawing reflects the 'terrible and terrifying hurry' with which Basquiat lived his short life. Although he is well known for his paintings, many critics have argued that Basquiat was in fact more accomplished at drawing. Executed with coloured oilsticks, the frantically drawn images, symbols, numbers, letters and crossings-out of this typically untitled work convey an intense and very primal sense of energy. Disquieting in its dizzy abundance of complex and confusing information, it reflects that peculiar collision of Expressionism and Pop Art that informs so much of Basquiat's best work.

PABLO PICASSO (1881-1973)
La femme qui pleure, I
etching, aquatint, drypoint and scraper, 1937, third state (of seven)
signed
P. 27⅜ x 19⁹⁄₁₆ in. (69.5 x 49.7 cm.)
New York, 3 November 1997, $552,500 (£331,500)

The image of the weeping woman dominated Picasso's output during 1937. Seen either as part of a larger composition as in *Guernica* or as an isolated figure, as here, she personifies Spain, torn apart by civil war, weeping for her children.

Picasso printed two editions of *La femme qui pleure, I* in the third and seventh states of the plate. The impressions were never formally published and were distributed by the artist himself.

EDVARD MUNCH (1863-1944)
Der Kuss (The Kiss)
etching with drypoint and aquatint printed in grey-black, 1895
signed
P. 13 x 10 in. (34.6 x 27.6cm.)
London, 27 June 1997, £66,400 ($110,224)

PAUL GAUGUIN (1848-1903)
Tahitienne nue de dos, assise
traced monotype, grey in black ink, *circa* 1902
S. 13⅝ x 9¼ in. (34.7 x 23.6 cm.)
Property from the Collection of the Marquis de Gonet (1872-1925)
New York, 3 November 1997, $266,500 (£159,900)

The Kiss is one of the best known and most re-worked motifs in Munch's oeuvre. He first tackled the subject of a couple embracing in a drawing made in 1891-2, and subsequently translated it into drawings and paintings, and into the graphic media of etching, drypoint and aquatint. This etching is the first print Munch made on the subject. It is directly based on a pencil drawing of a nude couple made in 1894-5, now in the Munch Museum in Oslo. By placing the couple in a room in front of a window overlooking a busy street, he makes this one of the more anecdotal of his works on the subject. Yet, by showing the couple naked and by blending their faces together, he transcends the purely narrative.

This powerful traced monotype is closely related to the seated figure in *L'appel* of 1902, now in the Cleveland Museum of Art. The prepared paper which Gauguin used to produce this monotype had clearly been used before, as a standing female nude can be seen horizontally across the lower back of the woman.

PABLO PICASSO (1881-1974)
La suite des Saltimbanques
etchings and drypoints, 1905
a complete set, from the de luxe edition
London, 27 June 1997, £276,500 ($458,990)

In *La suite des Saltimbanques*, Picasso treats the most important subjects which preoccupied him at the beginning of his career. Bohemianism, destitution and the theatre are all themes that pervade his work during the Blue and Rose periods. 1905 was a seminal year for the artist, representing the transition between these two phases. His artistic output rose as the company of poets, most notably Apollinaire whom he had met at the beginning of the year, enabled him to put away the sentimentality of the Blue period in favour of the impersonality of theatrical gesture and expression.

The subject of the Saltimbanques had preoccupied the artist since he first encountered these travelling acrobats in the Places des Invalides in about 1904.

EDGAR DEGAS (1834-1917)
En attendant le client
monotype, *circa* 1879
P. 6 x 8 (16.2 x 21.2 cm.)
London, 9 December 1997, £58,700 ($96,855)

Degas discovered monotypes nearly twenty years after he completed his first etchings, in the early 1870s. The facility and the freedom of the monotype was a revelation for the artist, the slow-drying ink allowing him to work and re-work the image. These small black and white depictions of intimate subjects had been known only to a close circle of artists, friends and collectors, and a number of them were destroyed before the series of studio sales.

En attendant le client, a recently re-discovered monotype, relates not only to the artist's love of experimentation and chance, but to his overriding concern for '*la vie moderne*'. The brothel scene, a major theme in Degas' work, reflects his own experience in these Parisian establishments. The small size and monochrome palette tie the image to illustration and photography.

By late 1904 Kandinsky's printmaking style had softened considerably and had moved away from the Jugendstil patterning which had dominated it earlier. The carefully considered combination of paper and watercolour, rather than ink, results in an image printed in the style of a monotype, brilliantly evoking a misty hillside.

WASSILY KANDINSKY (1866-1944)
Hugellandscaft
woodcut in colours, 1904
signed and inscribed on the support sheet
overall 10⅛ x 16⅜ in. (25.7 x 41.6 cm.)
New York, 13 May 1997, $151,000 (£93,620)

Schlemihls Begegnung mit dem Schatten is the seventh and final image of the series of woodcuts produced for *Peter Schlemihls wundersame Geschichte*, based on the novella by Adelbert von Chamisso, first published in 1814.

Produced before the artist entered a sanatorium in November 1915, this series is profoundly autobiographical. Peter Schlemihl sells his shadow to the devil, and is used by Kirchner as a metaphor for his own self-betrayal when he volunteered for military service. In July 1915, Kirchner started military training but the horrors of war had such a devastating impact on him that he was discharged from the army suffering a physical and nervous breakdown. Back in his studio and living under the constant threat of recall, Kirchner produced an astonishing amount of work, including the Schlemihl woodcuts, which are remarkable for their striking and richly applied colours as well as their deeply personal subject matter.

In this final woodcut in the series, Schlemihl tries in vain to align his feet with those of the shadow that he had once sold. Kirchner's attempt to regain his previous life as an artist similarly failed.

Kirchner inked and rolled all his prints himself. The present impression is extremely rare and is among the artist's finest works based on wartime experiences.

ERNST LUDWIG KIRCHNER (1880-1938)
Schlemihls Begegnung mit dem Schatten
woodcut printed colours, 1915
signed and inscribed
L. 12 x 11 in. (30.5 x 29 cm.)
London, 9 October 1997, £58,700 ($95,094)

This striking image is one of Heckel's best known and most important prints. Created shortly after the end of the first world war, this self-portrait with its contemplative, gaunt features not only stands as a representation of the artist's own depressed state of mind but also of a universal malaise. When Heckel retreated to the rural quiet of Osterholz near Bremen in 1919, he was physically and emotionally weak. He wrote to his friend and fellow artist Lyonel Feininger: 'Here everything is finally turning green. It is good for both of us [Heckel and his wife Siddi] to be able to live in the peace of this quiet simple country life. Nonetheless all those memories from the war years now emerge even more intensely in me again, but maybe they will lose their depressing effect in time'.

ERICH HECKEL (1883-1970)
Männerbildnis (Selbstbildnis)
woodcut printed in black, blue, ochre and green, 1919
signed and dated
L. 18 x 12 in. (46.1 x 32.3 cm.)
London, 9 October 1997, £62,000 ($100,440)

JASPER JOHNS (b. 1930)
Cicada
set of six screen-prints in colours, 1981
signed and dated, from an edition of 5
all S. 22 x 18 in. (56 x 46.1 cm.)
Sold from the Victor and Sally Ganz Collection
New York, 10 November 1997, $409,500 (£241,605)

The inspiration for this extremely rare set of screen-prints is the development of a cicada from a pupa into a winged insect. It is the cicada's emergence from its tough skin at birth and also its distinctive, repetitive call which Johns has translated into the cross-hatched surfaces which seem to vibrate.

In using screen-print for this series, Johns departed from his customary techniques of etching and lithography. He employed the screen-printing process to overprint repeatedly and build up a layering of colours which the other techniques could not provide. In all, nineteen screens were used in the production of each image.

WILLIAM SCOTT, R.A. (1913-1989)
Gaelic Landscape, 1961-62
signed, oil on canvas
63 x 68½ in. (160 x 174 cm.)
London, 30 May 1997, £58,700 ($96,033)

From the late 1950s Scott returned to pure abstraction in his work. His paintings became richer in form, stronger in colour and larger in scale, reaching 63 x 68 in. – proportions which he came to favour (and the size of *Gaelic Landscape*). The squarish shape of the canvas was in keeping with his earlier predilection for 'table-like' picture planes, which had been particularly appropriate for his still lifes.

LAURENCE STEPHEN LOWRY, R.A. (1887-1976)
Industrial Landscape
signed and dated, oil on panel
21 x 24 in. (53.3 x 61.3 cm.)
Painted in 1944
London, 27 November 1997, £364,500 ($608,350)

Industrial Landscape, previously in the collection of the writer Dame Rebecca West, who had purchased it from the artist in 1945, was first sold in these rooms by her Estate in November 1983. The picture contains the quintessential vocabulary of Lowry paintings: narrow Salford streets filled with 'matchstick' figures rushing along, bent forward against (one presumes) biting northern winds, tall buildings and factories and the ubiquitous smoking chimney-stacks. The picture realized the second highest auction price for a work by Lowry.

SIR STANLEY SPENCER, R.A. (1891-1959)
Angels of the Apocalypse
oil on canvas
24 x 36 in. (61 x 91.4 cm.)
Painted in 1949
London, 27 November 1997, £628,500 ($1,048,966)

While working on a commission from the War Artists' Advisory Committee to paint a series of shipyards in Port Glasgow (1940-1946), Spencer developed an idea for a Resurrection series which would celebrate the joy and sense of community that he had experienced among the shipyard workers. The sense of belonging he had felt there so moved him that Port Glasgow replaced Cookham in his artistic imagination. Originally he planned to paint one canvas, some fifty feet in length, depicting Christ seated at the top of a hill surrounded by hovering angels and with a newly-resurrected crowd of people climbing up the hill towards Him. In the end he chose to paint nine canvases, including *The Resurrection: The Hill of Zion* (1946); *The Angels of the Apocalypse* (1949); and *The Resurrection, Port Glasgow* (1947-50). He wished to emphasize the joy of the Resurrection, so instead of depicting the angels of the Apocalypse with their vials of wrath, meting out punishment to those whom Christ had judged, he chose to show 'angels assisting God in fertilizing the earth with distributory seeds'.

JOHN LUKE, R.U.A. (1906-1975)
Landscape with Figures
signed and dated, tempera on board
16¾ x 23¼ in. (42.5 x 59cm.)
London, 21 May 1997, £194,000 ($321,070)

John Luke's *Landscape with Figures* (1948) realized a world record price for the artist at auction when it was offered in Christie's annual sale of Irish Art in May 1997. It was executed during the late 1940s, when the artist, at the height of his career, had developed his use of tempera, a time-consuming method of producing powerful colours with oil glazes. Between 1943 and 1948 Luke produced some of his finest works, undertaking lengthy commissions for patrons in his native Belfast. He produced his last work, *The Rehearsal*, for the Belfast Museum and Art Gallery in 1950, after which ill-health brought his career to a premature end.

JACOB HENDRIK PIERNEFF (1886-1957)
Transvaal Landscape
signed and dated 1929, oil on canvas
32¼ x 44 in. (81.9 x 111.8 cm.)
London, 10 April 1997, £58,700 ($96,444)
A record auction price for the artist and for a 20th century South African painting

This is an outstanding work by the leading landscape painter in South Africa in the first half of the 20th century. The work dates to the apogée of his career, a year before he started work on a commission to produce 32 monumental South African landscape views to decorate the concourse of the Johannesburg Railway Station.

The second Exploration and Travel sale included five paintings by Edward Marston, the official artist on Shackleton's Imperial Trans-Antarctic Expedition of 1914-16. Shackleton had set sail from South Georgia in December 1914, intending to make the first crossing of Antarctica. His expedition never reached the continent; the *Endurance*, finding herself beset by ice in the Weddell Sea in January 1915, drifted for the following ten months. She was crushed and finally sank in November, the crew abandoning ship and making their now legendary escape in three open boats.

GEORGE EDWARD MARSTON (1882-1940)
The 'Endurance' crushed in the Ice of the Weddell Sea,
October 1915
oil on canvas, unframed
22¼ x 30¼ in. (56.6 x 76.9 cm.)
London, 10 April 1997, £49,900 ($80,788)

Born in Trinidad, the child of a 'free-coloured' family originally from the French West Indies, Cazabon studied in Europe before setting up his studio in Port of Spain in 1848. He won the patronage of the Governor, Lord Harris, and of the wealthy local planters, and his career developed in response to their demands, his work consisting mainly of local scenes in watercolour. In 1862 he moved to Martinique in search of new patrons but had little success, returning at the end of the 1860s to Trinidad, where he died, a forgotten figure, in 1888. The present work is the only extant oil of Martinique by the artist.

MICHEL-JEAN CAZABON (1813-1888)
The coast at Le Carbet, Martinique, with the Trou Caraïbe,
looking towards St. Pierre
signed, oil on canvas
17½ x 21¾ in. (44.5 x 55.3 cm.)
London, 10 April 1997, £67,500 ($108,810)
A record auction price for the artist

This is an exceptional watercolour by Alexander, the official draughtsman to the first British Embassy to China, which was led by Lord Macartney in 1793-94. Alexander's Chinese views, exhibited at the Royal Academy and published as engravings, created a sensation, presenting the British public with their first eye-witness pictorial account of the Chinese mainland.

WILLIAM ALEXANDER (1767-1816)
Pingze Men, the Western Gate of Peking
signed, watercolour
11⅜ x 17¾ in. (29 x 45.6 cm.)
London, 10 April 1997, £36,700 ($59,417)

This is one of a group of seven watercolours by Baines included in the April sale, all taken in the field during Chapman's Zambezi expedition of 1861-64. The view depicts the trading station of Charles John Andersson (1827-1867), an Anglo-Swedish explorer and author, at Otjimbingwe (in present day Namibia): it was from here that Chapman and Baines set off for the Zambezi and Victoria Falls.

THOMAS BAINES (1820-1875)
Otjimbingwe, Damaraland, 1861
pencil and watercolour, heightened with white
13 x 19⅜ in. (33 x 49.2 cm.)
London, 10 April 1997, £31,050 ($50,269)

CHARLES ALEXANDRE LESUEUR (1778-1846)
Animaux de La Nouvelle Hollande
signed, watercolour, goldleaf and silverleaf on vellum
8¼ x 10 in. (21 x 25.5 cm.)
Executed in 1807
Melbourne, 26 August 1997, A$211,500 (£94,773)
A record auction price for the artist

In 1800 the French admiralty, with the blessing of the First Consul, Napoleon I, launched an important voyage of discovery of the Pacific for 'the honour of the Nation and the progress of science'. Lesueur, an accomplished draughtsman, joined the voyage initially as an assistant gunner but he and Nicholas-Martin Petit were later promoted to official artists of the expedition. This small painting has been described as a 'Noah's Ark' of Australian flora and fauna. The depiction includes certain species which are now extinct.

BRETT WHITELEY (1939-1992)
The Pond at Bundanon
signed, oil on canvas
90½ x 54⅛ in. (230 x 137.5 cm.)
Painted in 1976
Melbourne, 26 August 1997, A$332,500 (£148,993)
A record auction price for the artist

The view is that from the window of Arthur Boyd's residence at Shoalhaven, New South Wales. The subject matter, the blue and gold palette so favoured by Australian collectors, and the connection with Arthur Boyd, another illustrious Australian artist, no doubt led to the record result achieved for this painting.

1997 marked 50 years since India's Independence, but it was long before 1947 that Indian artists began to break away from the academic schools established by the British and began to define an Indian artistic identity. Christie's second sale of Indian Contemporary Art traced the history of this struggle from the turn of the century to the present day with a wide selection of works by India's most important artists.

Raza's geometrical work, *Tree of Life*, is rooted in Indian metaphysical thought. The circle symbolizes the *bija* (seed) from which the tree grows, with the diagonals radiating from a point depicting the branches. The five primary colours, used in combination in this composition, represent the five elements (*pancha attavas*) which make up the universe.

SYED HAIDER RAZA (b. 1922)
Tree of Life
signed and dated 1996
acrylic on canvas, 47¼ x 47¼ in. (120 x 120cm.)
London, 4 June 1997, £8,625 ($14,093)

The startling diversity of Indian contemporary art can be seen by comparing Raza's abstract composition (above) with this figurative work by Bendre. Using rich earth colours and two dimensionality to represent his Indian heritage, Bendre captures daily life in the textile centre of Kutch in the state of Gujarat.

NARAYAN SHRIDHAR BENDRE (1910-1992)
Quilt from Kutch
oil on canvas, 47½ x 71 in. (120.6 x 180.3 cm.)
Painted in 1983
London, 4 June 1997, £23,000 ($37,582)
A record auction price for the artist

WALTER SPIES (1895-1942)
Tierfabel (Animal Fable)
oil on canvas
31⅞ x 25⅝ in. (81 x 65 cm.)
Painted in 1928
Singapore, 30 March 1997, S$828,750 (£348,075)

Spies was born in Moscow, the son of a German diplomat, and developed a particular interest in painting, music, dance and nature. He went to Batavia in 1923 and was captivated by the beauty of the Indonesian landscape, people and culture, which became a primary source of inspiration for his painting. He soon learnt the native language and translated Balinese fairytales. In 1927, he settled in the village of Ubud on Bali, and in 1928 was commissioned by his patron, Victor, Baron von Plessen, to paint *Tierfabel*, which evokes the Balinese legend of the battle between the animals.

RADEN SARIEF BUSTAMAN SALEH (1807-1880)
Lions and a Snake fighting outside a Grotto
signed and dated, oil on canvas
47⅜ x 69⅛ in. (121 x 175.5 cm.)
Singapore, 30 March 1997, S$1,983,750 (£833,175)

In 1829 Saleh arrived in Holland from his native Java. There he received training from the distinguished painters, Cornelis Kruseman and Andreas Schelfhout. He collected prints and books illustrated with tigers, lions and horses, and was inspired by reproductions of works by the French Romantic painter, Delacroix. In 1836 he met the circus-master Henri Martin, who allowed him to study and sketch his lions. He executed several well documented lion and tiger compositions between 1836 and 1839. The present picture, dated 1839, is probably the last he painted in the Netherlands before leaving for Dresden in May 1839.

There is no item more characteristic of Tamayo's pictorial vocabulary than the watermelon. In *Sandías y naranja* the three slices of watermelon seem to float in space, without the limitations of a bowl or plate; only the glowing sphere of the orange acts as an anchor for the composition. The form and composition suggest European influences, but the textures and bold, warm colours are a tribute to Tamayo's Mexican roots.

RUFINO TAMAYO (1899-1991)
Sandías y naranja (Melons and Orange)
signed and dated, oil on canvas
39⅜ x 31⅞ in. (100 x 81 cm.)
Painted in 1957
New York, 24 November 1997, $497,500 (£294,379)

From the late 1960s to the mid-1970s, the Chilean artist produced a series of enigmatic paintings which demonstrate, in both subject and form, important links with contemporary art in the United States and Europe as well as with Old Master painting. The trompe-l'oeil *Paquete azul* is a perfect example of Bravo's technical virtuosity and ability to suggest tantalizing mystery. The 'package' paintings were the subject of Bravo's first exhibition in New York in 1970 and introduced Bravo's very personal brand of realism to a Manhattan audience.

CLAUDIO BRAVO (b. 1936)
Paquete azul (Blue Package)
signed and dated, oil on canvas
74⅞ x 58⅞ in. (190 x 149.5 cm.)
Painted in 1967
New York, 28 May 1997, $585,500 (£359,202)

MARIO CARREÑO (b. 1913)
Patio colonial
signed and dated, oil on canvas
40⅝ x 31¾ in. (103.2 x 78 cm.)
Painted in 1943
New York, 28 May 1997, $442,500 (£271,472)

FERNANDO BOTERO (b.1932)
Princesa Margarita
signed and dated
oil on canvas
66 x 63½ in. (168 x 160 cm.)
Painted in 1977
New York, 24 November 1997, $662,500 (£392,012)

A major preoccupation of the 1940s generation of Cuban modernists was the pictorial exploration of the island's Spanish colonial architecture. In *Patio colonial* Carreño treats the Cuban interior patio in a charming, almost naïve manner, inspired by various European sources ranging from Renaissance and Baroque to Renoir and Picasso.

Probably the best-known and best-loved Colombian artist, with a highly distinctive 'naïve' style, Botero has made something of a speciality of parodies of Old Master paintings.

Princesa Margarita is clearly based on Velázquez's portrait of the Infanta Margarita, daughter of Philip IV of Spain, whom he painted at different stages of her life. The Infanta's head, the position of the arms, her oblique look and the flower in her hair indicate that Botero was drawing mainly on the most celebrated representation of the Infanta, in the work known as *Las Meninas*, painted *circa* 1656, now in the Prado, Madrid, but the design and colour of the dress and the medallion across her chest correspond to one of Velázquez's portraits of the Infanta as an adolescent.

ANTONIO BERNI (1905-1981)
La gallina ciega ('Blind Man's Buff')
tin, plastic containers, painted wood, fibreglass and oil on panel
63¾ x 78¾ in. (160.5 x 200 cm.)
New York, 24 November 1997, $607,500 (£359,467)
A record auction price for the artist

At the end of the 1950s, Berni created two fictional characters who would dominate his subject matter for over twenty years: Juanito Laguna, a boy from the slums, and Ramona Montiel, a prostitute. *La gallina ciega* of 1973 depicts Juanito's friends at play in the streets of a typical Buenos Aires neighbourhood. This work was presented for the first time in Mar del Plata in a one-man show in 1974 and was also included in the two most important retrospectives of the artist's work, both of which were held in Buenos Aires in the Museo Nacional de Bellas Artes, in 1984 and in 1997.

JOAQUÍN TORRES-GARCÍA (1874-1949)
Peinture Constructive
signed and dated
oil on canvas
29½ x 21¾ in. (75 x 55.2 cm.)
Painted in 1931
New York, 28 May 1997, $464,500 (£284,969)

JOAQUÍN TORRES-GARCÍA (1874-1949)
Ritmos, curvos y oblicuos en blanco y negro
signed and dated
tempera on board
32 x 19¾ in. (81.3 x 50.3 cm.)
Painted in 1938
New York, 24 November 1997, $332,500 (£196,746)

Born in Montevideo of a Catalan father and Uruguayan mother, Torres-García left South America at the age of seventeen to study mural painting in Spain, where he remained almost twenty years. He returned to Montevideo in 1910. After two years in New York in 1920-22, he went back to Europe, discovering Futurism in Italy. In 1924, he settled in Paris, allying himself with the abstract avant-garde. In 1930, in collaboration with the artist and critic Michel Seuphor, he founded the influential review *Cercle et Carré (Circulo y Cuadrado)*. In 1932 he returned definitively to Uruguay, where he established an art school and wrote works on art theory, promoting in particular Constructivist and Kinetic art.

Peinture constructive dates from his Paris period and is an example of what Torres-García called 'Constructive Universalism', a style which united the austerely geometrical forms of neoplasticism with human and figurative elements.

The composition of *Ritmos, curvos y oblicuos* occupies the enigmatic territory between abstraction, representation and symbolism. The irregular forms stacked up in horizontal registers evoke not only Inca stone walls and pre-Columbian pottery but also biomorphic fragments and even machined volumes. There are no doubt echoes of Léger *circa* 1912-14 and of Malevich, but Torres-García has fused his sources of inspiration to create his own unique style.

A River Nymph
[one of three terracotta figures]
French or Italian, 18th century
17 in. (43.2 cm.) high
London, 1 July 1997, £23,000 ($38,180) for set of three

Furniture, Sculpture
& Carpets

ARTS OF FRANCE

THE cultural force of France has been all-pervasive over the last three centuries. When Massialot, the great writer on gastronomy, wrote at the beginning of the 18th century that 'there is no one who would not dine *à la française*,' he was referring not only to food prepared in the French manner, but also to the French manner of serving that food in tureens and dishes of French manufacture, in an entirely French ambience. This is somewhat paradoxical, given that, for two centuries, at least half of the countries of Europe were at some point at war with France. The demand for all things French has been insatiable and now, at the end of the 20th century, the tradition of collecting the arts of France still flourishes.

NICOLAS LANCRET (1690-1743)
La halte de chasseurs
oil on canvas
39⅜ x 44½ in. (100 x 113cm.)
New York, 21 October 1997, $816,500 (£500,920)

17th century style fabrics and hung with pictures from the period.

Paintings attracted some of the highest prices, including three new artists' auction records, one of them for Nicolas Lancret's *La halte de chasseurs*, a well-documented work lost for most of this century. The very embodiment of the rococo, this picture shows Lancret to be perhaps the most stylish follower of Watteau. Watteau's own *Fête Champêtre: La Musette*, similarly fresh to the auction block (its last appearance had been in 1913), greatly exceeded estimate and realized $475,500. Record prices were also set for Charles Meynier and for Jean-Baptiste Huet: the latter's *A Pride of Lions*, a feline portrait com-

However, the spectacular dispersals of the late 18th century, when Versailles itself was put on the auction block, and the 19th century, such as the Christie's sales of the Watson-Taylor collection in 1825 and of works of art from Hamilton Palace in 1882, are a thing of the past. Last fall it was left to Christie's international team of specialists to bring together, in New York, a carefully chosen selection of the finest French furniture, paintings, sculpture, silver and porcelain, to evoke something of the scope and magnificence of those past sales. Presented together, instead of in specialized sales, such works of the fine and decorative arts could be seen as they were intended, as a part of the rich tradition of the golden age of France.

In other respects, too, the 'Arts of France' sale broke new ground. Its lavish catalogue, edited by Dr. Alain Gruber, departed from the usual practice and adopted a chronological rather than generic approach. The pre-sale exhibition, arranged under the direction of M. Hubert de Givenchy as a series of room settings, also enabled one to consider the objects in context. For example, a superb collection of Louis XIV Boulle furniture, which sold for nearly $2 million, was displayed in an *enfilade* of rooms decorated with

memorating the birth in 1802 of two female lion cubs at the Paris zoo, set a new record at $442,500.

The most expensive piece of the day, however, was not a picture or a piece of furniture, but a magnificent clock from the workshop of André-Charles Boulle, of bronze embellished with ormolu, tortoiseshell and ebony, which sold for $992,500. Its monumentality and vigorous decoration are rooted firmly in the baroque classicism of the end of Louis XIV's reign, but the asymmetry of the feminine figure surmounting it looks forward to the daintier forms of the ensuing decades. Two other versions of this model are known, one in the Wallace Collection and the other at Waddesdon Manor. It was consigned by the American collector Mrs. Nancy Richardson, who was also the owner of the second most expensive lot of the day, a ravishing commode by Benneman, which had been delivered as a pair to Louis XVI while his family was confined to the Tuileries in 1792. A mere three years later the pair was sold at auction in one of the great dispersals of treasures that followed the fall of the *ancien régime*. In 1997 it sold for $937,500, while the total for the day was just over $16 million.

A Louis XIV ormolu-mounted patinated bronze, tortoiseshell and ebony Mantel Clock
André-Charles Boulle, Paris, *circa* 1715
31½ in. (80cm.) high, 20 in. (51cm.) wide, 10 in. (25.5cm.) deep
New York, 21 October 1997, $992,500 (£608,896)

ADAM AND CHIPPENDALE:
A UNIQUE COLLABORATION

THE illustrious pair of sofas and armchairs designed by Robert Adam and made in 1765 by Thomas Chippendale for Sir Lawrence Dundas' town house at 19 Arlington Street were the first examples of Chippendale furniture fully documented in an original bill to be auctioned in London since July 1992, when Christie's sold a ravishing pair of silvered girandoles commissioned for Harewood House and a handsome pair of neoclassical marquetry commodes formerly at Burton Constable. For furniture connoisseurs, the chance to acquire, from a descendant of the original owner, a part of this celebrated suite was the event of the year, if not the decade, and prices were correspondingly high, the chairs fetching £1.7 million and the sofas £1.54 million.

Sir Lawrence Dundas, who belonged to the younger branch of an old Scottish family, amassed a huge fortune from lucrative army contracts: according to Boswell, he was 'a cunning, shrewd man of the world'. He was also a man of culture, who displayed great discernment as a patron, employing a constellation of important cabinet-makers, including Vile & Cobb, France & Bradburn, Fell & Turton, Thomas Chippendale, Samuel Norman, Pierre Langlois and James Lawson, to furnish his many properties.

Chippendale's bill invoices furniture for 19 Arlington Street and Aske Hall, Yorkshire, between July 1763 and January 1766, amounting to £1,123. The most expensive ensemble, a suite consisting of eight armchairs and four sofas, was ordered for the Great Room at the London house. Its exceptional quality is underlined by the price – each chair (excluding the luxurious crimson silk damask covers which Sir Lawrence supplied) cost £20, which is exactly twice the figure Chippendale charged for the most expensive chairs at Harewood House. The sofas cost £54 apiece. The entry in Chippendale's account reads: '9 July 1765. To 8 large Arm Chairs exceeding Richly Carv'd in the Antick manner & Gilt in oil Gold Stuff'd and covered with your own Damask and

A pair of George III giltwood Armchairs, 1765
Designed by Robert Adam (1728-1792) and made by
Thomas Chippendale (1718-1779)
London, 3 July 1997, £1,706,500 ($2,832,790)

strong Castors on the feet £160. / 4 large sofas Exceeding Rich to Match the chairs £216'.

When the documentation proving Chippendale's authorship of the suite was first discovered thirty years ago, what excited furniture historians was the existence, in the Sir John Soane's Museum, of a drawing by Robert Adam for one of the sofas, dated 1764. This was the first firm evidence that Chippendale ever executed furniture after a design supplied by the leading neoclassical architect, and at present it remains a solitary instance of such collaboration between the two men. Adam of course charged patrons for designs (on this occasion Dundas paid £5), while Chippendale provided them free to potential customers.

In 1764 the neoclassical style was still a novelty in England, and Sir Lawrence must have been convinced that only a professionally trained architect, such as Adam, who had studied ancient remains in Rome, rather than Chippendale (regarded at the time as a mere tradesman), was competent to handle the 'Antick' style. Chippendale, however, rapidly mastered the new idiom, and there is abundant evidence that his skill as a furniture designer soon earned him the respect of Robert Adam, who was happy for him to furnish some of his most splendid interiors. Letters show that the two men worked harmoniously together at Nostell Priory and Harewood House, although Adam expected, as a matter of courtesy, to be consulted about proposed furnishing schemes for rooms he had designed.

The unique Adam/Chippendale suite survived intact until the historic Arlington Street sale, held at Christie's on 26 April 1934, when one sofa and four chairs were sold for 360 guineas, the rest being taken to Aske Hall, where they remained together until the recent sale.

CHRISTOPHER GILBERT, F.S.A.
CHAIRMAN OF THE FURNITURE HISTORY SOCIETY
AND PRESIDENT OF THE CHIPPENDALE SOCIETY

A pair of George III giltwood Sofas, 1765
Designed by Robert Adam (1728-1792) and made by Thomas Chippendale (1718-1779)
86 in. (218.5 cm.) wide; 45½ in. (116 cm.); 36 in. (91.5 cm.) deep
The Property of the Marquess of Zetland and the 3rd Marquess of Zetland's Will Trust
London, 3 July 1997, £1,541,500 ($2,558,890)

A Louis XVI ormolu and patinated bronze-mounted mahogany Commode,
circa 1787, by Guillaume Benneman (d.1811), *maître* in 1785
38¼ in. (97 cm.) high; 65 in. (165 cm.) wide; 25 in. (63.5 cm.) deep
The Property of Nancy Richardson
New York, 21 October 1997, $937,500 (£571,875)

This magnificent commode, along with its pair, which is now in the Louvre, was delivered in 1787 to Madame Thierry de Ville d'Avray for her bedroom in the *Garde-Meuble*, now the Hôtel Crillon. In 1783, her husband purchased the position of *intendant et contrôleur général des meubles de la couronne*, which involved responsibility for the furnishing and upkeep of the royal châteaux. The commode was subsequently used in Louis XVI's *Cabinet du Conseil* at the Tuileries in 1792.

Guillaume Benneman, *ébéniste au service de la couronne* from 1786 to 1792, was one of the finest cabinet-makers of his day. Chosen by the *Garde-Meuble* as a less expensive alternative to the *marchand-mercier* Dominique Daguerre, he worked almost exclusively for the crown, supplying furniture to the palaces of Versailles and Fontainebleau.

A Charles X bronze and Roman micro-mosaic Centre Table, dated 1828
The micro-mosaic and marble top by Michelangelo Barberi (1787-1867)
42½ in. (108 cm.) diameter; 29 in. (74 cm.) high
London, 12 June 1997, £287,500 ($469,488)

Michelangelo Barberi was one of the most famous *mosaicisti* in Rome in the early 19th century, establishing his reputation with *Il trionfo d'Amore*, a mosaic bought by Tsar Nicholas I in 1827, which marked the beginning of a long trading relationship with Russia. The Bacchic theme of the table top, with its portrait of the Roman god of wine, is continued in the bronze panther-pelt used as a stretcher cloth and the amphorae-fashioned leg supports.

THE DUC D'AUMONT'S PORPHYRE GRIS VASES
A pair of Louis XVI ormolu-mounted porphyre gris and jaspe vert Vases
The design attributed to François-Joseph Bélanger (1744-1818), the mounts by Pierre Gouthière (1732-1814), *maître* in 1758
13¾ in. (35 cm.) high
London, 2 December 1997, £133,500 ($224,280)

These vases were made for the celebrated collection of ormolu-mounted hardstones formed by the duc
d'Aumont who, while responsible for the *Menus-Plaisirs*, commissioned magnificent works of art for his
collection. For the *Menus-Plaisirs*, the duc retained the services of both the designer François-Joseph Bélanger
and the most famous of all French 18th-century *ciseleurs-doreurs*, Pierre Gouthière, who executed the ormolu
mounts for these vases.

At the duc d'Aumont's astonishing nine-day sale in December 1782, the vases were bought by Paillet on
behalf of Queen Marie-Antoinette. In 1793 they are recorded in the first catalogue of the *Musée du Louvre*.
Their subsequent history is somewhat obscure, but they may well have been sold in the Directoire sales of
1798. They reappeared in Paris in 1837, when they were bought by the duc de Cambacérès.

THE CHÂTEAU D'EU VASES-CLOCHES
A pair of Louis XVI ormolu and Sèvres *bleu nouveau* porcelain *Vases-Cloches*,
circa 1772, designed by Jean Dulac (1704-1786)
and stamped with the château d'Eu inventory mark
17¾ in. (45 cm.) high, closed
London, 2 December 1997, £353,500 ($593,880)

These *vases-cloches* are possibly those designed and supplied by the *marchand-bijoutier* Jean Dulac to Madame du Barry before 1774 for the château de Louveciennes. They may have been sold during the Revolution and were recorded in the collection of the former Second Consul to Napoleon, Jean-Jacques Régis de Cambacérès in 1808. In 1814 he was exiled and his hôtel and its contents were sold to the duchesse d'Orléans. In 1821 the duc d'Orléans, later King Louis-Philippe, inherited almost all the furniture, most of which he sent to the château d'Eu, and these vases bear the inventory mark of a crown above the stamp 'EU'. In 1857, three years after the death of Louis-Philippe, the vases, along with the rest of his possessions, were sold at Christie's in London on 17 June, to Nieuwenhuys for £245.

Jean Dulac, *marchand-gantier-parfumeur* by 1740, was a successful *marchand-mercier* and specialized in the commercialization of Sèvres porcelain. He was appointed *marchand privilégié du Roi* on 16 May 1753 and, following that, *marchand-bijoutier*.

A Louis XVI Clock, *Les Porteuses*
circa 1790, by Pierre-Philippe Thomire (1751-1843) and Jean-Antoine Lépine (1720-1814)
25¼ in. (64 cm.) wide; 21 in. (53.5 cm.) high; 7¼ in. (18.7 cm.) deep
Monaco, 13 December 1997, FFr.892,500 (£90,876; $152,862)

This superb clock was acquired in about 1790 by Jean Grillon des Chapelles (1732-1813) and stood on the mantelpiece of the *grand salon* of his hôtel on the rue d'Anjou Saint Honoré in Paris. In 1803 he donated the *hôtel* to his children, and the clock, retained by his eldest son, was later moved to the château des Chapelles, Indre, where it remained until its recent sale. Both the design, which was possibly inspired by an engraving by Herbert Robert in *Recueil des griffonis,* published by l'abbé de Saint Non in 1771-1773, and the execution of this clock, have been attributed to the celebrated *fondeur doreur* Pierre-Philippe Thomire.

THE HENRY HOPE WRITING-TABLE

A Regency ormolu-mounted and brass-inlaid rosewood, ebony and parcel-gilt Writing-Table, *circa* 1805,
almost certainly designed by Thomas Hope (1769-1831), and attributed to George Oakley (1773-1840)
52¼ in. (132.5 cm.) wide; 29½ in. (75 cm.) high; 27 in. (68.5 cm.) deep
London, 3 July 1997, £221,500 ($370,500)

This table was almost certainly designed by the connoisseur Thomas Hope, the influential pioneer of the French Grecian style, for his brother Henry Hope (1774-1839), a philanthropist who lived at 3 Seymour Place, Mayfair. Its exotic woods and classical motifs show the contemporary fascination with classical ornament and design, popularized by Thomas Hope in his *Household Furniture and Interior Decoration* of 1807. The execution is attributed to George Oakley, a fashionable London cabinet-maker, who worked with exotic veneers and was a pioneer of 'Buhl' inlay. This table was acquired, along with some of the contents of 3 Seymour Place, when the house was bought in the second quarter of the 19th century by an ancestor of the present vendor.

A George I burr-walnut Bachelor's Chest
42¼ in. (107.5 cm.) wide; 34¾ in. (88 cm.) high; 16 in. (40.5 cm.) deep
Sold from The Parry Collection
London, 24 April 1997, £265,500 ($430,906)

The collection of English walnut and Welsh oak furniture assembled by John and Norma Parry was one of the most fascinating to have been formed in the latter half of the 20th century. The most vivid demonstration of the rigorous focus of the collection was its sixteen walnut bachelor's chests, each significantly different from the others and, as a group, illustrating the full spectrum of design and construction. Their aged walnut surfaces contrasted with the deep reddish-brown 'Dragon's-blood' patina of the Welsh oak.

THE WELLER-POLEY SUITE
A set of sixteen early George III mahogany Dining-Chairs,
circa 1760, in the manner of Mayhew and Ince
36½ in (93 cm.) high
The Property of the Trustees of the J.H. Weller-Poley Will Trust
London, 3 July 1997, £375,500 ($628,212)

This set of sixteen dining or 'parlour' chairs was almost certainly supplied to George Weller-Poley of Boxted Hall, Bury St Edmunds, Suffolk in about 1760. Highly sophisticated in design, this remarkable suite displays a rare mix of design, decorative detail and supreme quality of carving. The French rococo-inspired splats of interlaced and arcaded form, coupled with the square leg with unique fretwork of bells, rosettes and foliate scrolls, show the original and creative nature of furniture design in London in the 1750s and 1760s. The entire suite, comprising sixteen dining-chairs, four stools and a pair of card-tables, realized £507,600 ($842,616).

THE BELLINTER TABLES
A pair of George II white-painted Side Tables,
circa 1740, in the manner of William Kent (1684-1748)
61 in. (156.5 cm.) wide; 34 in. (87 cm.) high; 29 in. (75.5 cm.) deep
London, 17 April 1997, £595,500 ($967,092)

According to a family tradition, these magnificent marble-slabbed side tables were probably supplied to John Preston (d. 1753) in about 1740, for the Hall at Bellinter House, County Meath, the house designed for him by the celebrated Irish Palladian architect Richard Castle. The eagle and dolphin are emblematic of the Roman god Jupiter and the goddess Venus, and the theme was echoed in the statues that stood in niches above these tables. The design of the eagle-supported pier table is associated with Lord Burlington's protégé, William Kent, who featured Roman eagles in his illustrations for Alexander Pope's translation of the *Odyssey*. The marble tops inlaid with pietra dura are intentionally 'Roman' in design with their Apollonian sunbursts and Greek-key surround. They were almost certainly executed in the same workshops as the table tops from Lord Burlington's magnificent side tables at Chiswick House, which were sold from the Bute Collection at Christie's, London in July 1996 and which have now returned to Chiswick House.

THE SPENCER HOUSE PALM ROOM CHAIRS
A pair of George II giltwood Armchairs, *circa* 1758
Attributed to John Vardy (1718-1765) and John Gordon (fl.1748-96)
41½ in. (105 cm.) high
New York, 17 October 1997, $717,500 (£444,850)

These magnificent armchairs form part of a suite created for the Palm Room at Spencer House, London, the culmination of the architect John Vardy's elaborate decorative scheme for the house that he created for John, 1st Earl Spencer (1734-83) and his wife Georgiana Poyntz. The palm, considered a symbol of peace and victory, was associated with both Apollo and Venus: palm-trees with interwoven branches were symbolic of love and marriage, while the palm of victory was an Apollonian attribute. Vardy's project at Spencer House revolved around the symbolic and emblematic resonances of the palm.

The execution of the chairs can be attributed to John Gordon, a fashionable cabinet-maker who supplied furniture to Earl Spencer at Althorp in the 1770s.

A German ivory-inlaid walnut and marquetry Bureau-Cabinet,
Mainz *circa* 1740-1750
55 in. (140 cm.) wide; 79 in. (201 cm.) high; 25½ in. (65 cm.) deep
London, 30 October 1997, £122,500 ($204,575)

This ivory-inlaid walnut bureau-cabinet shows the fluidity of shape, pierced angle volutes and scrolling angles flanking the writing-slope characteristic of Mainz cabinet-making in the mid-18th century. An unusual feature of this cabinet is the fine ivory inlay depicting scenes of the Annunciation and the Assumption of the Virgin, a decorative effect more usually associated with cabinets made in Frankfurt and Braunschweig. This bureau-cabinet relates in details to a small number of master drawings from the years 1742-47 by cabinet-makers such as Joseph Wimer, Jakob Weinheimer and Joseph Hoffmann.

MASTERPIECES OF AMERICAN FURNITURE

GRACEFUL, elegant and masterfully carved, the Classical parcel-gilt rosewood card table made by Charles Honoré Lannuier (1779-1819) in New York City, *circa* 1815, was one of the most unusual and highly coveted 19th century objects in the American furniture sales this year.

Lannuier arrived in New York in 1803 from Paris, where he received his training as a cabinet-maker at the time when Europe's élite were embracing the Classical style. He opened a workshop on 60 Broad Street, lower Manhattan, and quickly gained renown for furniture designs which strongly relied on Greek and Egyptian motifs, such as caryatid supports and Greek-key borders on tables. Along with Duncan Phyfe (1769-1854), he designed and produced the best examples of furniture in the Classical style

A Chippendale carved mahogany Armchair
New York City, 1760-1780
40 in. (101.5 cm.) high; 30 in. (76.2 cm.) wide; 23 in. (58.5 cm.) deep
New York, 8 October 1997, $387,500 (£240,250)

private collections, will be exhibited. Christie's is proud to be a sponsor of this exhibition, the first retrospective devoted to Lannuier.

18th century furniture made in New York is rare, owing to the devastating fires which have swept through the city in the course of its history. Important furniture, such as the Lannuier card table, rarely appears on the market. Christie's discovery of a lavishly carved and decorated armchair, made for the New York merchant, Samuel Verplanck (1739-1820), inspired tremendous enthusiasm and led to a record price of $387,000. The consignor of the armchair, Gwendoline Verplanck, is an eighth-generation descendant of Samuel Verplanck, a prominent banker and leading member of New York society. More than any other colonial city, New York imitated English

in America. Christie's established the record for any piece of 19th century American furniture in January 1991, when a pier table branded by Lannuier sold for $704,000.

The card table, sold on 17 June 1997, has a companion piece which was discovered in an English country house and sold on 21 January 1996, in New York, for $310,000. Christie's example, separated from its companion piece two generations ago, turned up in a direct descendant's summer house on Rhode Island. The table sold for $497,500 to the same collector. These two masterpieces by Lannuier, who along with Duncan Phyfe, is considered to have been the premier American classical furniture designer of his time, have thus been reunited.

A major exhibition of the work of Lannuier will open in New York at the Metropolitan Museum of Art, in March of 1998; *Charles Honoré Lannuier: Cabinetmaker from Paris*. These tables, along with many other documented works from both public and

designs of the period: this armchair relates to a design by Robert Manwaring, published in 1765.

The highlight of the 1997 sale season was the magnificent Bliss family Chippendale chest-on-chest made in Boston in 1770-1785. Diminutive in proportions and surmounted by a superbly carved water-gilt eagle, this chest-on-chest passed down the family of Jonathan Bliss, a loyalist who fled from Boston to New Brunswick, Canada and became the province's first Chief of Justice. Discovered by Christie's in the home of a direct descendant living in London, this chest-on-chest sold for $297,000 in 1985 and was consigned by the purchaser in January 1997, when it sold for $1.2 million, a record for a chest-on-chest.

JOHN HAYS
HEAD OF THE AMERICAN FURNITURE AND DECORATIVE ARTS
DEPARTMENT, CHRISTIE'S NEW YORK

The Bliss Chippendale carved and blocked mahogany Chest-on-Chest
Boston, 1770-1785
85¼ in. (216.2 cm.) high; 39½ in. (100.3 cm.) wide; 21 in. (53.3 cm.) deep
New York, 18 January 1997, $1,212,500 (£730,422)

A classical carved and parcel-gilt rosewood Card Table
labelled by Charles Honoré Lannuier (1779-1819), New York City, *circa* 1815
30 in. (76.2 cm.) high; 36 in. (91.5 cm.) wide; 18 in. (45.8 cm.) deep
New York, 17 June 1997, $497,500 (£303,354)

The 1st Viscount Cobham commissioned Michael Rysbrack (1694-1770) to carve, between 1728 and 1730, a series of seven statues of the Saxon gods who gave their names to the days of the week, to adorn a rustic tempietto in the park at Stowe. Six were full-length and only Sunna, the Sun god, was half-length, in accordance with the iconographic description of *Sunna* in Richard Verstegan's *A Restitution of decayed Intelligence in Antiquities* (1605): 'Half a naked man, the face ringed by fire; he holds a burning wheel to signify his course round the world'. Cobham, imbued with Whiggish, liberal convictions, believed that the Saxons had championed a democratic spirit in public affairs. He also believed he could trace his own ancestry back to the Saxons.

A carved Portland stone half-length figure of the god Sunna
circa 1728-1730, by Michael Rysbrack (1694-1770)
34¾ in. (88.3cm.) high
London, 1 July 1997, £133,500 ($222,011)
Now in the Victoria and Albert Museum.

Johann Christoph Ludwig Lücke belonged to a dynasty of sculptors, whose greatest achievements were in the field of ivory carving. He was arguably the most distinguished member of the clan, although his inability to remain in the same place for more than a few years strongly suggests that he was a difficult character. First documented at the porcelain factory at Meissen, he later worked at Dresden, Höchst, Fürstenberg, Vienna and London. His production was impressively wide-ranging, but it is above all as a satirically acerbic portraitist that he is most admired. In the present piece, the protagonist is carved in the round and shown full-length. It is an unusually ambitious display of virtuosity, in which the almost sneering quality of the facial expression is entirely typical.

A carved ivory group of a ruler, probably Friedrich Christian, Elector of Saxony, by Ludwig von Lücke
mid-18th century
10⅛ in. (25.7cm.)
London, 1 July 1997, £45,500 ($75,667)

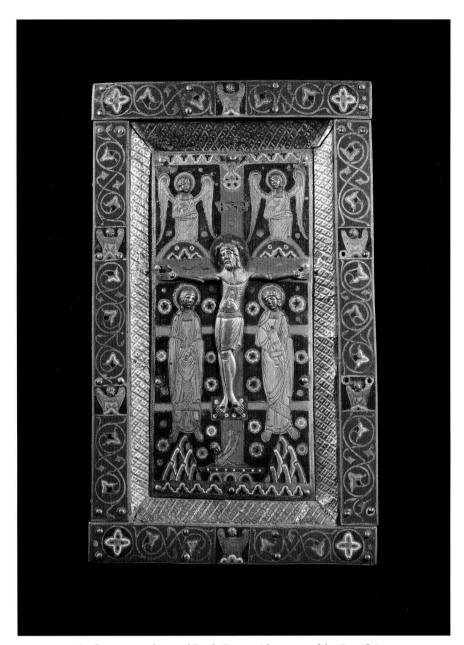

A gilt-copper and enamel Book Cover with a scene of the Crucifixion
by the Master G. Alpais
12⅞ x 7⅞ in. (32.9 x 20cm.)
Sold from the Property of the Giannalisa Feltrinelli Foundation
London, 1 July 1997, £276,500 ($459,820)

Only about 200 Limoges book covers are known, varying in quality and state of preservation. This late 12th century example is unusually complete, still mounted on its original wooden board and retaining its original outer border. Indeed, earlier this century when it was in the possession of Grand Duke Karl Alexander of Saxe-Weimar-Eisenach, it even had the plaque that adorned its back cover, but this has since disappeared. The Master G. Alpais was responsible for one of the greatest *chefs d'oeuvres* of Limoges art – a ciborium of about the same date as this plaque, signed with his name and now in the Louvre. By a simple but ingenious expedient, four of the nails used to attach the cover to its support double as the nails that hold Christ to the cross.

A gilt-bronze Statuette of a horse
Florentine, early 16th century
8¾ in. (22.25 cm.) high, 8 in. (20 cm.) wide, above a later ebonized wooden base
New York, 29 January 1997, $684,500 (£417,545)

This gilt-bronze statuette is one of the finest Renaissance sculptures to appear on the market in recent years. Cast solid, the bronze was made in Florence during the first quarter of the 16th century. The anonymous artist derived the pose of the horse from Leonardo's designs for the monument to Francesco Sforza and based the mane on that of Verrocchio's monument to Bartolomeo Colleoni in Venice. The detailing and chasing is of jewel-like quality, and the horse is animated with extraordinary vitality and vigour.

An important American white marble Figure of Sardanapalus, last of the great Assyrian kings
by William Wetmore Story, signed and dated 1883,
82 in. (233.5cm.) high, overall
London, 2 October 1997, £155,500 ($250,510)

Achieving the highest price since 1990 for a single-figure 19th century marble sculpture at auction in London, *Sardanapalus* was a major rediscovery of a lost work by Wetmore Story (1819-1895). The sale of the marble established a world record price for the sculptor, the most celebrated American working in Rome during the second half of the 19th century. Acquired directly from Wetmore Story's studio by Cyril Flower, later Lord Battersea, *Sardanapalus* was originally placed in the vestibule of the latter's Marble Arch residence, Surrey House. Thought to represent Ashurbanipal, the fortieth and last of the great Assyrian kings, *Sardanapalus* was one of the last in the series of Story's works which took as their subjects the mysterious, tragic characters of the pre-Greek civilizations, unearthed by Sir Austen Layard and his successors in the valleys of the Nile, Tigris and Euphrates and the deserts of the Holy Land.

A pair of French ormolu and *pietra dura*-mounted ebonized, brass and tortoiseshell 'Boulle' marquetry Cabinets-on-Stands
by Monbro Aîné, Paris, mid-19th century
65 in. (165cm.) high
London, 2 October 1997, £35,600 ($57,352)

This fine pair of cabinets-on-stands, in the Louis XIV style and by the celebrated Parisian *ébéniste*, Monbro Aîné, was the highlight of a collection of eight pieces sold on 2 October 1997 on behalf of a European princely family and formerly belonging to the second daughter of Tsar Nicholas I, Olga Nikolaevna, Grand Duchess of Russia and Queen of Württemberg.

An Agra Carpet
North West India, late 19th century
23 ft. x 14 ft. (701 x 444 cm.)
New York, 17 December 1997, $239,000 (£147,530)

The most popular design of Agra carpets is directly descended from a 17th century Isfahan prototype, already copied in India at the time. This carpet has exactly that design but a most unusual and attractive green background colour. Both colour and condition are important factors in making this carpet perfect for today's decorator's taste.

A Star Ushak Carpet
West Anatolia, late 16th century
15 ft. 9 in. x 8 ft. 1 in. (479 x 246 cm.)
London, 24 April 1997, £91,700 ($148,554)

left:

This carpet is an exceptional example of one of the best known types of 16th century carpet. It has a very unusual border design: while at first sight it appears totally symmetric, a closer examination of the minor motifs reveals an inventive variation on a theme. Early Ushak weavers often incorporated minor motifs – typical of village weaving – into carpets destined for export to the West.

near right:

In 1902 the great art dealer Joseph Duveen lent this carpet to Westminster Abbey to be used on the dais beneath the throne on which King Edward VII was crowned. It is also a carpet of considerable interest to scholars, showing a version of a design which was very popular in carpets made in the capital, Isfahan, but less common in the distant provinces. Particularly interesting is the motif of Khorassan parrots rather than Isfahan peacocks.

far right:

Within the Islamic world, it is in Mughal India that one finds the greatest interest in natural motifs. Many painted studies of single flowers have survived, and this interest spread to many art forms as shown in this carpet. A number of carpets showing flowers on a red ground exist, the majority of which were in the collection of the Maharaja of Jaipur at Amber. Inventory details on labels on the reverse of the carpets there show dates of acquisition which go back to 1632, although the majority in this style were purchased in the 1650s. The present example shows a rarer variation on the theme, in which floral sprays are enclosed within a lattice.

King Edward VII's Coronation Carpet
Khorassan, North East Persia, 17th century
22 ft. 1 in. x 9 ft. 10 in. (670 x 299 cm.)
Sold from the Collection of Yves Mikaeloff
London, 16 October 1997, £111,500 ($180,630)

A Mughal Carpet
Northern India or Lahore, mid-17th century
18 ft. 11 in. x 8 ft. 1 in. (576 x 246 cm.)
London, 24 April 1997, £150,000 ($243,000)

A Sultanabad Carpet [detail]
Central Persia, third quarter 19th century
17 ft. 5 in. x 13 ft. 8 in. (531 x 417 cm.)
New York, 17 December 1997, $178,500 (£110,185)

In the second half of the 19th century carpet dealers from Western countries began themselves to travel to Persia to select carpets suitable for export. The Manchester-based firm of Ziegler and Co. soon realized that they could commission weavers, particularly in Sultanabad, to make carpets which met the specific needs of their European clients.

This is a good example of such a carpet designed for a Western market: the soft palette is particularly un-Persian. The taste of that period is once again in fashion, which, together with the excellent condition of this carpet, explains the very high price it realized.

A German rococo jewelled and gold–mounted
hardstone presentation Snuff–Box
circa 1775
3¼ in. (82 mm.) wide
Geneva, 19 November 1997, SFr.97,000 ($69,840)

SILVER, OBJECTS OF VERTU, JEWELLERY, PORCELAIN AND DECORATIVE ARTS

A Victorian silver Soup-Tureen, Cover and Stand
Maker's mark of John Mortimer and John S. Hunt, London, 1841
stand 24½ in. (62.2 cm) long, 519 ozs. (1,6147 gr.)
New York, 15 April 1997, $277,500 (£172,050)

above:
This massive tureen, originally one of a pair, was probably commissioned to commemorate the 1st Marquess of Westminster's creation as Knight of the Garter in 1841. The sculptural ornament is enriched by the applied armorials, including the Marquess' coronet on the cover and the hound-form supporters, which also serve as the tureen's handles.

left:
The design of these wine-coasters, decorated with heavily cast grapevines, was first introduced by Benjamin Smith II, around 1805. Most coasters of this type, including the present set, were retailed by Rundell, Bridge and Rundell, the Royal Goldsmiths, and remained popular for about ten years. It is extremely rare to find a set of eight wine coasters of this model, which were usually made in pairs or sets of four.

A set of eight George III silver-gilt Wine-Coasters
Maker's mark of Benjamin Smith II, London, 1807
5⅜ in. (13.7 cm.) diam., 199 oz. (6,201 gr.) gross
New York, 20 October 1997, $629,500 (390,290)

A George II silver Soup-Tureen in the form of a green Turtle (*Chelonia Mydas*)
Maker's mark of Paul de Lamerie, London, 1750
18⅝ in. (47 cm.) long, 161 ozs. (5,018 grs.)
London, 9 July 1997, £815,500 ($1,373,302)

This recently re-discovered tureen, made in 1750, shortly before the death of Paul de Lamerie (1688-1751), the greatest English goldsmith, is a significant addition to the surviving body of his work. This piece is now believed to have been commissioned by John Hill (1689-1753) of Thornton Dale, County Yorshire, Commissioner of Customs and MP for Higham Ferris. The only other recorded English 18th century tureen incorporating silver in the form of a turtle appears to be that made by Paul Crespin (1694-1770), also of 1750, now in the collection of the Marquess of Bath at Longleat. Lamerie and Crespin retailed each other's work, although this arrangement seems to have been confined to the 1720s.

This Italian inkstand, made by one of the leading Turinese silversmiths, Lorenzo Lavy (1720- 1789), is engraved with the arms of the House of Savoy, Kings of Piedmont-Sardinia. Lavy trained in the workshop of François-Thomas Germain in Paris, before returning to Turin where he became Silversmith to the Court in 1750. The design for this royal inkstand reflects his French training and can be related to the work of one of the leading sculptors of his day, Francesco Ladatte (1706-1787), who was himself influenced by the French rococo designer Juste-Aurèle Meissonnier (1695-1750).

An Italian silver-gilt Inkstand
Maker's mark of Lorenzo Lavy,
assaymaster Bartolomeo Pagliani, Turin, *circa* 1760
33 cm. (13 in.) long, 1469 gr. (47 oz.)
Geneva, 19 and 21 May, SF355,500 (£153,232)

This rare soup-tureen strongly resembles another work attributed to Giambattista Boucheron, which bears the same assay-master's marks and is now in the Hermitage, St. Petersburg. Boucheron was appointed royal goldsmith in 1763 and director of the royal collection of silver in 1775. He studied Roman antiquity and was influenced by the work and stylistic repertoire of Piranesi, as seen in this soup tureen.

An Italian silver Soup-Tureen and Stand
Attributed to Giambattista Boucheron,
1st assaymaster Matteo Promis,
2nd assaymaster Guiseppe Fontana, Turin, *circa* 1790
stand 59 cm., 8,150 gr.
Rome, 30 April 1997, Lit.199,050,000 (£71,089)

This cadinett, which was used to hold the monarch's eating accessories, comprises a closed compartment for salt, pepper and other spices, and a flat tray on which was placed the king's bread and napkin. This cadinett is one of only six examples of its kind to survive. It was originally part of a dinner service commissioned by Augustus the Strong of Augsburg, presumably for the wedding of his son, the Electoral Crown Prince, Fredrich Augustus and the Archduchess Maria Josepha, daughter of the Emperor Josef I, on 13 September 1719.

A German silver-gilt Cadinett
Attributed to Gottlieb Mentzel, Augsburg, 1718
21.2 cm (8⅜ in.) wide, 1172 gr. (37 oz.)
Geneva, 19 and 21 May 1997, SF212,500 (£91,584)

This secular casket is applied with the enamelled arms of Pedro de Meras, great-grandson of Sancho Garcia de Meras, who married Aldonza Martinez de la Plaza, sister and heiress of the celebrated Asturian captain Garcia Fernandez de la Plaza. The arms are charged with symbols commemorating Garcia Fernandez de la Plaza's valour during the 1535 campaign led by the Emperor Charles V. In Tunis, he captured and beheaded the elder Barbarossa brother and four of his captains. Queen Joanna the Mad and her son, the Emperor Charles V, subsequently granted him permission to bear representations of the five heads on his coat-of-arms.

A Spanish enamelled silver Casket
Unmarked except for later French control marks,
circa 1650
30.5 cm (12 in.) high, 4292 gr. (138 oz.) gross
Geneva, 19 and 21 May 1997, SF256,500 (£110,295)

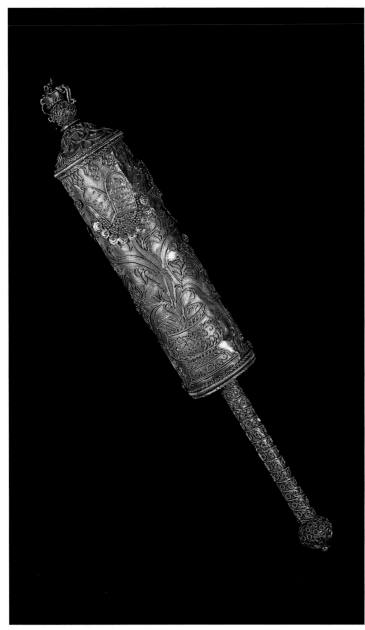

A rare Italian gold Scroll of Esther Case
probably Venice 17th century
8½ in. (21 cm.) long
Amsterdam, 25 November 1997, Nlg. 714,984 (£214,495)

An important silver and silver-gilt German Jewish Torah Ark with copper back
maker's mark of Johann Christoph Müller, Breslau, 1746-1758
24 cm. (20⅞ in.) high
Geneva, 17 and 19 November 1997, SFr. 718,500 (£308,955)

The scroll of Esther is one of the ceremonial objects used on the Purim holiday, which celebrates Queen Esther's success in preventing the extermination of the Jews by Haman. This antique Italian gold case, which contains a later handwritten text, was previously owned by various families of Jewish scholars in Northern Italy. It later came into the possession of the Montefiore family and then passed by descent to the last owner.

This exceptionally rare Torah ark, previously in the collection of the late Nathaniel Meyer Victor Rothschild, third Baron Rothschild, is the earliest of the four known arks of this kind. It is reminiscent of the numerous magnificent carved, wooden, polychrome and gilded arks which formed an indispensable part of East European (mainly Polish) Jewish art, and which were almost completely destroyed during the Second World War. The meticulous attention to detail, the elaborate foliate decoration and the shape and style of the present example, denote a strong Polish influence.

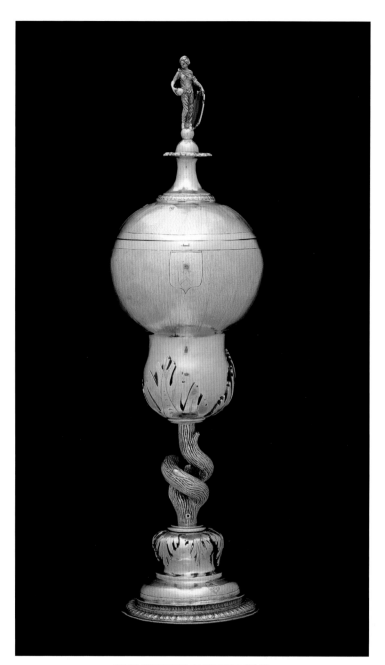

A Dutch silver dish
Middelburg, 1629
29.7 cm. (11.5 in.) diam., 494 gr.
Amsterdam, 25 November 1997, Nlg. 276,768 (£83,030)

THE TUCKER-DAYRELL CUP
An Elizabeth I parcel-gilt Cup and Cover
Maker's mark IE above three pellets, London, 1598
New York, 20 October 1997, $376,500 (£233,430)

This octagonal *puntschotel* is one of the rarest items of Dutch silver to appear on the market in recent years. Only eight of these dishes are known, all dating from before 1640. Five were made in Amsterdam, one in Utrecht and two in Middelburg. These Dutch *puntschotels* were already prized in the 17th century. The present example was exhibited at the Fries Museum, Leeuwarden in 1927, before being sold at auction as part of the Smulders Collection in The Hague in 1937.

The gourd-form cups enjoyed a brief period of popularity in England between 1570 and 1610. The twenty known examples of this distinctive shape are based on German designs, probably brought to England by immigrant silversmiths. This cup is believed to have been commissioned on the occasion of the marriage of George II Tucker, Prime Searcher of the Port of Gravesend, to Mary Dayrell of Kent, in 1598.

JEAN-ÉTIENNE LIOTARD (1702-1789)
The Prince of Wales, future King George III
enamel on copper, *circa* 1753-55
oval, 1⅞ in. (49 mm.) high
London, 21 October 1997, £128,500 ($209,664)

JEAN-BAPTISTE-JACQUES AUGUSTIN (1759-1832)
Charles-Ferdinand de Bourbon, duc de Berry
watercolour on ivory
oval, 3¹¹⁄₁₆ in. (94 mm.) high
London, 15 April 1997, £43,300 ($70,232)

The recently-discovered enamel miniature by Liotard is an outstanding addition to the group of five enamels painted by the Swiss artist during his first sojourn in London in 1753-55.

Charles-Ferdinand de Bourbon, duc de Berry, was a nephew of King Louis XVI of France. He settled in England in 1801, marrying Amy Brown; his family refused to recognize this union and forced him to marry Marie-Caroline de Bourbon-Siciles in 1816. He was murdered in 1820, the year this miniature was painted by Jean-Baptiste Augustin. Augustin was the most celebrated portrait miniaturist in France in the early 19th century.

The portrait, dated 1579, by Hilliard the most distinguished limner of the 16th century, demonstrates the transition from the illuminated manuscript to the Tudor portrait miniature. The coat-of-arms, painted on the reverse, would suggest that it represents Francis Lawley, High Sheriff of Shropshire.

NICHOLAS HILLIARD (1547-1619)
A young Gentleman, believed to be Francis Lawley
watercolour and bodycolour on vellum
rectangular, 4⅞ x 4¼ in. (125 x 111 mm.)
London, 21 October 1997, £73,000 ($119,574)

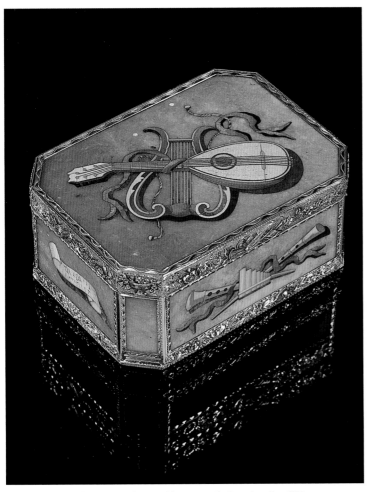

An Italian vari-colour gold-mounted *pietra dura* Snuff-Box
Florence, Opificio delle Pietre Dure, *circa* 1800
3⅛ in. (80 mm.) wide
Geneva, 21 May 1997, SFr. 223,500 (£96,105)

A Saxon hardstone and gold Snuff-Box
by Johann-Christian Neuber, Dresden, *circa* 1780
3½ in. (87 mm.) wide
Geneva, 21 May 1997, SFr. 333,500 (£143,405)

This snuff-box, inlaid with trophies of music in various hardstones, is one of two known examples with this particular design. It is a fine example of *pietra dura* mosaic produced by the Florentine Grand-Ducal workshop, the Opificio delle Pietre Dure, first established in the Casino di San Marco by Francesco I de' Medici in 1580.

This snuff-box is decorated with a portrait miniature of Elector Friedrich-Augustus III (1750-1827), son of Crown Prince Friedrich-Christian of Saxony and his wife Princess Maria-Antonia of Bavaria. Friedrich-Augustus III succeeded his father as Elector of Saxony in 1763 and was styled the first King of Saxony in 1806, by order of Napoleon I. He and his family were Neuber's most important patrons.

This writing set was commissioned by the Empress Elizabeth Petrovna (1709-1762) and bears the Imperial cypher. The daughter of Peter the Great, she succeeded to the throne in 1742, and during her reign the Empress enlarged the collections and embellished the palaces of her forbears.

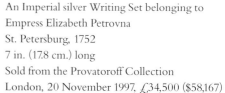

An Imperial silver Writing Set belonging to
Empress Elizabeth Petrovna
St. Petersburg, 1752
7 in. (17.8 cm.) long
Sold from the Provatoroff Collection
London, 20 November 1997, £34,500 ($58,167)

This *nécessaire* is a particularly fine example of the craftsmanship typical of the firm of Fabergé. On the death of Michael Perchin in 1903, Henrik Wigstrom took over as Fabergé's master craftsman, retaining the position until 1917, when he returned to his native Finland. The *nécessaire* was bought from the London showrooms of Fabergé in 1916 by Mrs. Psimenos, subsequently passed into the collection of the late Sir Charles Clore and was sold at Christie's Geneva in 1985.

A gold and guilloché enamel gemset *Nécesssaire*
by Fabergé, workmaster Henrik Wigström,
St. Petersburg, 1908-1917
3⅛ in. (8 cm.) long
Sold from the Kazan Collection
New York, 15 April 1997, $255,500 (£156,748)

A pair of monumental two-handled Campana Vases
by the Imperial Porcelain Factory, St. Petersburg, period of Nicholas I, 1840
37⅜ in. (95.5 cm.) high
London, 12 June 1997, £485,500 ($792,821)

These monumental vases are painted with Italianate landscapes, one after a painting by Jan Dirksz Both (1610-1652), the other possibly after the same artist or his brother, Andries Both (1612-1650). As the porcelain factory was part of the domain of the Emperor they were painted with copies of paintings in Imperial collections at the Winter Palace, the Hermitage and other residences.

A gold and silver-gilt mounted guilloché enamel Frame with Portrait Miniature
by Fabergé (1846-1920), workmaster Michael Perchin (1860-1903),
St. Petersburg, *circa* 1890
4⅜ in. (11.2 cm.) high
Sold from the Kazan Collection
New York, 15 April 1997, $365,500 (£224,233)

In its original box with the original label, this frame was probably bought by Harold F. MacCormick for his wife, Edith Rockefeller MacCormick, during their honeymoon in 1895. The daughter of John D. Rockefeller, Sr., Edith MacCormick was doyenne of Chicago society and a noted philanthropist. In 1913 she became a follower of Jung and lived for many years in Zurich.

FILIPP ANDREEVICH MALIAVIN (1869-1940)
Portrait of a Russian Peasant Girl
oil on canvas
42⅛ x 33¼ in. (107 x 87 cm.)
London, 20 November 1997, £56,500 ($95,259)
A record auction price for the artist

Born in Moscow, Maliavin was sent to study as an icon painter on Mount Athos. He abandoned his religious training, however, and returned to Russia, where he became a student to I. E. Repin at the St. Petersburg Academy of Arts from 1892 to 1899. He emigrated in 1925 and died in Nice in 1939. He is known particularly for his distinctive depictions of Russian peasantry and rural life. This early work attracted a high price as pre-Revolution portraits rarely appear on the market.

A diamond ring
24.46 carats, D colour, VVS2 clarity
Geneva, 20 May 1997
SFr.1,301,500 (£559,645)

An unmounted
pear-shaped fancy intense
blue diamond
5.15 carats, VS1 clarity,
potentially flawless
Geneva,
17 November 1997
SFr.1,433,500 (£616,405)

An unmounted
heart-shaped fancy blue
diamond
3.20 carats, VVS1 clarity,
potentially flawless
Geneva,
17 November 1997
SFr.839,500 (£360,985)

An Art Deco fancy coloured diamond pendent brooch,
circa 1925
London, 18 June 1997
£441,500 ($721,850)

An unmounted
circular-cut diamond
22.13 carats,
D colour, flawless
Hong Kong,
4 November 1997
HK$14,320,000 (£1,145,600)

An unmounted square-cut diamond
30.21 carats, D colour, internally flawless
New York, 27 October 1997
$1,927,500 (£1,179,620)

A diamond ring
by Repossi
37.85 carats, D colour, VVS2
clarity
Geneva, 20 May 1997
SFr.2,808,500 (£1,207,655)

A fancy intense yellow
diamond ring by Graff
46.47 carats, VS1 clarity
Geneva, 20 November 1997
SFr.993,500 (£427,205)

A fancy intense yellow diamond
cluster ring by Harry Winston
20.73 carats, VVS2 clarity
Geneva, 17 November 1997
SFr.1,873,500 (£805,605)

THE DEEPDENE DIAMOND
A treated yellow diamond
104.53 carats, VS1 clarity
Geneva, 20 November 1997
SFr.993,500 (£427,205)

A pair of fancy yellow diamond ear-pendants
by Bulgari
total weight of yellow diamonds 58.41 carats
Geneva, 20 November 1997
SFr.619,500 (£266,300)

A fancy intense yellow diamond
flower brooch
yellow diamond 23.35 carats, VS1 clarity
New York, 27 October 1997
$684,500 (£418,910)

A Burmese ruby ring
ruby 15.04 carats
St. Moritz, 19 February 1997
SFr.641,500 (£275,845)

A Burmese star ruby and yellow
diamond ring by Carvin French
ruby 11.88 carats
Hong Kong, 4 November 1997
HK$1,500,000 (£120,000)

A ruby and diamond ring
mounted by Cartier,
circa 1935
London, 18 June 1997
£9,200 ($15,040)

A Burmese ruby and diamond bracelet
Geneva, 20 May 1997 SFr.1,103,500 (£474,505)

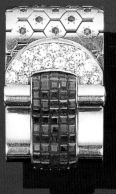

A pair of invisibly-set ruby and diamond
'Ludo-Hexagone' clip brooches by Van Cleef & Arpels,
circa 1936
London, 18 June 1997 £19,550 ($31,960)

An Art Deco ruby and diamond brooch
by Cartier, *circa* 1930
London, 18 June 1997
£16,100 ($26,320)

A pair of sapphire and diamond ear-pendants
by Van Cleef & Arpels
Geneva, 20 May 1997
SFr.86,000 (£36,980)

The Beaumont sapphire and diamond bracelet by Van Cleef & Arpels, *circa* 1935
Geneva, 20 November 1997
SFr.905,500 (£389,365)

A Kashmir
sapphire ring by
Van Cleef & Arpels
12.85 carats
Geneva, 20 May 1997
SFr.399,500 (£171,785)

A sapphire and
diamond ring
57.69 carats
New York, 9 April 1997
$178,500 (£109,910)

A Burmese
sapphire ring
21.27 carats
St. Moritz,
19 February 1997
SFr.289,500 (£124,485)

A jadeite and diamond jabot pin
Hong Kong, 29 April 1997
HK$1,780,000 (£142,400)

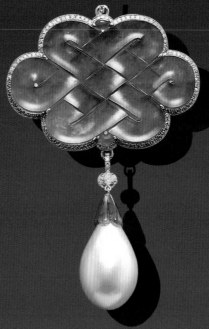

A jadeite diamond and pearl pendant
Hong Kong, 29 April 1997
HK$5,300,000 (£424,000)

A pair of jadeite Huaigu and
diamond ear-pendants
Hong Kong, 29 April 1997
HK$636,000 (£50,880)

A jadeite ring
Hong Kong, 29 April 1997
HK$3,540,000 (£283,200)

A jadeite and diamond bracelet
Hong Kong, 29 April 1997 HK$437,000 (£34,960)

A single-strand jadeite bead necklace from the stone "Doubly Fortunate"
Hong Kong, 6 November 1997 HK$72,620,000 (£5,809,600)

A pair of pearl and
diamond ear-pendants
Geneva, 20 November 1997
SFr.245,500 (£105,565)

A Belle Epoque pearl and diamond
girandole brooch/pendant, *circa* 1910
Geneva, 20 November 1997
SFr.74,750 (£32,143)

THE NINA DYER BLACK PEARL NECKLACE
Geneva, 17 November 1997
SFr.1,268,500 (£545,455)

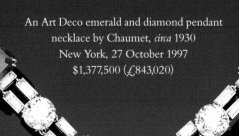

An Art Deco emerald and diamond pendant
necklace by Chaumet, *circa* 1930
New York, 27 October 1997
$1,377,500 (£843,020)

A pair of emerald and diamond ear-pendants
emeralds 51.21 and 52.68 carats
Geneva, 20 November 1997
SFr.509,500 (£219,085)

An Art Deco emerald and
diamond lapel watch by
Janesich, *circa* 1925
St. Moritz, 19 February 1997
SFr.69,000 (£29,670)

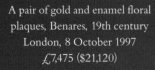

A pair of gold and enamel floral
plaques, Benares, 19th century
London, 8 October 1997
£7,475 ($21,120)

An antique diamond, ruby, emerald and
enamel Jigha
London, 8 October 1997
£62,000 ($100,440)

An antique Mughal Karnphul
(one of a pair)
London, 8 October 1997
£155,500 ($251,910)

A collection of Mughal-cut diamonds,
16th/17th century
London, 8 October 1997 £243,500 ($394,710)

An Art Deco red coral, diamond and onyx
pendent watch by Cartier,
circa 1925
Geneva, 20 November 1997
SFr.80,500 (£34,615)

A red coral and diamond "carnival" clip brooch by
Cartier, *circa* 1950
Geneva, 20 November 1997
SFr.74,750 (£32,142)

An Art Deco diamond, coral, hardstone and enamel vanity case
by Black, Starr & Frost, *circa* 1925
New York, 9 April 1997 $101,500 (£62,500)

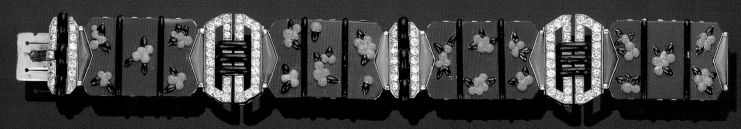

An Art Deco jasper, enamel, turquoise and diamond bracelet by Boucheron, *circa* 1925
London, 18 June 1997 £41,100 ($67,200)

A Belle Epoque sapphire, emerald
and diamond pendent necklace,
circa 1900
London, 18 June 1997
£47,700 ($77,990)

An Art Deco gem-set "Giardinetto"
brooch by Cartier, 1922
Geneva, 20 November 1997
SFr.63,250 (£27,197)

An Art Deco diamond and
gem-set flower basket lapel watch
by Lacloche, *circa* 1925
New York, 28 October 1997
$32,200 (£19,250)

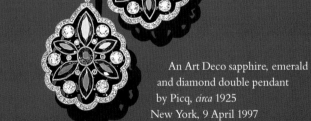

An Art Deco sapphire, emerald
and diamond double pendant
by Picq, *circa* 1925
New York, 9 April 1997
$51,750 (£31,870)

A Belle Epoque sapphire and diamond necklace by Koch, *circa* 1910
Geneva, 17 November 1997 SFr.108,000 (£46,440)

A Louis XIV rose-cut diamond and
petitot enamel pendant, *circa* 1680
London, 16 December 1997
£43,000 ($70,500)

A diamond, pearl, enamel and
gold pendant, 19th century
New York, 28 October 1997 $18,400 (£11,000)

A gold and enamel marriage bracelet by Boucheron,
circa 1875
London, 18 June 1997
£16,100 ($26,320)

A cameo pendant, *circa* 1620
London, 8 October 1997
£7,475 ($12,120)

A Queen Anne diamond bracelet, *circa* 1710

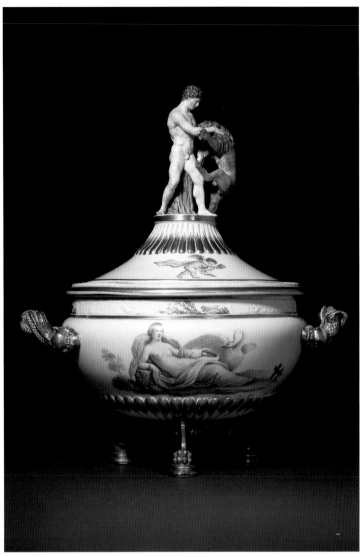

A Naples (*Reale Fabbrica Ferdinandea*) ormolu-mounted circular two-handled Soup-Tureen and Cover from the 'Ercolanese' Service
circa 1781-1782, painted by Giacomo Milani and Antonio Cioffi
13¾ in. (35cm.) high, 12¼ in. (31cm.) wide
London, 7 July 1997, £44,400 ($74,769)

A Meissen ormolu-mounted Model of a Peacock
the porcelain *circa* 1730, the Louis XV mounts *circa* 1740
7 in. (19 cm.) high
London, 24 February 1997, £38,900 ($63,290)

The 'Ercolanese' (Herculaneum) service was commissioned in 1781 by Ferdinand IV, King of Naples and the Two Sicilies as a gift to his father Charles III, King of Spain (1716-1788). It was the first service to be produced by the Naples factory under the directorship of Domenico Venuti, erstwhile Superintendant of Antiquities for Naples. The design of the tureen and cover were inspired by illustrations in *Le Antichità di Ercolano esposte*, published in five volumes from 1757 to 1798, documenting the artefacts and wall paintings excavated at Herculaneum from 1738 onwards.

This peacock was probably created by Georg Fritzsche and inspired by Japanese models in Arita porcelain. It resembles other Meissen models of Japanese birds which date from the 1720s and 1730s and is made of a similar, hard, white paste and decorated in brilliant enamel colours.

There are five known similar models, all of which are in the Residenz in Munich: two are mounted in a clock and three have similar ormolu mounts to this example. It has not been possible to remove the mounts from the present example, but it is likely that it bears the same caduceus mark (found on Meissen ware in the early 18th century) on its base as the Munich peacocks and that it too formed part of the larger group.

A Worcester (Flight, Flight & Barr) part Dinner-Service
circa 1791-2 and *circa* 1805
London, 24 February 1997, £67,500 ($109,822)

Commissioned in January 1790 by the Duke of Clarence, later William IV (1765-1830), the entire Hope Service, of which this is part, took a year to produce and cost £700. The original service consisted of 260 pieces, which were sold at Christie's on 11 May 1893 by Charles, 20th Earl of Erroll, who had inherited the service from his grandfather who had married Elizabeth FitzClarence, William IV's daughter. Every piece is painted with figures *en grisaille* by John Pennington, who was related to the family of Liverpool porcelain manufacturers of the same name and who had previously been employed at the Wedgwood workshops in London.

Two gilt-metal mounted Chantilly chinoiserie Pagoda-Figures
circa 1735
8 in. (21.1 cm.) high overall
New York, 21 May 1997, $129,000 (£78,690)

These figures are possibly based on representations of Budai, one of the Seven Gods of Felicity in Daoist tradition. Capitalizing on the taste for chinoiserie in France, Chantilly produced several models of this God of Happiness and Contentment, modelling him with his body pierced as a pot pourri vase or seated holding a pot pourri vase and cover between his knees. Parisian *marchands-merciers* used Chantilly figures of Budai in assembling ormolu-mounted clocks, inkstands and other examples of decorative arts. The present figures are noteworthy for their bright Kakiemon decoration and for having retained their original mounts.

LE SERVICE DE L'ARCHICHANCELIER
Sèvres *fond pourpre* fable and topographical Plates,
and part Dessert-Service
New York, 21 May 1997, $104,650 (£63,837)

The complete dessert-service was presented as a gift by Napoleon I to his archchancellor Jean-Jacques Régis de Combacérès (1753-1824), on the occasion of the wedding of Stéphanie de Beauharnais, Napoleon's niece by marriage, to Karl Friedrich, Grand Duke of Baden on 7 April 1806. Combacérès is best remembered as the leader of the commission which drafted the *Code Napoléon* in 1804, still the cornerstone of French jurisprudence. Although few painter's marks appear on the plates, careful study of the payment records have made it possible to attribute most of the painted scenes to specific painters: Caron, Lebel, Robert and Swebach. Many of the topographical scenes are based on engravings found in *Voyages pittoresques de Naples et de Sicile* by the abbé de Saint Non and *Vues d'Italie* by Charles Bourgeois.

THE PINK LOTUS LAMP

THE *Wrigley Pink Lotus* lamp by the Tiffany Studios is the most splendid and important leaded glass lamp to have been offered at auction. Of the two known extant examples, it is the more elegantly proportioned and accomplished.

Its originality derives from the two-tiered structure of the 'shade' and its beauty from the delicacy and superb colours of the flowers and foliage.

The chasing of the gently curling, veined lotus foliage of the base gives a convincing impression of three-dimensionality, enhanced by the exquisite green tesserae. The single-column bronze stem, with its reeded, naturalistic detail, branches at the top into sixteen chased bronze tendrils, eight of which terminate in Favrile glass globes, delicately modelled to suggest pendulous lotus blossoms, in vibrant shades of pink and soft white; the other eight tendrils arch gracefully and descend to support the large leaded glass shade, creating a beautiful domed effect of bending lotus flowers. Here Tiffany's genius in interpreting nature is seen at its most refined. The assemblage of glass set into a leaded frame creates an undulating frieze of open and budding lotus blossoms, against a swath of *ombrelle*-like leaves.

The glory of the lamp resides in the glowing tints of the glass: ranging from bright pink to orange and reds to waxy greens and whites; the flowers are set against mottled emerald, moss-greens and blues, shaded to suggest curling leaf edges.

The original price of the *Lotus* lamp gives an indication of the quality and complexity of the workmanship. In the Tiffany Studios 1906 price list, the *Lotus* lamp model was priced at $750, by far the most expensive lamp they produced, substantially more than the next most costly lamps, the *Cobweb* and the *Butterfly*, both priced at $500. The highly prized *Wistaria* and *Pond Lily* were considerably less costly at $400.

Louis Comfort Tiffany's use of the lotus motif probably owes less to the Art Nouveau movement than to his reverence for nature. In his early work, he sought inspiration in the arts of Japan, Egypt and Byzantium, but by 1900 he looked far more to nature to furnish him with themes.

The *Lotus* lamp belonged until recent years to the Wrigley family. Family tradition has it that the original order was placed by Ada Wrigley, wife of William Wrigley, Jr. (1861-1932), founder of the Wrigley chewing-gum company in Chicago. The Wrigley name remains a well-respected one in Chicago, not only for chewing gum, but also for the Wrigley Field, Chicago's park for professional baseball, and the Wrigley building of 1921, still a distinctive feature of Chicago's skyline.

NANCY McCLELLAND
HEAD OF THE INTERNATIONAL DEPARTMENT OF
20TH CENTURY DECORATIVE ARTS, CHRISTIE'S

THE PINK LOTUS LAMP
A leaded glass, bronze and mosaic *Lotus* Lamp
by Tiffany Studios, *circa* 1900-1910
34¾ in. (88.3 cm.) high, 28 in. (71.1 cm.) diameter
New York, 12 December 1997, $2,807,500 (£1,684,500)

État d'Angle
An ivory and ebony inlaid amboyna *Encoignure*
by Jacques-Émile Ruhlmann, 1916
50⅛ in. (127.3 cm.) high, 32⅝ in. (82.9 cm.) wide, 20½ in. (52 cm.) deep
New York, 12 December 1997, $662,500 (£397,500)
A record price for an Art Deco piece of furniture
A record price for Ruhlmann at auction

Ruhlmann's creation of this three-legged corner-cabinet defined him as the quintessential designer and craftsman of the Art Deco period, while his use of 18th century materials, techniques and forms earned him the reputation as an *ébéniste*. His beautiful, exotic veneers and marquetry work and his use of line as decoration also placed him at the forefront of the period: his employment of a stylized oval floral pattern was considered a modern interpretation of the traditional 'flower and urn' design.

Ruhlmann and his contemporaries, such as Paul Iribe, chose to stylize the rose. The *Iribe rose* was popularized in 1910, preceding the International Exhibition of 1911 in Turin, where flowers, specifically roses, covered stencilled walls, burst forth from bas reliefs and adorned capitals of pilasters. From 1916 to the mid 1920s, Ruhlmann elaborated on the use of the stylized rose in his *État d'Angle* and *État Rect* cabinets, rejecting the naturalistic floral interpretations of the Art Nouveau period.

Ivory enjoyed a revival under Ruhlmann, who employed it for its colour and ornamental quality. In this case, the application of the white ivory in the floral design accentuates the warm honey-coloured amboyna ground, while the contrast of the black ebony with the veneered ground is striking and bold.

Two painted deal Chairs
designed by William Morris, painted by Dante Gabriel Rossetti with
William Morris, 1856-57
55 in. (141.5 cm.) high
London, 29 October 1997, £333,000 ($552,780)

A chromed steel and leather 'Barcelona' Chair, Model MR 90
designed by Ludwig Mies van der Rohe in 1929, manufactured by
Berliner Metallgewerbe Josef Müller, Berlin, 1929-30
28¾ in. (73 cm.) high; 29⅛ in. (74 cm.) wide; 30 in. (76 cm.) deep
London, 29 October 1997, £122,500 ($203,350)

The highlight of the year was 'The Chair', a sale intended to trace the development, interpretation and design of the chair from the early 19th century to the present day. The theme of 'The Chair' crossed the usual chronological and technical categorizations, with juxtapositions, both in the catalogue and the viewing, producing sharp contrasts and suggesting unusual affinities between pieces.

The highlights of the sale were undoubtedly two unique 'Mediaeval' chairs designed by William Morris and painted by Dante Gabriel Rossetti with Morris in 1856-7. It was at the suggestion of their mentor Rossetti that Morris and his friend Edward Coley Burne-Jones moved into unfurnished rooms at 17 Red Lion Square, London, an event that was to mark the beginning of Morris's development as the master of the decorative arts in the latter half of the 19th century. Amidst a background of passion for the medieval and devotion to the principles of the pre-Raphaelite movement, the three artists set to painting the raw furniture made to Morris's designs with scenes taken from Morris's own poetry. Although Morris wrote texts drawing on many of Rossetti's later paintings, the chairs seem to be the only works the latter based on pre-existing Morris work. Of the several elaborately decorated pieces they produced, only these two chairs appear to have survived and can definitively be ascribed to that interior. They have belonged to the same family since the time they were purchased from William Morris in 1866, and their rediscovery provides a fascinating insight into the earliest days of the artistic association between the three artists.

The rare, early example of Mies van der Rohe's 'Barcelona' chair (illustrated) stands in complete contrast to the Rossetti chairs. In exceptional condition and sold with its original cushions, the chair was first created as part of Mies's project for the German Pavilion at the Barcelona World Fair in 1929. Although its radical design has the purest of forms, the laborious production process led to a very high unit cost. It was priced at 540 Reichsmarks, even at a time of worldwide recession. Doubling its top estimate, it was the pick of a string of chairs by designers such as Wagner, Hoffmann, Guimard, Van de Velde, Breuer, Rietveld, Eames, Kuramata and Arad that fetched exceptional prices.

An ebonized and inlaid Cabinet
designed by Mackay Hugh Baillie Scott, made at the
Dresdener Werkstätten für Handwerkskunst, 1902-3
43⅜ in. (110.8 cm.) maximum width closed;
84 in. (210 cm.) width open
London, 1 May 1997, £133,500 ($217,605)

La Vieille
A gold, enamel and rock crystal centre-piece
by Falize Frères, *circa* 1900
12½ in. (32 cm.) long; 9⅞ in. (25.1 cm.) wide; 6½ in. (16.5 cm.) high
London, 1 May 1997, £128,000 ($208,640)

The spring sales exemplified the unusual and varied nature of objects sold in London. They featured an important private collection of sculpture and Art Nouveau glass with a wide range of the finest quality pieces by Daum and Gallé. Certain individual pieces fetched spectacular prices, and all the sculpture sold strongly, with a world record price achieved by *Les Girls*, a Chiparus sculpture.

There were two particularly important and recently re-identified works in the Decorative Arts sale. The ebonized and inlaid cabinet is a fine example of M.H. Baillie Scott's most creative association with Germany, in particular with the Dresdener Werkstätten. Of all British designers of the Arts and Crafts movement, he had the closest affinity with the ideal of the Modern Movement there, and his gold medal at the 1902 *Haus eines Kunstfreundes* competition, organized by his tireless advocate, the architect Herman Muthesius, marked his widespread acceptance. This cabinet from the Ladies' Drawing Room, exhibited in 1903, encapsulates the qualities of unity and *Innigkeit* so admired by his German peers with its elegant restrained exterior and more complex but equally elegant interior.

La Vieille, a magnificent centre-piece was also until recently untraced despite contemporary documents recording its display at the Exposition Universelle in Paris in 1900. It was the first time Falize Frères had exhibited under their new company name following the death of their father Lucien, but it is not impossible that the conception of *La Vieille* owed something to their father. The jury noted 'the richness of the materials used....and the beauty of colour and workmanship....evidently inspired by the Japanese, but of truly Parisian design and execution'. The art and craft of Japan had been a telling inspiration for Lucien Falize, and his sympathy with the Japanese passion for nature, shown here to such good effect, marks him out as a significant precursor to the Art Nouveau movement.

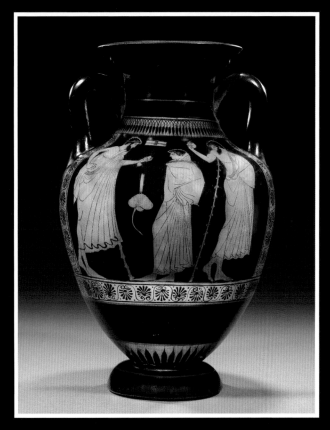

An Attic red-figure pottery Amphora
attributed to the Pig Painter, *circa* 480-470 B.C.
16½ in. (42 cm.) high
Property from the Collection of Charles Eyre (d.1855)
London, 25 November 1997, £84,000 ($141,372))

ANTIQUITIES, ISLAMIC
& ORIENTAL ART

A Roman parcel-gilt silver figure of a Bull
circa 1st century B.C./A.D.
5½ in. (14 cm.)
New York, 30 May 1997, $107,000 (£65,644)

The number of sculptures made of precious metal which survive from the ancient world is relatively small. The intrinsic value of the metal resulted in these sculptures being melted down in later periods. During times of turmoil, when the availability of precious metals was limited, sculptures in precious metals were often converted into currency. When sculptures in precious metals do survive, it is usually due to catastrophe, man-made or natural. In the wake of an invasion, fleeing owners often buried sculptures, intending, but failing, to retrieve them once the danger had passed. The eruption of Mount Vesuvius on the 24 August in A.D. 79 buried the Roman towns of Pompeii and Herculaneum, preserving them intact until their rediscovery in the 18th century.

The superb parcel-gilt silver figure of a bull was originally discovered at Pompeii between 1780 and 1790. It was later in the collection of Maria Cristina di Savoia and was subsequently inherited by Tomaso di Savoia, and then his daughter Maria Adelaide di Savoia. Superbly crafted, the bull is at once stylized and realistic, embellished with lively detailing such as the projecting ears, the bulging eyes, incised eyelashes, the poll of thick curling locks, the tasseled tail and the sagging flesh of the underbelly.

Photo: Werner Forman

THE CONSTABLE-MAXWELL CHARIOT *SKYPHOS*
A Roman white cameo and blue glass *Skyphos* (enlarged detail)
1st century A.D.
3¼ in. (8.1 cm.) high
London, 25 November 1997, £496,500 ($835,610)
A world record auction price for an ancient cameo

The 'Constable-Maxwell' Chariot *skyphos* (drinking-cup) is one of the most important Roman glass vessels ever to have been sold at auction. Roman cameo vessels are exceedingly rare, only twelve known to have survived from the ancient world, including the famous 'Portland Vase' now in the British Museum. Of these, only this *skyphos* and a perfume flask still remain in private hands, the *skyphos* having formerly been in the renowned glass collection of Mr. and Mrs. Andrew Constable-Maxwell. The *skyphos* epitomizes the extremely high quality glass which was produced during the early Roman Imperial period (*circa* 25 B.C. - 70 A.D.). The vibrant scene on the *skyphos* is unique in ancient cameos, with a racing charioteer on one side, the reverse with a second charioteer restraining his horses by leaning back and pulling on his reins. It has been suggested that the motif may derive from a scene in Homer's *Iliad*, where, during the funeral games in honour of Patroclus, Antilochus whips up his horses to race past Menelaus, who is forced to rein in as both chariots approach a narrow gully. The *skyphos* would have been commissioned by a wealthy patron. It is tempting to consider that it was commissioned by the Emperor Nero, who is known to have had a passion for chariot-racing.

THE BRONZE DEER OF CORDOBA

IN April, this highly important bronze fountainhead in the form of a hind sold in London for £3.6 million, establishing a new world record for an Islamic work of art at auction.

The bronze sculpture is almost certainly the companion piece to a bronze stag, now in the Archaeological Museum of Cordoba, which was found in the ruins of the palace of Madinat al-Zahra, formerly the seat of the caliphal court of 10th century Muslim Spain. The two animals would have been placed together on one of the fountains in the palace. The 16th century historian, al-Maqqari, describes a marble basin in the reception hall of the palace, surrounded by twelve gold animal statues encrusted with jewels which spouted water from their mouths. These animals had been made in the royal workshop and included a lion, gazelle, elephant and deer. Visitors to the Alhambra palace in Granada can still see in the Patio de los Leones a similar medieval fountain, surrounded by stone carvings of lions.

Under the Caliph Abd al-Rahman III and his son al-Hakam, who reigned from 912 to 976 A.D., Cordoba became one of the wealthiest and most brilliant cities of the early medieval world. Arts and sciences flourished under the patronage of the Muslim rulers, and luxurious objects, textiles and manuscripts poured from the royal workshops. Particularly notable are a group of marvellous ivory boxes, including two dated pyxides engraved in relief with paired animals including deer, griffins and lions. Abd al-Rahman was responsible for building a city palace near Cordoba, along the lines of the early desert palaces of his Umayyad forebears in Syria and Jordan. Perched on high ground, Madinat al-Zahra was a huge complex of public and private rooms linked by gardens and parterres. The position of the Caliph as temporal and spiritual leader of the Islamic world is reflected in the great hall of the palace linked to the gardens with their fountains, symbolic of paradise.

The Cordoba stag is of slightly larger size and more robust form than this hind. Like her, he is covered with incised roundels containing palmettes and also has a central roundel on the chest, though of slightly different form. It is as if the animals are covered with a form of cloth, perhaps reflecting the importance of textile design, which by the 11th century had become a highly developed industry in Spain. The hind typifies the way in which animals are treated in Islamic art: whether from the eastern reaches of the region such as Iran or from Europe, the animal is highly stylized, but the essence of the subject is captured. Here the textile design covering the body, the curious almond-shaped eyes, the tasseled mane and the delicately conceived mouth reflect a high degree of abstraction.

Both the hind and the stag are cast in the same way, so that the water rises through the pipe into the hollow pedestal, up the legs into the hollow body, and thence out of the mouth. The hind appears to have been cast in one piece, possibly by the lost wax method. The lower plate and pipe would have been cast separately. A metallurgical analysis of the deer performed by the Department of Materials in Oxford showed a bronze alloy remarkably rich in copper, but with no lead and only very small quantities of tin and zinc. While very much at variance with the proportions found in other Islamic bronzes, this mirrors results found in at least two other pieces attributed to Muslim Spain, the famous griffin of Pisa and a lion, sold at Christie's in 1993, both tested at the same laboratory. These sculptures are considered to be of later date than the deer and probably date from the 11th or 12th centuries. The lion, which sold for £2.4 million, was previously the most expensive work of Islamic art sold at auction.

It is difficult, therefore, to exaggerate the importance and rarity of this fascinating survival from 10th century Spain.

DEBORAH FREEMAN
SENIOR SPECIALIST, ISLAMIC DEPARTMENT,
CHRISTIE'S LONDON

A bronze Fountain-head in the form of a Hind
from Cordoba, Umayyad Spain, mid-10th century
17½ in. (44.5 cm.) high
London, 25 April 1997, £3,631,500 ($5,890,293)

A Safavid *Qur'an*
made in Shiraz, mid-16th century
15 x 9½ in. (38 x 24 cm.)
London, 25 April 1997, £58,700 ($95,211)

An illuminated Manuscript of the Khamseh of Nizami
written in Bokhara in AH 1064-6/ 1653-6 A.D.
9¼ x 5½ in. (23 x 14 cm.)
London, 25 April 1997, £89,500 ($145,169)

This beautifully preserved and illuminated *qur'an* is an excellent example of the type of manuscript produced in the middle of the 16th century at the Safavid workshops in Shiraz. It is written throughout in a very fine cursive script, highlighted with lavish use of gold, cobalt blue and turquoise, a typical colour combination. Its quality suggests that it was prepared for a royal patron though, rather unusually, the calligrapher has not signed or dated the manuscript.

This manuscript is a copy of a famous work which influenced many artists of the Persian courts from the 15th century onwards. It was produced in a provincial court in Central Asia. In these paintings we see a remarkable blend of Mughal Indian and Iranian painting styles and a daring use of colour. This particular manuscript is dedicated to Abd al-Aziz Khan, the last great ruler of Bokhara, who reigned from 1645 to 1680. He is mentioned twice in the manuscript, both in the colophon and in an inscription contained within one of the miniatures.

A Mamluk silver- and copper-inlaid brass Bottle
Syria or Egypt, late 13th century
3¼ in. (8.3 cm.) high
London, 25 April 1997, £62,000 ($100,564)

A Kashan Lustre Bowl
Central Persia, 13th century
7¼ in. (18.5 cm.) diameter
London, 25 April 1997, £34,500 ($55,959)

above left:

This small piece is interesting in that it identifies the Mamluk *amir* for whom it was made, one Fakhr al-Din, and in that most of the very fine engraving and inlay has survived. The decorative detail around the centre shows typical scenes of courtly life, with seated rulers flanked by courtiers, musicians and people drinking. The epigraphic frieze round the neck contains a blazon in the form of a wing-shaped shield, a device normally associated with Western heraldry but which had been adopted to some degree by the aristocracy of the Mamluk Empire.

above right:

This lustre bowl is exceptionally rare, as few undamaged 13th century pieces exist. This is a particularly fine example, with a delicately drawn horse and rider in the centre and a very well preserved glaze.

right:

This is an exceptionally fine 12th century jug with very high quality inlay and unusual detail such as the vase motif on its body. The scrolling arabesques on the rounded panels on the cover show the Khorassan School at its most fluent.

A Khorassan silver and copper inlaid bronze Jug
made in North East Persia, late 12th century
10¾ in. (27.2 cm.) high
London, 14 October 1997, £54,300 ($87,966)

GREAT MING PORCELAIN

An early Ming blue and white Moonflask, *Bianhu*
Yongle period (1403-1425)
9½ in. (24 cm.) high
Hong Kong, 28 April 1997, HK$4,200,000 (£336,000)

IN Europe, the term 'Ming' has long been synonymous with porcelain of great rarity and beauty. Important examples of 14th and 15th century blue and white porcelain illustrate above all the elusive qualities which the Qing Emperors attempted to reproduce in a wide range of 18th century pastiches. What the later porcelains could not capture was the boldness of spirit inherent in these inspired works. Apart from the qualitative elements of the fine clay, potting, painting and, most of all, the vibrant colour of the cobalt under a rich, yet very fine grained glaze, the best of Ming underglaze-porcelains possess a jewel-like brilliance which great ceramic traditions elsewhere sought in vain to emulate.

Among the wealth of masterpieces that appeared in 1997, pride of place must go to the underglaze copper-red pear-shaped vase (see back cover), which remains one of the very few intact pieces of its kind. This was a magnificent example of Hongwu period (A.D. 1368-1398) copper-red, at its finest. Since copper, as a glaze, is a difficult medium to control, the ability to fire this vase to such a high quality of reddish hue, varying from crushed-raspberry to salmon-pink, is a remarkable feat of Chinese late 14th century technology. It had previously appeared in our London rooms in 1984, selling then for a record price of £421,000. Its import-

ance was reaffirmed when it made a house record for Chinese porcelain and a world record price for underglaze-decorated Chinese porcelain (HK$22,020,000).

This was a year particularly rich in splendid early Ming blue and white specimens, among which none was more outstanding than a Xuande-marked stembowl (1426-1435), of peerless quality. The decoration on this stembowl demanded an excellent control of the brush and would have been executed by artisans working at the Imperial kilns of Jingdezhen. The contrast betweeen the dark blue of the dragons and rocks and the delicately pencilled light blue ground of breaking waves is one of the most delightful and dramatic effects to be found in this period. Simplicity and quietude are the marks of the Chenghua era, and the 'Palace' bowl, sold in the 'Imperial Sale', is the most successful and flawless example of its kind. The underglaze-blue painting is finely outlined and shaded with a thicker brush, leaving some white areas, which give an element of depth to each flower blossom.

Another highlight was a very rare moonflask of Islamic form and design, embellished with a complex geometric star pattern.

ANTHONY LIN
MANAGING DIRECTOR, CHRISTIE'S HONG KONG AND TAIWAN

An early Ming blue and white *Anhua*-decorated 'dragon' Stembowl
Xuande six-character mark and of the period (1426-1435)
6 in. (15.3 cm.) diameter
Hong Kong, 27 April 1997, HK$10,140,000 (£811,200)

A Ming blue and white 'Palace' bowl
Chenghua six-character mark and of the period
5¾ in. (14.7 cm.) diameter
Hong Kong, 27 April 1997, HK$8,820,000 (£705,600)

The clarity of the glaze and fine build-up of the enamelling are distinctive qualities, setting this vase above other examples of its type. The quality of the painting and fine texture of the enamels combine to create an unusual harmony between design and ceramic form.

A *Famille Rose* nine-peach globular Bottle Vase
Qianlong seal mark and of the period (1736-1796)
20½ in. (52.1 cm.) high
Hong Kong, 5 November 1997, HK$8,490,000 (£679,200)

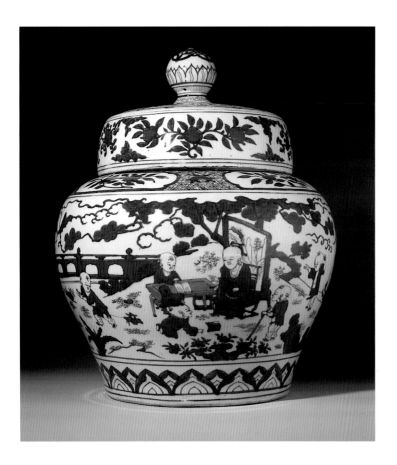

The rich jewel-like cobalt blue of this jar is characteristic of its period. The painted decoration revives a 'Boys-at-play' theme, which originated from Chinese paintings of the Southern Song court (1127-1279). The auspicious 'Boys' imagery was thought to be particularly pertinent to the Emperor Jiajing, who was anxious to produce male heirs to the throne. It is rare to find a cover accompanying a jar of this design and exceptional size.

A Ming blue and white 'Boys' Jar and Cover
Jiajing six-character mark and of the period (1522-1566)
18½ in. (47 cm.) high
Sold from the Jingguantang Collection
Hong Kong, 5 November 1997, HK$4,200,000 (£336,000)

This representation of an enlightened being is notable for both the finely carved facial expression of peaceful benevolence and the crisply realized robes and drapery. The subject of a *bodhisattva* seated on Mount Potala's rocky shore was a favourite theme of Song sculptors. Unlike the figure of the Buddha, who renounced all wordly goods and who is usually depicted without ornamentation, the *bodhisattva* wears a foliate diadem, a jewelled necklace, armbands and bracelets. The fact that the *bodhisattva* is shown as an elongated and rather youthful figure suggests that it may belong to the Southern Song period.

A wood Figure of a *bodhisattva*
Song Dynasty (960-1279)
19½ in. (49.5 cm.) high
New York, 20 March 1997, $266,500 (£162,565)

This ritual bronze food vessel is notable for both its very large size and its fine condition. It would have been used by Chinese royalty or nobility during the Western Zhou dynasty for ceremonial occasions. The closest known comparable *ding* is in the Idemitsu Museum of Arts, Tokyo. The bulbous body of the present vessel is encircled by a decorative band cast in high relief, with three pairs of dragons confronted on a notched flange, each pair separated by an animal mask positioned over one of the three massive, waisted legs. Each of the legs has on its upper section a large mask with coiled ram's horns and is divided by a prominent flange. Although the original significance of these animal symbols has been lost, they still emanate a sense of power and energy today.

A massive bronze ritual tripod Vessel, *Ding*
Western Zhou Dynasty (1100-771 B.C.)
22½ in. (57.2 cm.) high
Sold from the Jingguantang Collection
New York, 20 March 1997, $1,652,500 (£1,041,075)

THE PICCUS COLLECTION

CLASSICAL Chinese furniture of the late Ming and early Qing dynasties (16th-early 18th centuries) was first collected earlier this century, largely by Americans and Europeans resident in China. Although interest dropped after the 1949 change of government in China, Hong Kong witnessed a revival in the market in the 1960s, which has continued to the present day. The Museum of Classical Chinese Furniture Collection, sold at Christie's New York on 19 September 1996, was perceived by many to mark the coming of age of this field, heralded by a series of exhibitions, sales, scholarly articles and books on the subject. This opinion was confirmed when the Mr. and Mrs. Robert P. Piccus Collection of Fine Classical Chinese Furniture was offered for sale at Christie's New York on 18 September 1997.

Robert and Alice Piccus formed the largest part of the collection in Hong Kong over the past three decades, when the material was becoming more and more readily available. Characterized by simple form, elegant proportions and beautiful wood, the resulting group of furniture was not only of high quality, but was also made up of items which were individually handsome and interesting. The collectors lived with the furniture, which they studied, researched and sometimes published, thereby contributing in no small measure to our knowledge of the field.

The Piccuses did not wish to form an encyclopaedic collection, preferring to acquire lots that were both usable and attractive. They favoured certain types and themes: for example, there were six round-cornered, tapered cabinets, each one slightly different in size, wood and detail, but all variations of the same design. The tallest, with exquisitely matched doors above a narrow horizontal panel, sold to a London dealer for $79,500; a shorter pair, also with a lower horizontal panel, but in *jichimu* and *nanmu* and with fluted frame members, sold for $25,300 to a private collector making his first purchase of Chinese furniture. Another round-cornered, tapered cabinet, without the lower horizontal panel, in an unusual combination of *huanghuali* on the sides and *zitan* in front, sold for $57,500. A much smaller *huanghuali* version of this design, meant for use on a *kang* bed, sold to an American decorator for $23,000.

Another form that attracted the Piccuses was the recessed-leg table. A rare example, entirely in *huanghuali* except for the unusually wide *nanmu* top panel, and with the ribbed, slightly splayed legs inset from the table ends, sold for $74,000 to a Hong Kong dealer. The phoenix-form spandrels flanking each leg below the apron were repeated in another recessed-leg *huanghuali* table,

albeit in a more stylized manner. Each phoenix was created from a single piece of wood, and the table assembled in such a way that the crest of the bird overlapped the apron above, thereby maintaining the integrity of the individual motif. This table sold for $46,000 to a private Italian collector. A smaller and most interesting variation of the recessed-leg table was a demountable *huanghuali* wine table, its two recessed trestle legs readily removable, to allow the long aprons to fold flush under the top. This lot, an excellent example of the portability and versatility of Chinese furniture, sold for $46,000 to a private collector.

Undoubtedly, the highlight of the sale was the rare and important pair of brass mounted *huanghuali* folding stools, with each slatted top hinged in half to enable the stool to collapse to a flat form. Only two other examples are recorded, one in the Tianjin Museum and the other in a private Asian collection. The flurry of bidding on this lot came from European, American, and Asian private and trade clients, both on the telephone and in the room. The final bid was $321,500.

Another important lot was the 17th century *huanghuali* three-shelf bookcase of unusually wide proportions, and acknowledged by many to be one of the finest extant examples. The successful buyer paid $244,500.

Yet another notable lot was the *huanghuali* waistless side table with corner legs, which fetched $140,000. The severity of the *simianping* or 'four sides flush' frame-like design, pleasingly modified by details such as the hoof feet, very slightly protruding top and rounded corners between legs and apron, lent a Bauhaus look to the piece, which attracted many Western connoisseurs.

An interesting aspect of the sale was the strong demand for the large group of forty or more scholastic objects such as scroll boxes, seal chests and brush pots. These had been purchased in the 1960s, when large items of good furniture were unavailable in Hong Kong. It is therefore a tribute to the Piccuses' foresight that the smaller objects which attracted their initial interest sold just as well in their category as the more important pieces that were acquired later.

The sale of ninety-nine lots totalled $2.4 million (£1.5 million).

THEOW TOW
SENIOR VICE-PRESIDENT AND INTERNATIONAL HEAD,
THE CHINESE WORKS OF ART DEPARTMENT,
CHRISTIE'S NEW YORK

A view of the exhibition of the Mr. and Mrs. Robert P. Piccus Collection of
Fine Classical Chinese Furniture, New York, 18 September 1997

Attributed to HU TINGHUI (14th century)
Portraits of Fan Zhongyan (989-1052) and Fan Chunren (1027-1101)
scroll, ink and colour on silk
85 x 50 in. (216 x 127cm.)
New York, 19 September 1997, $68,500 (£42,470)

Dated 1306, this is a rare and beautiful example of Yuan dynasty portraiture. The refinement and high quality of the work would suggest that these portraits were commissioned by the family of a high-ranking official. The scroll would have been displayed during ancestral worship rites.

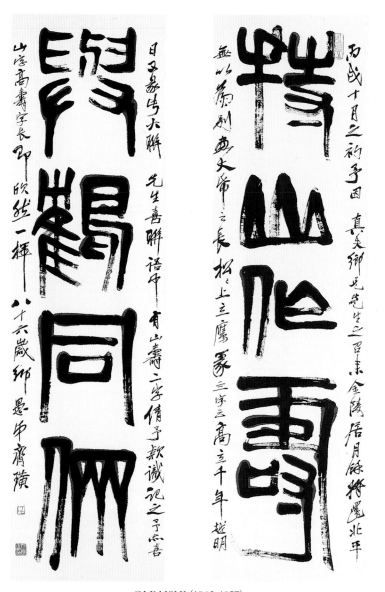

QI BAISHI (1863-1957)
Seal Script Calligraphy Couplet (zhuan shu)
pair of hanging scrolls, ink on paper
each scroll 66½ x 16½ in. (168.9 x 41.9 cm.)
Painted in 1946
New York, 19 September 1997, $63,000 (£39,060)

One of China's most famous 20th century artists, Baishi was born into a poor peasant family. His grandfather taught him the few Chinese characters which he knew, by drawing the forms in the dirt with a stick; having mastered these, Baishi excelled at script writing while at school. He worked as an artist during one of the most turbulent periods of modern Chinese history, from the decline and fall of the Qing dynasty to the Sino-Japanese war and the Communist revolution of 1949.

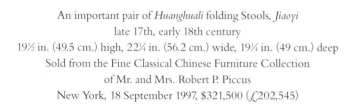

An important pair of *Huanghuali* folding Stools, *Jiaoyi*
late 17th, early 18th century
19½ in. (49.5 cm.) high, 22¼ in. (56.2 cm.) wide, 19¼ in. (49 cm.) deep
Sold from the Fine Classical Chinese Furniture Collection
of Mr. and Mrs. Robert P. Piccus
New York, 18 September 1997, $321,500 (£202,545)

A late Ming blue and white Jar, *Guan*
Jiajing six-character mark in underglaze-blue in a line
and of the period (1522-1566)
21⅞ in. (53 cm.) high
New York, 18 September 1997, $250,000 (£157,500)

To date, only four *huanghuali* examples of this type of stool have been recorded, including the present pair. One of the other examples is currently in the Tianjin Museum of Art in China. The stools have a unique construction which allows the seat to fold upwards with pivoting frame members, allowing them to be folded flat for efficient storage. The excellent workmanship is clear not only from the finely carved dragons on the seat frames but also from the quality of the *baitong* mounts.

A number of Jiajing or Wanli-marked jars of this type exist, but few can compare with this example in the boldness of painting and strength of vivid violet-blue tones. The dragon, with its fringed lashes, bulging eyes and furrowed brow, is typical of the Jiajing period imagery. Also characteristic of the period are the symbols of longevity decorating the jar, including the *lingzhi* fungus and the *shou* characters, reflecting the Jiajing emperor's preoccupation with attaining eternal life.

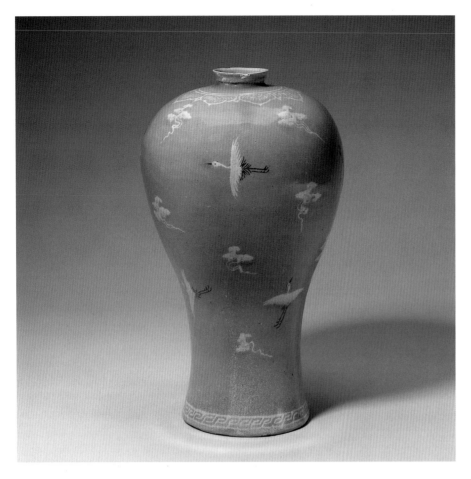

The 'cranes-among-clouds' design is the most popular motif on Korean celadons. During the Koryo dynasty (918-1392) the crane was the symbol of immortality. Here the celadon ground represents the sky through which the cranes are flying.

Korean potters were achieving beautiful celadon glazes by the first half of the 12th century. The earliest appearance of the inlay *sanggam* technique has been the subject of controversy, but there is general agreement that the technique reached maturity by the second half of the 12th century.

The expressive and lively design and the full form of the body infuse this vase with a vitality that is typical of Korean ceramics. The shape and surface design are expertly harmonized.

An inlaid celadon *Maebyong*
Koryo Dynasty, 12th century
13⅝ in. (34.6 cm.) high
New York, 24 April 1997, $717,500 (£440,184)

Korean 15th century blue and white wares are extremely rare. It has been suggested that the blackness of the cobalt in this case was an intentional attempt to achieve an ink-like quality in the decoration rather than a result of impurities in the cobalt. A Korean official document, dated 1481, states that artists from the Academy of Painting frequently painted decoration on porcelain made for the royal house. The painterly quality of this water dropper (used by scribes to dissolve dried pigment to make ink) suggests that it was decorated by such a painter.

An underglaze-cobalt-decorated peach-form Water-Dropper
Choson period, 15th century
3¼ in. (8.2 cm.) high; 3⅝ in. (9.3 cm.) diameter
New York, 24 April 1997, $816,500 (£500,920)

A large white porcelain Jar
Choson period, 17th century
21½ in. (54.7 cm.) high
New York, 25 November 1997, $827,500 (£489,645)

During the early Choson era (1392-1910), white ware was one of the most desirable types of porcelain, since it was made exclusively for the Korean court. Later its use spread, and many types of storage jars began to be made. In the 17th century, large, elegant baluster-form jars were less common than the round moon jars of comparable size. A blue-white cast to the glaze adds to the beauty of this piece.

JAPANESE EXPORT LACQUER

A folding Missal Stand
Momoyama Period, late 16th/early 17th century
13 in. (35.1 cm.) high
London, 19 June 1997, £87,300 ($142,299)

BY the mid-16th century, Japan had suffered more than two hundred years of civil war, but during the 1560s Oda Nobunaga (1534-82) began to emerge as the most powerful of all the *daimyo*, or regional war-lords, establishing his authority in Kyoto and central Japan. Toyotomi Hideyoshi (1537-98), Nobunaga's top general, built on his success and achieved effective control over most of the country. His colourful and megalomaniac career came to an end with his death in 1598. He was succeeded by Tokugawa Ieyasu (1542-1616), the strongest of his vassals, who laid the foundations for an era of stability that would last until the middle of the 19th century.

The period from about 1540 to 1640 was known as the 'Christian century', because of the presence of the Portuguese in Japan. The widespread dissemination of Christianity followed the arrival of St. Francis Xavier in 1549. Having flourished under Nobunaga, the Society of Jesus had, however, a more difficult time under Hideyoshi who, in 1587, suddenly ordered that all missionaries be banished from Japan. Nevertheless the number of converts is believed to have been around 300,000. In 1612 Ieyasu ordered his Christian retainers to apostatize. His son Hidetada intensified the persecution. The Catholic church recognizes 3,125 martyrdoms in Japan between 1597 and 1660, a figure which does not include tens of thousands massacred during the 1637 Shimabara rebellion in Kyushu. By this date the Japanese were forbidden under pain of death to travel abroad and soon after-wards, Chinese and Dutch traders were confined to the port of Nagasaki.

The internationalization of Japan during the 'Christian century' introduced new motifs into Japanese decorative art, especially items made for export. Elements of late Ming (1368-1644) Chinese design, as well as the Korean style of bold mother-of-pearl inlay, are seen in most export lacquer of the period. These elements, and others drawn from the craft traditions of the other Asian cultures with which the Portuguese were in contact, combined with new lacquer techniques of purely Japanese origin to produce the style known as *Namban shikki*, 'southern barbarian lacquerware', which is most commonly found in the form of trunks and cabinets. Much rarer are pieces such as the host-box or pyx, the portable shrine and the folding missal stand. The shape and construction of the missal stands almost certainly derive from Goanese carved wood originals, perhaps themselves based on Islamic prototypes.

JOE EARLE
CONSULTANT, JAPANESE WORKS OF ART DEPARTMENT,
CHRISTIE'S LONDON

An export lacquer Pipe Holder
Edo Period, late 17th century
75.3 cm. long
London, 19 June 1997, £45,500 ($74,165)

A miniature export lacquer Coffer
Edo Period, mid-17th century
6 x 3⅛ x 2⅞ in. (15.3 x 8 x 7.2 cm.)
London, 7 April 1997, £18,400 ($29,992)

An incense set (*kodogu*) in lacquer Cases
Edo Period, early 19th century
New York, 19 March 1997, $107,500 (£67,725)

A 'red-cornered' lacquer incense Box (*Sumiaka Chinkobako*)
Edo Period, early 17th century
3⅞ x 3⅝ x 3⅛ in. (10 x 9.2 x 7.9 cm.)
New York, 17 September 1997, $63,000 (£39,690)

A complete incense set with matching gold lacquer utensils was a part of every aristocratic lady's dowry. In the 'incense game', a variety of incenses is burned in succession, and the guests attempt to identify them. An incense spoon is used to place a small incense wood chip on the centre of a mica plate. Thus positioned, the incense is heated and gives off a fragrance. Each guest used a tag to identify the fragrance as the incense burner was passed around.

This small box was part of a large dowry set for the grand-daughter of Tokugawa Ieyasu, the founder of the shogunate. In 1633 Kamehime, the seven-year-old daughter of Iemitsu, the third shogun, married Maeda Mitsutaka, head of the Kanazawa branch of the Tokigawa family. A complete dowry set was an impressive sight as it included not only cosmetic utensils but also items such as an incense ceremony set, a tea ceremony set, boxes for shell games, stationery and writing boxes, clothing boxes and food utensils.

Anonymous (second quarter 17th century)
A Potuguese Trading Ship arrives at a Japanese Port
six-panel screen; ink, colour and gold leaf on paper
46½ x 136¾ in. (118 x 369 cm.)
New York, 24 April 1997, $442,500 (£274,350)

This screen is a rare example of *Namban*, or 'southern barbarian', art produced in Japan during a brief, dynamic period of interaction between East and West. Portuguese merchants and Jesuits could be seen in the streets of Nagasaki from 1571 until 1640, when the shogun put into effect a seclusionist policy. The 'southern barbarians', as these foreigners were called, arrived annually in a carrack that had set off from Goa, the capital of the Portuguese empire in Asia. The costumes and physiognomy of the Portuguese and their black slaves, considered strange and exotic, caused much wonderment in Japan and became the subject of numerous screen paintings by anonymous artists in Kyoto during the 17th century.

This screen is unique for the liveliness and originality of its anecdotal detail. The great ship, its sails already dismantled, is dramatically silhouetted against an expanse of gold. Cargo is being off-loaded onto small craft and ferried ashore, where the captain-major is shown parading through the town with a parasol held over his head. His welcoming committee includes some Franciscans in brown hoods and a large group of Jesuits from the local mission in long black cassocks. In the central upper section, there is a fortified mansion where a local feudal lord receives a group of foreigners who sit humbly on his veranda. The street life is fascinating: Portuguese bring exotics peacocks as well as Chinese silk, ceramics and carved lacquer, which they trade for Japanese silver. Amidst these scenes of commerce are amusing elements of local colour – a samurai grimaces as a barber shaves his head, for example, and a Portuguese sailor buys a skewer of sweet rice balls at a food stall.

A Nabeshima Dish
Edo Period, *circa* 1700
8⅛ in. (20.2 cm.) diameter
New York, 24 April 1997, $90,500 (£56,110)

A Ko-Imari Bottle
Edo Period, late 17th century
10 in. (25.5 cm.) high
London, 18 November 1997, £32,200 ($54,418)

Porcelains made for the Nabeshima lords represent the finest porcelain production of Arita and are now amongst the most desirable Japanese ceramics known for their sober elegance. Cherry blossom and wooden rafts are classic motifs.

The first written record of enamelled ware from Arita occurs in the tea diary of the priest Horin in 1652. This bottle, with its combination of iron red, green and yellow enamels, is an illustration of early enamelled ware. It was made for the domestic market and is in the form of a Japanese tea whisk.

A Goto Ichijo Tsuba
signed *Kiju o Hakuo saku*
late Edo Period, 19th century
3¾ in. (8.1 cm.) wide, 3 mm. thick
Sold from the Lundgren Collection of Japanese Swords and Sword Fittings
London, 18 November 1997, £13,800 ($23,322)

Japanese sword fittings (*kanamono*) have often been described as the soul of the samurai, his most precious possession. When the Japanese government abolished the wearing of swords in 1897, large quantities of *kanamono* came onto the market, their beautiful craftsmanship drawing the attention of westerners.

Mr. Lundgren, the notable Swedish connoisseur, gathered avidly and widely, choosing only the best examples of *tsuba* (sword guards), *kozuka* (the handles of small utility knives) and *fuchi-kashira* (pommel and ferule). His collection constituted a history of the development of Japanese sword furniture from the 8th to the 19th century.

A Bizen Kanemitsu *Wakizashi* with *Koshirae* by Ishiguro Masayoshi
Mei: Bishu Osafune Kanemitsu and dated 1356
12⅞ in. (32.7 cm.) long
Sold from the Lundgren Collection of Japanese Swords and Sword Fittings
London, 18 November 1997, £62,000 ($104,780)

A Benin bronze Head *(Uhunmwun-elao)*
circa 1550-1580
9 in. (23 cm.) high
New York, 20 November 1997, $662,500 (£390,875)

Bronze heads such as this were displayed on the ancestral altars in the city of Benin. The present head dates from the Middle Period of Benin bronze casting, in the mid- to late 16th century. During this period more than fifty bronze heads were cast, of which nine (including the present head) form an early sub-group distinguished by their smaller size, fine quality casting and the presence of iron inlaid *ikao* marks on the forehead. They were probably cast by Oba Orhogbua for the great king Esigie in about 1550 or by Ehengbuda for Orhogbua in about 1580. Most of the Benin bronzes known in Western museums and collections were taken at the time of the Benin Punitive Expedition of 1897. The present head was collected in Nigeria by William Charles Giffard Heneker, who does not appear to have taken part in the expedition: he was in Nigeria shortly afterwards, working for the Niger Coast Protectorate, and is known to have assisted in the transfer of the deposed *oba* (or king) of Benin to his exile in Calabar (present-day Nigeria).

A jeroboam of Le Pin 1982
Pomerol. Château-bottled
In original wooden case
London, 9 October 1997, £17,600 ($29,216)

An Italian 'Export' Sallet
circa 1450–1460
9¼ in. (23.5 cm.) high
South Kensington, 12 December 1997, £106,000 ($176,172)

OTHER DEPARTMENTS

Rosa Centifolia prolifera foliacea.   La Cent feuilles prolifere foliacé.

S. J. Redouté pinx.   Imprimerie de Remond.   Victor sculp.

PIERRE-JOSEPH REDOUTÉ (1759-1840)
and CLAUDE-ANTOINE THORY (1759-1827)
Les Roses
Paris: Firmin Didot, 1817-1824
3 volumes, large folio (553 x 359 mm.)
contemporary English red half morocco gilt
London, 30 April 1997, £276,500 ($449,865)

left:

Redouté, one of the most celebrated of flower painters, held several important positions, including draughtsman to the Cabinet of Marie-Antionette and *maître de dessin* at the Musée National d'Histoire Naturelle. He also enjoyed the patronage of the duchesse de Berry and the Empress Joséphine. *Les Roses* is rightly considered the most remarkable of Redouté's printed works. This copy is the largest-paper copy of the first edition of his most famous work, with the plates in two states and finished by Redouté himself.

below:

John Gould is justly celebrated for his important monographs on birds. His reputation, rivalled only by that of Audubon, is based on his combination of industry, commercial intuition and passionate love of his subject. In partnership with his wife, Edward Lear, Nicholas Vigors, Henry Richter, Joseph Wolf, William Hart and Richard Sharpe, Gould published a series of magnificent works such as *A Monograph of the Trochilidiae, or the family of Humming-Birds* and *The Birds of Asia*. This fine set of the ornithological folios in contemporary bindings achieved the second highest auction price ever for Gould's works.

JOHN GOULD (1804-1881)
[*Works.*] London: [1830]-1888
11 works in 43 volumes,
folio (approximately 550 x 370 mm.)
near-uniform green morocco
by Zaehnsdorf and others
London, 30 April 1997, £507,500 ($825,702)

MARCUS ANNAEUS LUCANUS (A.D. 39-65)
Pharsalia. Ed. Aldus Manutius (1452-1515)
Venice: Aldo Manuzio and Andrea Torresano, July 1515, Aldine octavo (166 x 90mm.)
Parisian gold-tooled fawn marbled morocco of *circa* 1540-43, bound by Jean Picard for Jean Grolier
London, 26 November 1997, £95,000 ($158,555)

above:

Jean Grolier (1479-1565) is the most famous bibliophile of the French Renaissance. His patronage of the leading French bookbinders was second only to Henri II, perhaps the greatest patron in the history of bookbinding. This marbled morocco binding by Jean Picard is in very fresh condition and one of the finest Grolier bindings to have appeared at auction in many years. Picard, a bookseller as well as a bookbinder, and Grolier, were closely involved with the Aldine Press of Venice in the marketing of its productions in France.

right:

A fine, rare association copy of the first issue of the first edition of the most celebrated illustrated book of the French Renaissance, which argued strongly for the use of the French language rather than Latin. Tory was an artist, author, classicist, translator, editor, bookseller and publisher. The *Champ fleury* is his principal work on language and letter design. This copy was owned by Jacques Thiboust de Quantilly (1492-1556), a contemporary of Tory and fellow native of Bourges. Thiboust shared Tory's passionate interest in the vernacular, spelling reform and the art of writing, and both were closely connected to the royal court of François I and Marguerite de Valois.

GEOFROY TORY (c. 1480-1533)
Champ fleury. Au quel est contenu Lart & Science de la deue & vraye
Proportion des Lettres Attiques…proportionnees selon le Corps & Visage humain
Paris: printed for the author and Gilles Gourmont, 28 April 1529
Small folio (250 x 170mm.), blind-tooled calf by the royal binder Simier
London, 25 June 1997, £55,600 ($94,129)

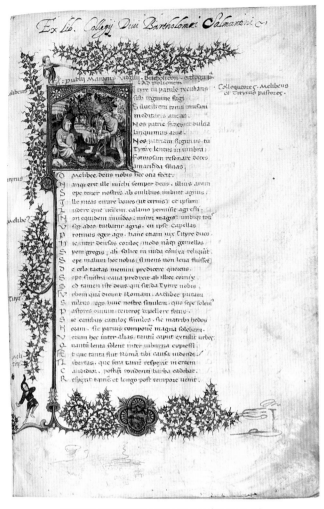

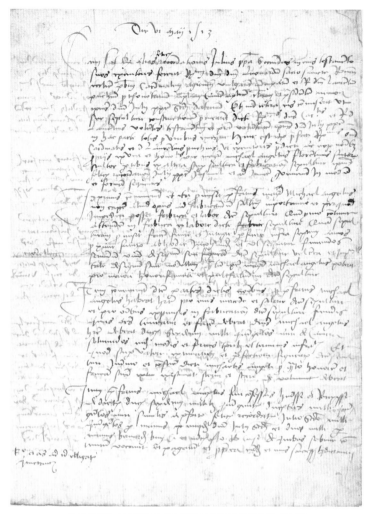

PUBLIUS VERGILIUS MARO (70-19 B.C.)
Eclogues, Georgics, Aeneid, written by Umberto Decembrio and
illuminated by Tomasino da Vimercate, Master of the Modena Hours
Illuminated manuscript on vellum. Milan, 1417 (335 x 230mm.)
early 19th century Spanish royal binding of mottled calf
From the Giannalisa Feltrinelli Library, Part Two
London, 3 December 1997, £771,500 ($1,296,120)

[MICHELANGELO BUONARROTI (1475-1564)]
FRANCESCO VIGOROSI (papal notary)
Autograph document signed, giving the terms of the contract with
Michelangelo for the tomb of Pope Julius II, Rome, 6 May 1513, in Latin
98 lines in brown ink on a bifolium, 295 x 215 mm.
autograph cancellations and corrections made by Vigorosi
From the Giannalisa Feltrinelli Library, Part Two
London, 3 December 1997, £84,000 ($141,120)

This important manuscript perfectly exemplifies early Renaissance humanism, combining scholarly interest in classical antiquity with a taste for the elegant and courtly in miniature painting. Both scribe and illuminator were employed by the Visconti court. By the 16th century the manuscript found its way to Spain and was transferred to the royal library in about 1800. On 21 June 1813 it was captured as booty from Joseph Bonaparte on his retreat from Vitoria; the following day it was presented to Arthur Wellesley, then Marquess of Wellington, later Duke of Wellington.

Pope Julius II summoned Michelangelo to Rome in 1505 to embark on an ambitious project for the construction of a magnificent tomb for himself. Julius died in 1513, but the project dragged on until 1545. It was originally conceived on the most grandiose scale, but was gradually whittled down in successive contracts with Julius' executors. The design of the tomb obsessed and tormented Michelangelo. The original intention was to have a free-standing monument, adorned with sculptures representing the liberal arts, surmounted by a bier bearing the Pope, supported by angels. The monument was never completed. The celebrated colossal figure of Moses survives in S. Pietro in Vincoli, whilst smaller sculptures are to be found in the Accademia in Florence and in the Louvre.

The double elephant folio edition of Audubon's *The Birds of America* is one of the greatest bird books ever produced. In 1803 Audubon avoided conscription into Napoleon's army by emigrating to America, where he devoted his life to recording the birds of his adopted country. This production, the culmination of meticulous observation and painstaking research, depicts birds with understanding and great naturalism, in their typical environment. The text is lively and scholarly, but it is the beauty and size of the plates that make this work one of the most sought-after natural history books.

JOHN JAMES AUDUBON (1780-1851)
The Birds of America
Volumes I-III [of 4]
London: published by the author, 1827-36, 3 volumes, double elephant folio, (985 x 660 mm. and smaller)
New York, 21 April 1997, $1,707,500 (£1,041,575)

The Works of Geoffrey Chaucer is the masterpiece of the Kelmscott Press and arguably the greatest book of the private press movement. This copy belonged to Sydney Cockerell, secretary and bibliographer of the Kelmscott Press, and contains his signature and two autograph inscriptions, each separately initialed and dated. The first of these records his purchase of the book in 1944 from Quaritch, many years after he had worked on its production and 'read every page in proof', and his delighted astonishment at finding and acquiring one of the rare vellum copies in mint condition. Its provenance makes this the most desirable association copy sold at auction this season.

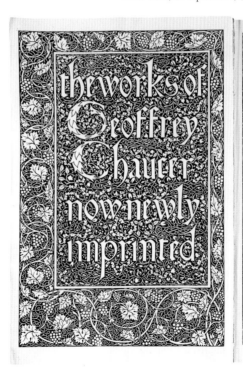

KELMSCOTT PRESS
The Works of Geoffrey Chaucer
edited by F.S. Ellis, Hammersmith, 1896, large folio (434 x 307 mm.)
one of 13 copies on vellum, from the edition of 438
original holland-backed blue paper over boards, covered in a printed chintz cotton
and linen chemise in the 'Rose' pattern designed by William Morris
New York, 21 April 1997, $607,500 (£370,575)

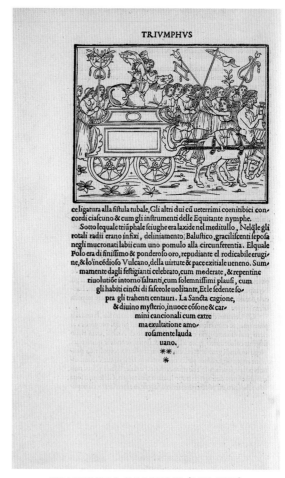

JOHN SIBTHORP, JAMES EDWARD SMITH and JOHN LINDLEY
Flora Graeca: sive plantarum rariorum historia, quas in provinciis aut insulis Graeciae
London: Richard, Arthur and John E. Taylor for John White,
White Cochrane and Payne & Foss, 1806-40 [plates watermarked 1847]
10 volumes, large folio (474 x 333 mm.)
contemporary green half morocco gilt
New York, 4 June 1997, $321,500 (£196,115)

FRANCESCO COLONNA (1433-1527)
Hypnerotomachia Poliphili [in Italian]
Venice: Aldus Manutius [for Leonardus Crassus], December 1499
folio (299 x 202 mm.)
mid-16th century blind-tooled dark brown calf over pasteboard,
by the Flemish binder Claus van Doermaele
From the Giannalisa Feltrinelli Library, Part One
New York, 7 October 1997, $266,500 (£162,565)

John Sibthorp (1758-96) succeeded his father as Sherardian Professor of Botany at Oxford in 1784 and soon after left for Vienna to study the Dioscorides manuscript known as *Codex Vindoboniensis*. He planned a botanical tour of Greece and persuaded the artist Ferdinand Bauer, whom he had met in Vienna, to join the expedition. Whilst Sibthorp worked on other projects, Bauer continued to prepare his drawings for publication. However, Sibthorp died of tuberculosis before the work could be published. The drawings were bequeathed to Oxford University with an endowment to provide for their publication. Sir James Edward Smith was appointed to write the text and had competed six volumes before his death in 1831. John Lindley finished the project. The ten volumes were published over a period of thirty-five years and is considered the finest botanical work produced in 19th century England.

This copy of the most celebrated illustrated book of the Italian Renaissance belonged to Franciscus Raphelengius (c.1568-1643), printer and Latinist, son of the philologist of the same name and grandson of Christophe Plantin. The anonymous text, an allegorical love story, echoes in form the medieval chivalric romances, but in substance expresses a humanist vision of classical art and aesthetics, strongly influenced by the works of Alberti and Vitruvius. The Renaissance binding is by Claus van Doermaele, who in 1533 moved to Antwerp, where he was made *Stadsboekbinder* following the death of Willem Vosterman in 1543.

HUGO GROTIUS
(1583-1645)
De jure belli ac pacis libri tres.
In quibus ius
naturae & Gentium: item iuris
publici praecipua explicantur
Paris: Nicolas Buon, 1625.
quarto (246 x 180 mm.)
first edition, third state
New York,
5 December 1997,
$63,000 (£38,430)

NICOLAES VISSCHER II (1649-1702) [and others]
Atlas minor, sive geographia compendiosa qua orbis terrarum
per paucas attamen novissimas tabulas ostenditura
Amsterdam: Nicolaes Visscher [1696 or later]
2 volumes, folio (532 x 335 mm.)
publisher's blind-stamped dark brown goatskin
New York, 5 December 1997, $101,500 (£61,915)

above right:

A fine composite atlas, belonging to the series of large atlases compiled and sold by the Visscher family of art dealers and cartographers in the late 17th and early 18th centuries. No two Visscher atlases seem to have been identical in content, and most contain, like this one, a selection of maps by the Visschers themselves as well as by other cartographers. This particularly extensive atlas, issued without the usual printed or manuscript index, was probably assembled and coloured to order for a German or Dutch customer, the first volume being devoted exclusively to Northern European maps.

above left:

Grotius was a statesman and thinker, whose influence on modern international law cannot be overestimated. He wrote this masterwork in 1623-24, having escaped from a sentence of life imprisonment in Holland. Writing a century before the Enlightenment, Grotius attempted to establish a principle of immutable law, outside the domain of the Church or Bible. His work was thus the direct precursor of 'Natural Law' in the 18th century and the first to express a fundamental axiom of modern law. The first edition is today of great rarity, particularly in such fine condition.

right:

One of Lincoln's most famous letters, acknowledged to be one of the greatest condolence letters ever written, was addressed to a young woman distraught after the death of her father, William McCullough. McCullough had been a clerk in an Illinois circuit court and was well known to Lincoln. When war broke out, he was rejected by the Union Army on medical grounds, having lost his right arm and sight in one eye – but the President intervened to obtain a commission for him. He was killed in a Confederate ambush near Coffeyville, Mississippi.

President ABRAHAM LINCOLN
Autograph letter signed, as President, to Miss Fanny McCullough,
of Bloomington, Illinois; Washington D.C., 23 December 1862
one full page, quarto (250 x 201 mm.)
New York, 5 December 1997, $442,500 (£269,925)

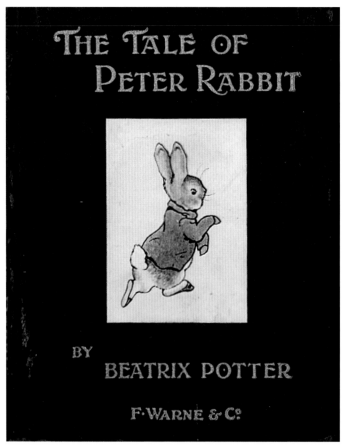

The Doris Frohnsdorff Collection of Beatrix Potter contained eleven important association copies belonging to Noël Moore, the son of Potter's close friend and former governess Annie Moore. It was to him that Potter wrote her famous letter on 4 September 1893, in which she first told the story of Peter Rabbit. This copy is signed and inscribed on the front free endpaper 'Noël C. Moore. See her letter dated to me in 1893'.

BEATRIX POTTER (1866-1943)
The Tale of Peter Rabbit
London: Frederick Warne and Co., [October 1902]
16mo, first Warne (and first commercial) edition, first issue
From the Doris Frohnsdorff Collection
New York East, 16 April 1997, $40,250 (£24,552)

Mental Photographs offers a new insight into the character of Oscar Wilde. It is a compilation of questions which, when answered, would be rather like a photograph album – a series of snapshots of the owner's identity. A photograph of Wilde, cut from a newspaper, has been attached to the front page. His witty answers to questions about his favourite flower, colour, or his views on men and women, marriage and friendship, are strikingly honest, and some of them foreshadow his later life.

OSCAR O'FLAHERTIE WILLS WILDE (1856-1900)
Mental Photographs, an Album for Confessions or Tastes,
Habits and Convictions. Ed. Robert Saxton
New York: Leypoldt & Holdt, 1870
4to, with a two-page entry by Oscar Wilde, dated 1877
South Kensington, 6 June 1997, £25,000 ($40,775)

This first edition of *De Aetna* is a Renaissance book *par excellence*: it recounts the humanist Bembo's youthful ascent of Mount Etna; it is the first Latin publication by the Aldine Press; and it employed for the first time the first roman type cut exclusively for Aldus by Francesco Griffo. This type is probably the most influential in the history of typography, inspiring Garamond and Granjon in the 16th century and Stanley Morison in our own, who immortalized it in his own 'Bembo' type.

PETRI BEMBI DE AETNA AD ANGELVM CHABRIELEM LIBER.

Factum a nobis pueris est, et quidem sedulo Angele; quod meminisse te certo scio; ut fructus studiorum nostrorum, quos ferebat illa aetas nõ tam maturos, q̃ uberes, semper tibi aliquos promeremus: nam siue dolebas aliquid, siue gaudebas; quae duo sunt tenerorum animorum maxime propriae affectiones; continuo habebas aliquid a me, quod legeres, uel gratulationis, uel consolationis; imbecillum tu quidem illud, et tenue; sicuti nascentia omnia, et incipientia; sed tamen quod esset satis amplum futurum argumentum amoris summi erga te mei. Verum postea, q̃ annis crescentibus et studia, et iudicium increuere; nósq; totos tradidimus graecis magistris erudiendos; remissiores paulatim facti sumus ad scribendum, ac iam etiam minus quotidie audentiores.

A

PIETRO BEMBO (1470-1547)
De Aetna
Venice: Aldus Manutius, February 1495-96
quarto (199 x 142 mm.)
Rome, 10 June 1997, Lit. 464,600,000 (£165,928)

Between 1768 and 1771 Captain James Cook made his famous voyage round the world in *HMS Endeavour*. He was accompanied by the naturalist Sir Joseph Banks, later President of the Royal Society, and by Daniel Solander, pupil of Linnaeus and later Keeper of the Natural History Department at the British Museum. Banks and Solander collected numerous specimens which were recorded by the expedition artist, Sydney Parkinson. The completed drawings were engraved by several artists between 1771 and 1784 on at least 743 copper plates but they remained unpublished and passed to the British Museum when Banks died in 1820. The present edition is the first printing from the original plates and was limited to one hundred copies.

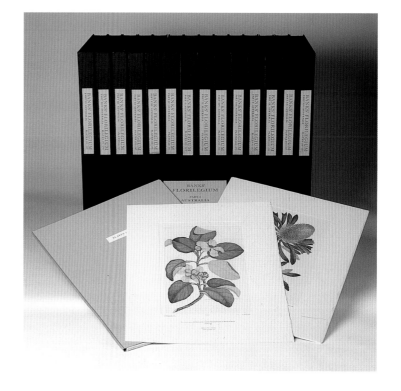

[CAPTAIN JAMES COOK] – SIR JOSEPH BANKS
Banks' Florilegium…copperplate engravings of plants collected on Captain James
Cook's first voyage round the world in H.M.S. Endeavour 1768-71
Parts I-XV Australia, London: 1980, large folio (724 x 556 mm.)
No. 25 of 100 sets only of the complete Australian
section of Banks's *Florilegium* comprising 337 coloured copper engraved plates
Melbourne, 17 August 1997, A$48,300 (£22,258)

KARL BLOSSFELDT (1865-1932)
Serratula Nudicaulis (Bare-stemmed Common Sawwort)
gelatin silver print, *circa* 1928
11¾ x 9⅜ in. (29.8 x 23.8cm.)
New York, 9 October 1997, $90,500 (£56,110)

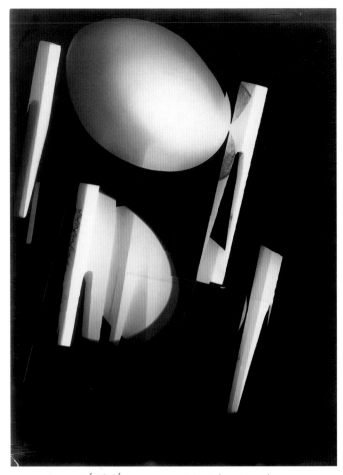

LÁSZLÓ MOHOLY-NAGY (1895-1946)
Fotogramm
unique gelatin silver print, signed and dated, 1925
New York, 9 October 1997, $90,500 (£56,110)

From 1898 to 1932, Blossfeldt taught sculpture at the Royal School of the Museum of Decorative Arts in Berlin. He strove to perfect the documentation of botanical specimens with macro-photography, using a camera of his own design. In his desire systematically to draw parallels between nature and art, Blossfeldt created a lexicon of forms, his efforts culminating in the landmark book *Urformen der Kunst*, published in 1928.

The recent discovery of this original *fotogramm* (photogram) adds to the definition of Moholy-Nagy's work in this medium. This photogram is one of a well-documented group of a dozen related works employing the same materials. It is not by accident that Julien Levy, the renowned Surrealist dealer, met Moholy-Nagy in 1931 and was immediately drawn to his photograms. The photograms which Moholy-Nagy produced between his arrival at the Bauhaus and his departure in 1928 differ significantly from the work of other photographers employing the same technique. Their plasticity of forms and insistent denial of any reference to reality differ markedly, for example, from Man Ray's auto-biographical and narrative works.

HIROMU KIRA (1898-1991)
Paper Bird
gelatin silver print, signed and dated, 1928
10⅜ x 13 in. (26.4 x 33cm.)

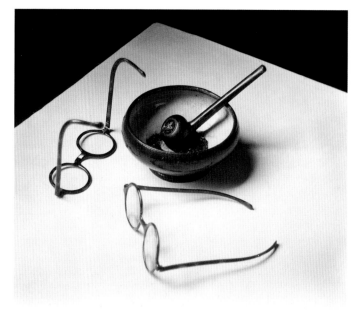

ANDRÉ KERTÉSZ (1894-1985)
Mondrian's Pipe and Glasses, Paris, 1926
gelatin silver print on postcard
3⅛ x 3⅝ in. (7.9 x 9.3cm.)
New York, 17 April 1997, $376,500 (£233,430)

Born in Hawaii and raised primarily in Japan, Hiromu Kira did not begin to develop an interest in photography until he settled in Seattle in the early 1920s. His passion for photography quickly grew and by 1924 he became a founding member of the Seattle Camera Club. Early in his career he was closely associated with the Pictorialist movement but, in 1926, when he moved to Los Angeles, Kira's work took on a new direction. After seeing several exhibitions of Edward Weston's work, Kira developed a new interest in still life.

This print was one of 21 postcards discovered in Kertész's New York apartment after his death in 1985. The gathered objects are emphasized and united by the harmony of their simple forms, offset by the plain white field on which they rest.

ROGER FENTON (1819-1869)
South Porch, Roslin Chapel, 1856
salt print
16 x 13⅞ in. (40.7 x 36.2 cm.)
A record auction price for the photographer
and for a 19th century British photographer
South Kensington, 30 April 1997, £58,700 ($98,480)

JOHN NICHOLAS TRESIDDER, FELICE BEATO,
DONALD HORNE MACFARLANE AND OTHERS
From an album belonging to J.N. Tresidder, *circa* 1857-63
South Kensington, 30 April 1997, £19,550 ($32,780)

In France, as early as 1851, the government commissioned the leading photographers to travel around the country to document important architectural sites for the *Mission Héliographique*. There was no similar patronage for architectural photography in Britain, so large-scale photographs of such subjects from this period are rare. Roger Fenton, one of the undisputed masters of the medium in the 1850s, travelled around Britain on his own initiative, photographing sites of architectural importance, and exhibited his prints to great acclaim. Such large-format prints, particularly signed salt prints, are now extremely rare, especially in such excellent condition as this one.

This remarkable album documents the period when J.N. Tresidder served as Surgeon General in the Northern Provinces of India *circa* 1858-1863. It contains about 1,000 images, several previously unattributed and many others which were exhibited at the time. It provides a unique insight into British life in India during the aftermath of the Indian Mutiny of 1857.

Schetky's depiction of Lord Anson's triumphant arrival at Spithead, exhibited at the Royal Academy in 1841, is of major historical importance as a celebration of a notable victory which earned Anson his peer-age and title of First Lord of the Admiralty. In the spring of 1747, intelligence reached the British Admiralty that two important enemy convoys, one bound for India and the other for North America, were being prepared in French ports. Anson and a sizeable squadron sailed from Spithead on 26 March for the Bay of Biscay where, by late April, he had gathered a considerable fleet. Meanwhile the French, knowing that Anson's fleet was at sea, decided to combine the two convoys as far as Madeira and assigned to them a strong escorting force under the joint command of Admirals Jonquière and St. Georges. As the two battle fleets drew together, two of Jonquière's armed East Indiamen broke formation, throwing the French line into confusion. Jonquière signalled his ships to retreat but, overwhelmed by the superior gunnery of Anson's fleet, both French commanders' flagships *Le Sérieux* (illustrated in Schetky's picture) and *L'Invincible*, were taken, among the enemy warships.

JOHN CHRISTIAN SCHETKY (1778-1875)
Lord Anson's Arrival at Spithead, 3 May 1747
signed and dated 1841, oil on canvas
48 x 66 in. (122 x 167.7 cm.)
Sold from the Collection of the Royal Institution of Naval Architects
South Kensington, 6 November 1997, £113,200 ($196,133)
A record auction price for the artist

The outstanding price achieved for J.W. Carmichael's *British Opium Schooner* was due, partly no doubt, to the timing of its sale. 1997 was the year when Great Britain's last great colony and trading post was handed over to the Chinese. From the moment the British took formal possession of the territory in 1841, it assumed an imperial role of the greatest importance, not only as a key base for the Royal Navy's far Eastern fleet but also as a major port for the immensely lucrative opium trade with China. Painted in 1843, this picture is an extremely early depiction of Hong Kong and possibly the first by a European artist. Although the topography is partially obscured by the shipping offshore, the bustling trading port is clearly visible beyond, prefiguring the future growth and prosperity of Hong Kong.

JOHN WILSON CARMICHAEL (1799-1868)
A sleek-hulled British Opium Schooner amongst other Shipping, off the Coast of Hong Kong
signed and dated 1843, oil on canvas, 23½ x 35½ in. (59.7 x 90.2 cm.)
South Kensington, 6 November 1997, £172,000 ($296,700)
A record auction price for the artist

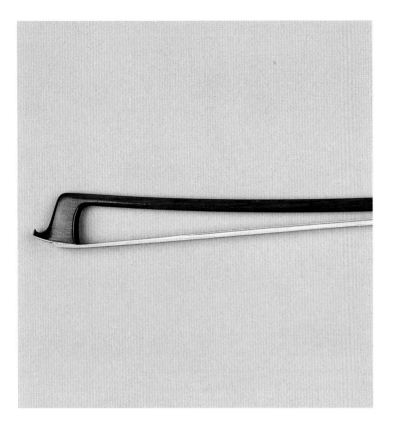

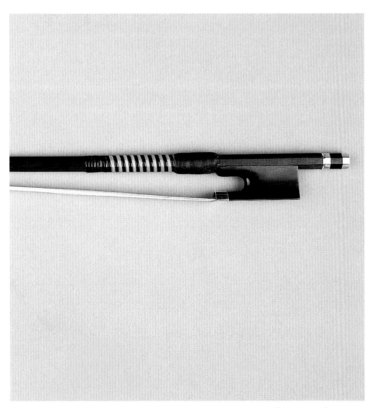

A silver-mounted Violin Bow by François Tourte (1747-1835)
circa 1780
South Kensington, 19 March 1997, £43,300 ($70,059)

An Italian Violin by Giovanni Francesco Pressenda (1777-1854)
labelled 'Joannes Franciscus Pressenda q.Raphael/fecit Taurini
anno Domini 1836'
the length of back 13¹⁵⁄₁₆ in. (35.4 cm)
South Kensington, 16 July 1997, £84,000 ($137,256)

A Queen Anne walnut month-going longcase Clock
Thomas Tompion, London, No. 365, *circa* 1705
7 ft. 10 in. (239 cm.) high
London, 2 July 1997, £331,500 ($550,290)

This clock was a wedding present from Queen Victoria to her first cousin once removed, Princess Frederika of Hanover, who married Baron Alfons von Pavel-Rammingen in 1880. The ceremony was held in the Private Chapel at Windsor Castle. Thomas Tompion (1639 1713) was born the son of a blacksmith in Northill, Bedfordshire. His horological education is totally unknown and the first mention of his name in any records is in 1671 when he became a Brother of the Clockmakers' Company. In 1674 he had established premises in Water Lane and had met the influential academic Dr. Robert Hooke, through whom he came to the notice of King Charles II. By about 1685, Tompion had earned a reputation for making clocks to a consistently higher quality than any other clockmaker and by 1700, he had completed several royal commissions and was universally regarded as the greatest clockmaker in the country. In 1703 he was made Master of the Clockmakers' Company; when he died in 1713, he was buried in Westminster Abbey.

A Charles II walnut bracket Timepiece
Joseph Knibb, London, *circa* 1685
11½ in. (29.2 cm.) high
London, 25 November 1997, £52,100 ($87,528)
A record price for a walnut timepiece by Joseph Knibb

A French mahogany two-day Marine Chronometer
Henri Motel, *circa* 1830
3 in. (78 mm.) dial diam.
London, 25 November 1997, £42,200 ($70,896)
A record auction price for a Marine Chronometer by Motel

Joseph Knibb (1640-1711), is thought to have been apprenticed to his cousin Samuel Knibb (1625 - c.1670) in about 1655. He moved to Oxford to join his brother John in about 1662 and became a Freeman of Oxford in 1668. In 1670 he moved to London, where he set up workshops at 'The Dial' in Fleet Street. Knibb made quite a large number of bracket clocks in this particular style. What sets this clock apart from other similar examples is Knibb's use of walnut: most of his clocks were veneered in ebony. Moreover, the walnut here is of an unusually attractive colour.

Jean-François Motel (1786-1859) was the son of a tavern keeper and farmer in Margny-les-Compiègne. Having studied at the École des Arts et Métiers in Châlons, he won a government scholarship to study in Paris alongside the great clockmaker, Louis Berthoud (1754-1813). He had scarcely finished his apprenticeship, when Louis Berthoud died. Motel stayed on at the workshops to oversee the completion of marine chronometers and watches, commissioned by the French Ministry of Marines.

In 1823 Motel received the highest accolade: he was made *Horloger de la Marine*. In 1817, he left the Berthoud workshop to set up his own business, initially undertaking occasional contract work for the great clock- and watchmaker Abraham-Louis Breguet (1747-1823) and also repairing chronometers for the French navy. By 1821 he was in full production, making his own chronometers, mainly for the French navy. Motel was known to use a springmaker by the name of 'M. Vincent': the present chronometer is signed, dated and inscribed 'Vincent Juin 1830 No. 107'.

UHRENFABRIK UNION; AUDEMARS PIGUET
An 18 carat gold hunter-cased minute-repeating, perpetual calendar,
split second chronograph keyless lever Watch with phases of the moon,
instantaneous minute recorder, flying fifths of a second,
grande and petite sonnerie Clockwatch,
signed, *circa* 1896
2¾ in. (71 mm.) diameter
Geneva, 19 May 1997, SFr. 663,500 (£285,305)

BREGUET
An 18 carat white gold tonneau-shaped
instantaneous perpetual calendar Wristwatch
with phases of the moon,
signed, *circa* 1929
1⅛ in. (29 mm.) long
Geneva, 17 November 1997, SFr. 498,500 (£209,370)

PATEK PHILIPPE
An important 18 carat gold openface keyless
one-minute lever tourbillon Watch
signed, *circa* 1920
2⅛ in. (53 mm.) diameter
Geneva, 17 November 1997, SFr.608,500 (£255,570)

PATEK PHILIPPE
An 18 carat gold minute-repeating hunter cased perpetual calendar keyless
lever Watch with phases of the moon and power reserve
signed, *circa* 1980
2¼ in. (53 mm.) diameter
New York, 29 October 1997, $107,000 (£65,644)

A platinum Wristwatch, ROLEX
signed Rolex and R.W.C. Ltd., model Prince Brancard,
model no. 971u, indistinct case no. 7.528, 1920s
1⅝ x 1 in. (42 x 25 mm.)
Sold from the Ravenborg Collection of Rolex Watches
London, 30 September 1997, £17,825 ($28,591)

EDWARD EAST
A crystal case verge fob Watch
signed, *circa* 1640
1⅞ x 1⅛ in. (48 x 30 mm.)
London, 26 March 1997, £17,250 ($27,945)

The most significant sale held by the Watch department for some years was the sale of the collection of Rolex wristwatches belonging to the German industrialist Hans Ravenborg.

Some 350 examples, representing a wide cross-section of Rolex's production from the 1910s to the present day, were included. This was the first time that such a large private collection of Rolex watches had been offered by any auction house. The sale attracted enormous interest worldwide and made £1.1 million with 94% of the lots being sold.

The sale catalogue has already become a reference work and price guide for collectors and dealers alike.

Fewer and fewer fine early pocketwatches appear on the market, so it was an horologist's delight to see this immaculate crystal-case verge watch by Edward East in Christie's salerooms.

A gilt-brass Ptolemaic armillary Sphere
13 in. (33 cm.) diameter of sphere
South Kensington, 9 April 1997, £771,500 ($1,252,916)

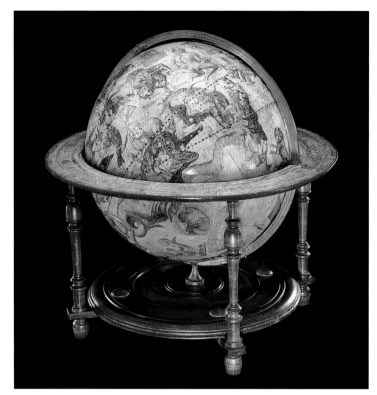

A celestial table Globe
by Jodocus Hondius, the Younger (1591-1629) and
Henricus Hondius (1597-1651), Amsterdam 1627
14 in. (35.5 cm.) diameter
South Kensington, 26 November 1997, £36,700 ($59,967)

This superb armillary sphere is no doubt a companion to the magnificent pair of terrestrial and celestial gilt-metal globes which were sold by Christie's in 1991. They are about the same size, have matching stands and were engraved by the same hand – and come from the same European private collection. The Latin inscription and the *turgha* (Ottoman cypher) on the globes indicate that they were made for Sultan Murad III (1546-95).

It is therefore almost certain that this sphere was also made for Murad III, who, shortly after he succeeded his father in 1574, built an observatory in Istanbul, which was completed in 1577. An Ottoman miniature depicts a room containing quadrants, an astrolabe and a large European globe. A European visitor, Salomon Schweygger, saw the observatory in 1578 and reported the existence of a pair of globes. The observatory stirred religious opposition, however, and was destroyed in 1579.

No other European artefacts of quality destined for the Ottoman court of the second half of the 16th century survive.

This very rare celestial globe was produced by Jodocus Hondius (1563-1612), one of the greatest cartographers of the Dutch 'Golden Age' of globe manufacture. A Protestant, he grew up in Ghent but, in 1584, in order to escape from the religious upheavals of the Low Countries he moved to London, where he produced both maps and globes. In 1595, he returned to the Low Countries, settling in Amsterdam.

Hondius published his second globe pair (his first of 14 inches in diameter) in about 1597, its distinction being that it used observations of previously unknown stars at the South pole, made by Pieter Dircksz. Keyser, Frederik de Houtman and other astronomers of the first Dutch expdition to the East Indies (1595-97). In response to competition from Willem Jansz. Blaeu (1571-1638), Hondius produced a new pair, showing superior astronomical information, with more attractive engravings in the style of Jan Pietersz. Saenredam.

Hondius died in 1612, but his business was continued by his wife Colette van der Keere and his son Jodocus, and later his brother Henricus. It was they who published this second state of the celestial globes in 1627. Only one other copy is known, now in the Bibliothèque Municipale of le Mans.

GRAND CRUS:
A SUPERLATIVE PRIVATE CELLAR

IN what was destined to be a highly successful year for the wine department, the month of September in the Great Room witnessed the most extraordinary auction of a quite remarkable private cellar – or to be more accurate, half of a private cellar, for the 19,000 bottles detailed in the cloth-bound catalogue comprised less than half of the owner's total wine collection.

The vendor, a highly successful European businessman, had never intended to sell his wines. Having been one of the most loyal and astute buyers at Christie's wine auctions for over a decade, he had consistently acquired the greatest wines, with the objective of drinking them. His parameters were broad: he would buy the greatest wines from all over the world, both young and mature, his absolute proviso being that he would accept only wines in the best possible condition and with the best possible provenance. An enthusiastic taster, generous host and bon viveur, he based his buying decisions on his extensive tasting experience.

However, it became apparent, when the total cellar exceeded 40,000 bottles, that he could never consume the wine even if he lived several life-times, and so discussions began about a sale to reduce this to a more manageable size. The result was the sale on 18 and 19 September which, apart from shattering many individual price records, set a new record for a single wine auction and for the sale of a single wine collection anywhere in the world.

What was extraordinary about the sale, and the reason why it so captured the attention of wine lovers the world over, was that it offered supreme quality, exceptional variety and unprecedented

A jeroboam of Château Mouton-Rothschild 1945
London, 18-19 September 1997, £71,500 ($114,614)
A record auction price for the wine, and the highest price
achieved for any bottle of wine since 1985

quantity. It included port from 1908 to 1992; claret from 1899 to 1994; Château d'Yquem from 1847 to 1990; champagne from 1959 to 1985; a superb array of Australia's Grange Hermitage from 1966 to 1991, as well as Rhônes and Cognacs. The quantities on offer of some of the very rarest wines had never previously been seen: 37 bottles of Château Mouton-Rothschild 1945 (up to £4,538 per bottle); 48 bottles of Château Cheval-Blanc 1947 (up to £41,800 per case); 14 cases of Château Latour 1961 (up to £15,400 per case). Younger wines were represented in even more extraordinary quantities, many 1982, 1986, 1989, 1990 first-growths being in quantities of up to fifty cases. Perhaps most remarkable of all were the 20 cases of Château Pétrus 1982 (up to £17,600 per case).

Another unique feature of the collection was the astonishing array of large formats, which attracted fiercely competitive bidding, thanks to their quality and scarcity. Examples included an impériale (8 bottles) of Château Mouton-Rothschild 1929 (£20,900); an impériale of Château Cheval-Blanc 1947 (£68,200) and a jeroboam (6 bottles) of Château Mouton-Rothschild 1945 (£71,500). The latter two bottles were the most expensive wines sold at auction since 1985.

The sale achieved a remarkable total of £7.04 million ($11.29 million) against a pre-sale estimate of just £4.2 million ($6.74 million). It is unlikely that such a comprehensive and extensive cellar will ever again appear on the market.

PAUL BOWKER
DIRECTOR AND HEAD OF THE WINE DEPARTMENT,
CHRISTIE'S LONDON

A case (12 bottles) of Château Latour-à-Pomerol 1961
London, 18-19 September 1997, £55,000 ($88,165)
A record auction price for the wine

An impériale of Château La Mission Haut Brion 1949
London, 18-19 September 1997, £28,600 ($45,845

WINE SALES:
ANOTHER RECORD YEAR

A collection of Château Mouton-Rothschild
vintages 1945 to 1994
London, 4 December 1997
£20,350 ($34,188)

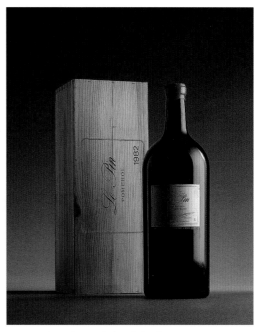

A jeroboam (6 bottles) of Le Pin 1982
London, 9 October 1997
£17,600 ($28,529)

IT has been a quite exceptional year all round in the wine market. The record for a private cellar sold at auction was broken no less than three times, in March, May and finally September, when the 'Grand Crus' sale realized £7 million.

There has been considerable, perhaps excessive, publicity about the influence of a relatively new group of wine lovers in the Asia-Pacific region upon wine prices and, conversely, concern about the possible effect of the economic uncertainties in this region. Whilst there is no doubt that a significant proportion of the finest wines have been heading east, the simple fact is that global demand for wine has never been greater. We enter 1998 with optimism tempered by realism: there will almost certainly be a levelling off of prices at the top level, but this must be seen as a very good thing.

One element which always, rightly, plays a significant part in the level of demand for wines is the provenance, and premium prices have consistently been paid for a number of excellent cellars with particularly good backgrounds. March saw the sale of the first *tranche* of an exemplary cellar from France, offered anonymously on behalf of a distinguished French businessman. The collection, which had been inherited, comprised almost exclusively Bordeaux from 1959 to 1990 and attracted highly competitive bidding. Châteaux Lafite and Latour from the great 1959 vintage achieved £6,820 and £7,480 per dozen respectively, and the whole cellar realized in excess of £400,000.

Another individual cellar which created enormous excitement was the pristine cellar of Sir John Plumb. Sir John, former Master of Christ's College, Cambridge, and a lifelong connoisseur, had built up a magnificent collection, which he kept in Christ's College's perfect cellars, over a period of some fifty years. The number of competing bids was exceptional, and the first bottle, Château Latour 1899, which sold for £2,530, set the tone for the whole sale, with the vast majority of the wines selling significantly over estimate. A total of £334,000 was realized, and Sir John has retained a sufficient number of great wines to ensure his continuing enjoyment.

The strength of the market, a considerable number of great cellars and, of course, the £7 million private cellar sold in September, all made 1997 the most successful year in wine auction history. In addition to sales in London and New York, successful auctions were held in Amsterdam, Geneva, Bordeaux, and Tokyo. The total value sold worldwide amounted to £33.8million, an increase of 51% on the previous year.

PAUL BOWKER
DIRECTOR, WINE DEPARTMENT, CHRISTIE'S LONDON

ZACHYS-CHRISTIE'S NEW YORK WINE SALES

GROWTH in Zachys-Christie's U.S. wine auctions continued unabated in 1997, with a sold total of over $17 million, surpassing even the $13 million achieved in 1996. The market continued to be driven by increases in the prices of Bordeaux, particularly important recent vintages including 1982, 1986, 1989, and 1990. As elsewhere, the United States Bordeaux resale market was pushed considerably by very strong demand for 1995 and 1996 Bordeaux futures, price levels of which were almost as high in some instances as the 1989 and 1990 vintages. By late in the year prices of the 1990 First Growths, except Lafite and Haut-Brion, were virtually equivalent to their 1982 counterparts. Demand from the Far East played a rôle but less significantly so than in London none of the top ten lots in the important September sale went to the Far East, though the sale was 99.7% sold and over the top end of the estimate.

Château Pétrus 1982
New York, 26 September 1997
impériale ($16,100) and jeroboams ($9,200 each)

Another notable feature was the increase in prices for top California red wines. The September sale saw prices in the $3,000 per case range for Dominus 1991 and 1994, as well as some of the rare boutique wines such as Harlan and Bryant Family Cabernets. A case of magnums of Heitz Martha's Vineyard 1974 brought $9,775, more than double the previous high. The high prices of Bordeaux are a factor in this increase, as American wine lovers decide to pay closer to one-half rather than one-sixth the price of First Growth Bordeaux for favoured Cabernets which sometimes perform at the same levels in blind tastings.

The highlight of the year was the single owner sale conducted on behalf of Tawfiq N. Khoury, one of America's foremost collectors. The auction, which totalled almost $3.2 million, comprised about 15,000 bottles of a collection that once exceeded 60,000 and was rich in the great classics: Burgundies from the Domaine de la Romanée-Conti, First Growths, Yquem from 1865 to the present, 'Super Tuscans', along with Heitz, Beaulieu Vineyards Private Reserve, and Opus One cabernets, and an extraordinary range of Madeira. Many of the wines appeared in rare oversize format. A case of magnums of Romanée-Conti 1971, in the original wood, sold for $32,200, and two cases of Montrachet DRC 1978, in the original wood, sold for $32,200 per case. Zachys Christie's were privileged to sell on behalf of two other distinguished collectors during the year: Haskell Norman, the late founder and amazingly energetic director of the Marin Chapter of the International Wine and Food Society; and Belle and Barney Rhodes, America's foremost collecting couple, who have acted as 'ambassadors' for the Napa Valley for over forty years. Northern California collections are noteworthy both for superb selection and the extraordinary condition of the wines. The Rhodes cellar included some of the finest bottles of German TBA's ever to appear at auction in the United States, with prices often exceeding $1,000 per bottle, and the Scharzhofberger TBA 1959 from Egon Muller topping the list at $4,025 for a single bottle.

The most important single lot offered during the year was a fifty-case lot of Mouton Rothschild 1982, in original wooden cases, offered on 26 April 1997. The lot sold for $420,500, or about $8,400 per case, a record price for the wine and for any lot of wine ever sold in the United States. The price reflected both the fine single-owner, single-source provenance and the rarity of such a large block of this wine in the marketplace.

The highly successful Zachys-Christie's partnership now extends to sales conducted throughout the United States, and the partnership's first sale in Los Angeles is to take place on 21 February 1998. 1998 will also witness an increase in the number of sales from five to eight conducted between the two locations, continuing the Christie's Wine Department's practice of offering clients more regular and widespread service than any other firm.

FRITZ HATTON
DIRECTOR, WINE DEPARTMENT, CHRISTIE'S NEW YORK

The Jaguar D-Type is generally acknowledged as one of the greatest classic sports racing cars ever produced. This model scored a hat trick of victories in the famous 24-hour Grand Prix d'Endurance at Le Mans in 1955, 1956 and 1957. This particular example had for many years lain undiscovered in a New England barn.

1956 Jaguar D-Type Sports Racing Car
chassis no. XKD 537, engine no. E2047-9
Pebble Beach, 17 August 1997
$1,014,500 (£608,700)

The 6C series of Alfa Romeos first appeared in 1925 and immediately proved a great success as a light, medium capacity car with brilliant performance. The engine was quickly developed to produce more power and, by 1927, a twin camshaft was introduced. The supercharged variance did particularly well in the sports car category events in 1928 and 1929. The ultimate development of the 6C series was the 1750 Supercharged Gran Sport Testa Fissa. The name *testa fissa* ('fixed head') refers to the engines.

It was a design that was used for only a few high performance race engines for the Alfa Romeo Works entries. This particular example is reputed to be the car that finished second in the 1931 Mille Miglia.

The Ex Count Johnny Lurani Alfa Romeo
6C-1750 (1931)
supercharged Gran Sport Testa Fissa
Sold from the Ben Rose Collection
New York, 26 April 1997, $651,500 (£397,415)
A world record price for the model

While Ferrari is perhaps most famous for their 12-cylinder engines, by 1952 they had successfully introduced a lighter, more reliable and efficient 4-cylinder engine for the Formula 2 category. This smaller engine model provided world championship titles for Alberto Ascari in 1952 and 1953. In 1953, the 625TF (Tipo Formula) Barchetta was announced. Only three examples were built, and this one is the sole known survivor. This model thus marks an important beginning in Ferrari 4-cylinder sports racing cars, from which evolved a number of highly competitive vehicles which won numerous events throughout the 1950s. This particular car was a factory team car and was raced by the late Mike Hawthorn.

The Ex Works Mike Hawthorn
1953 Ferrari 625TF Barchetta
coachwork by Vignale
Geneva, 22 May 1997, SFr. 1,235,500 (£531,265)

In 1955, the Maserati factory created the Tipo 300S, which was virtually a sports racing version of the 250F Grand Prix car. Similar to its sister car, the 300S had a reputation for superb road holding, and all drivers remember it with the utmost affection. The principal competition came from Mercedes-Benz, Ferrari, Jaguar and Aston Martin, all of whom provided better straight line speed. However, the 300S was invariably a better handling car and its long stroke 3 litre engine proved to have a good endurance record. During Christie's view, more of this car's history came to light: it was confirmed as a factory (Works) team car, and indeed Stirling Moss won the Venezuelan Grand Prix in this very vehicle in 1956. It is also thought that the car raced in several other events in South America during that time and, interestingly, the car was later sold to Juan Manual Fangio (the five times World Champion driver).

1956 Maserati 300S
chassis no. 3062, engine no. 3069
London, 14 July 1997, £441,500 ($746,135)

243

A Selection of Armour and Edged Weapons
Sold from a Private Collection
South Kensington, 12 December 1997, £717,500 ($1,192,485) for the whole collection

The December sale of Antique Arms and Armour totalled £1.2 million, with 97% sold. It included the finest group of early European armour and edged weapons to have come on the market since the Hever Castle sale in 1983, most of the pieces consigned by a private collector from the United States who was at his most active in the 1970s. The highest price achieved was £155,500 for part of an etched and gilt Milanese garniture for the field and tournament, ascribed to Emmanuel Philibert, Duke of Savoy (1528-1580). A portrait by Giacomo Vighi detto l'Argenta (c.1510-1573) in the Galleria Sabauda, Turin, shows Emmanuel Philibert wearing the garniture, of which the majority of pieces known to survive are in the Armeria Reale, Turin. Also illustrated above (far left and far right) are two 15th century sallets, one German and the other Italian, which sold for £73,000 and £106,000 respectively.

.600 (3 in. nitro express) double-barrelled 'Royal' hammer Rifle
by Holland & Holland, No. 19285
weight 15lb. 15oz., 14⅜ in. pull, 26 in. barrels, nitro proof
London, 17 December 1997, £37,800 ($61,992)

This exceptional rifle was made in 1909 for H.H. Prince Youssouf Kemal of Egypt. In the Holland & Holland records it is described as 'a best quality .600 bore Hammer Ejector Cordite Rifle', sighted 'to 25 metres only' and built so as to be well balanced and butt-heavy. It took eight months to make and was dispatched to Cairo in October 1909. Whilst it was designed to be built as a hammer ejector, the production only went so far as to cut the slots in the action-body and forend-iron for the ejector work, leaving it as a non-ejector, with provision for rapid conversion to ejector if needed.

The Tussauds' Collection of fairground art, recognized as one of the world's finest, was formed during the 1960s and 1970s by Lord and Lady Bangor, who had a little shop called 'Trad', in the Portobello Road, which was an Aladdin's Cave of unusual antiques. The Tussauds' Group purchased the bulk of the Bangor's collection in 1973, and it was subsequently displayed, with much imagination, at one of their former visitor attractions at Wookey Hole Caves, where it was auctioned by Christie's.

The Collection was made up of approximately 120 animals and 70 figurative pieces, many of which were extremely rare. The Heyn Hippocampus was a rare piece carved by Friedrich Heyn, of Neustadt near Dresden, who was Europe's most prolific producer of carved animals from 1870 onwards.

The Heyn Hippocampus
circa 1890
49 in. (124 cm.) wide
Sold from the Tussauds' Collection of Fairground Art
Wookey Hole, Somerset, 6 October 1997, £25,300 ($40,859)

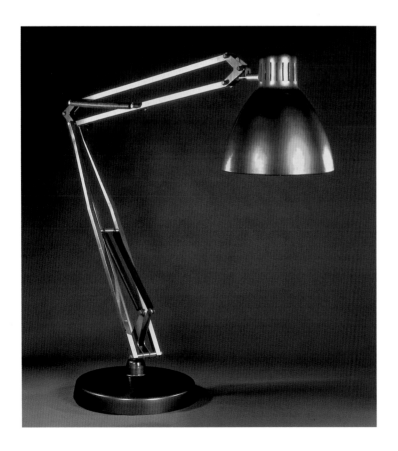

Architect and designer, Gaetano Pesce (b. 1939) was one of the most important Italian exponents of 'radical' or anti-design during the 1960s, influenced by American Pop artists, such as Claes Oldenburg. He made his name with his moulded polyester tables and 'Up' series of chairs (1969), made of brightly coloured compressed polyurethane foam, compressed to a tenth of their normal size, vacuum packed into boxes which, when opened, allowed the polyurethane to bounce into life.

Pesce has taught at many institutions, including the Carnegie Mellon University of Pittsburgh, Cooper Union School of Art and Architecture, Sao Paulo School of Architecture and the University of Strasburg.

The Moloch lamp, which looks on paper like a desk lamp, surprises one when seen 'in the flesh', because of its size: it is more than ten feet high and would be almost eighteen feet if fully extended vertically. The design is derived from the original by Naska Loris.

A Moloch anglepoise Floor Lamp
designed by Gaetano Pesce in 1970-71
213 in. (542 cm.) fully extended
South Kensington, 26 March 1997, £20,700 ($33,492)

This is one of the most sought-after of all Mickey Mouse tinplate toys. No more than ten examples of the rare five-fingered Mickey motor-cyclist are believed to exist. This is believed to be the only example with its original box.

A lithographed tinplate clockwork Mickey Mouse Motorcycle
by Tipp & Co., Germany, early 1930s
6½ x 9½ in. (16.5 x 24.1 cm.)
South Kensington, 16 June 1997, £51,000 ($83,385)
A world record auction price for a piece of its kind

1997 saw Christie's fifth annual Teddy Bear sale which, like its predecessors, was a huge success. Christie's devoted an entire section of the sale to Steiff bears in honour of Margarete Steiff's 150th Birthday.

Margarete Steiff, born on 24 July 1847, was a remarkable woman from an equally remarkable family, founders of the world's first soft toy company and creators of the world's most popular toy, the teddy bear. When Margarete Steiff died on 9 May 1909 at the age of 61 years, the trademark of the Steiff company had become a quality seal for the highest standards.

Christie's holds the world record for a teddy bear sold at auction with 'Teddy Girl', a Steiff teddy bear, which fetched £110,000 in December 1994.

A Steiff Teddy Bear
circa 1905
20 in. (51 cm.) high
South Kensington, 8 December 1997, £23,000 ($38,065)

Pandora's Box (1929)
A Nero-Film Poster, French
63 x 47 in. (160 x 119.4 cm.)
South Kensington, 19 May 1997, £8,500 ($13,923)

A velvet stage Shirt worn by Elvis Presley in 1956
South Kensington, 29 May 1997, £10,925 ($17,862)

An Album Cover for *Sergeant Pepper's Lonely Hearts Club Band*, 1967
signed by all four members of The Beatles
South Kensington, 29 May 1997, £6,900 ($11,247)

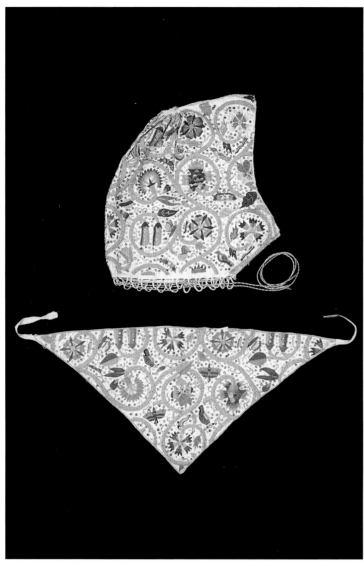

A Coif and forehead Cloth
linen embroidered in silk and gold thread
English, *circa* 1610
South Kensington, 10 June 1997, £24,150 ($39,461)

An Anglo-Indian open Robe and Petticoat
appliqué in gold thread and sequins with
chintz flowers and butterflies, *circa* 1785
South Kensington, 7 October 1997, £20,700 ($33,451)

This early 17th century lady's coif with forehead cloth is embroidered in brightly coloured silks. English needlework of this period is justly famous and very sought after. One very rarely finds examples in such fresh and vivid colours, including reds and pinks. The coif has retained its original tie strings and loops and matching forehead cloth. Earlier this century it was at Fingask, a Perthshire castle, which housed an important collection of needlework, including Jacobite work.

This superb 18th century open robe and petticoat is applied with motifs of Indian chintz, cut out and edged with gold fringe and sequins. The effect is similar to the 18th century patchwork coverlets called *broderie perse*.

The dress is beautifully made, retaining its tie strings, designed so that it could be worn *à la polonaise*. It is rare to find an 18th century dress in such good condition and totally without later alterations.

AT CHRISTIE'S

CHRISTIE'S GREAT ESTATES

CHRISTIE'S Great Estates, with its network of 350 real estate offices worldwide and more than 10,000 estate agents, completed a very successful year.

Selected as exclusive marketing agents for *The World of ResidenSea*, the world's first residential and most technologically advanced ocean liner, Christie's Great Estates introduced this remarkable new concept to clients seeking exclusive travel, adventure and accommodation. The liner boasts 250 spacious apartments, plus an extraordinary array of amenities and state-of-the-art business

facilities. Christie's Great Estates' network successfully sold a number of the apartments ranging in price from $1.2 million to $5.3 million.

The 958-foot luxury liner is the creation of Norwegian architects Petter Yran and Bjørn Storbraaten who, together with cruise industry leader Knut Kloster, Jr. and Captain Ola Harsheim, have been responsible for the majority of the finest cruise ships ever built. Upon completion, *The World of ResidenSea* will begin a continuous circumnavigation of the globe, with extended, scheduled stays in cities during events of international importance.

Following the successful sale of Douglas S. Cramer's Contemporary Art Collection in New York this year, Christie's

Great Estates successfully sold 'La Quinta Norte', Cramer's 100-acre estate in Santa Ynez Valley, California. The 20,000 square foot residence features views over the property's own vineyards and stunning interior treatments including Yosemite slate floors, a clay wine cellar, 15th century carved stone Celtic archways and built-in furnishings for every room. The estate was offered for sale at $8.5 million.

CHRISTIE'S EDUCATION

CHRISTIE'S Education runs a wide variety of specialized and non-specialized programmes in all aspects of the fine and decorative arts, opera and wine, for students of widely differing ages and academic backgrounds.

All periods are covered from classical antiquity to contemporary art, and courses range from diploma to evening courses. These are run in London, Scotland, Paris, New York and Australia. Each course makes full use of the collections and exhibitions available in each location and emphasizes the value of direct contact with works of art.

1997 saw the launch of a successful programme of lectures and classes in association with the 20th century sales at Christie's South Kensington. Further talks on modern design, studio pottery and 20th century jewellery are planned for 1998. Both Christie's Geneva and the new saleroom in Los Angeles offered educational lectures and seminars all of which were well attended. The inaugural Decorative Arts Summer School run by Christie's Education in New York was immensely popular and will be repeated in 1998. Oxford University and Christie's Education are launching a new Summer Programme on *Arts and Connoisseurship in the 18th Century*, at Christ Church, Oxford, in August 1998.

THE GARDEN
OF THE YEAR AWARD

THE superb gardens of Sudeley Castle near Winchcombe in Gloucestershire won this year's Garden of the Year Award, sponsored by the Historic Houses Association and Christie's.

In the 10th century, Ethelred 'the Unready' gave the manor of Sudeley to his daughter Goda on her betrothal to Walter de Maunt, but the castle of Sudeley dates from the 15th century. It passed to the Duke of Gloucester (the future Richard III) and Henry VIII's widow Katherine Parr (who is buried in the grounds). Sadly, the castle was largely destroyed in 1649, on the orders of Cromwell, and lay in ruins for 180 years. It was resuscitated by

the indefatigable Emma Brocklehurst, who in 1852 married John Coucher Dent. Sudeley's survival today is due to the sedulous efforts of the Dent Brocklehurst family.

The splendour and variety of the gardens today are due to the dedication and gusto of the present owner, Lady Ashcombe, assisted by Lanning Roper, Jane Fernley Whittingstall and Rosemary Verey.

The Queens' Garden, boasting over 800 roses, commemorates three queens associated with Sudeley: Katherine Parr, Lady Jane Grey and Elizabeth I. The gardens are divided into several smaller gardens, each with its own character: the Tithe Barn Garden, the White Garden, the Ruins Garden, the Mulberry Garden, the Dungeon Terrace and the recently created Knot Garden, inspired by a pattern in the 16th century Sheldon Tapestry, which hangs in the library at Sudeley.

NATIONAL ART COLLECTIONS
FUND EXHIBITION

IN January 1997 Christie's hosted a sumptuous exhibition of 150 works, drawn from over 50 public collections, all saved for the nation thanks to the support of the NACF, Britain's largest art charity. This represented 10% of the works acquired with the help of the Fund over the last 15 years.

Most visitors were astonished by the diversity and exceptional quality of the objects, which ranged from antiquities, paintings, drawings and sculptures to textiles, jewellery, ceramics, glass and furniture. Highlights included a masterpiece of Sienese *trecento* art, the exquisitely solemn *Crucifixion*, attributed to Duccio; El Greco's shadowy, sensual and enigmatic canvas, known only as *An Allegory*; Claude's infinitely mysterious *The Enchanted Castle*; Nicholas de Largillière's *Anne Throckmorton as a Nun*, a quiet miracle of 18th century portraiture at its most subtle; van Dyck's sensitive study of the infant daughters of Charles I, Princess Elizabeth and Princess Anne (illustrated below); a charming Zoffany portrait of John Wilkes, gazing fondly at his plain daughter. Less familiar objects included an 18th century dress, destined for a lady with the most slender of waists; a very rare carved, 12th century unicorn's horn; the astonishingly well preserved Bronze Age dirk, a ceremonial dagger, dating from *circa* 1200 B.C.; the exquisite 15th century Middleham jewel; and the very ornate 18th century silver-gilt toilet service of the Countess of Kildare.

Included in the exhibition were works of art recently acquired with lottery funds - two Renaissance drawings by Marco Zoppo; an ebonized pine table with pearl inlay by Charles Rennie Mackintosh; works from the Penrose Collection of Dada and Surrealist art; Ken Howard's *Ulster Crucifixion*; a Paula Rego *Self-portrait*; and the 12th century Limoges casket, known as the Thomas à Becket *châsse*.

The exhibition served as a highly persuasive exhortation to visit, or re-visit, museums and collections outside the capital.

Christie's International plc

Directors

The Lord Hindlip

Chairman; A. N. G. Annesley, *Deputy Chairman*

C. M. Davidge, *Chief Executive*

C. J. Burge; F. P. Curiel;

S. S. Lash; C. R. Balfour;

P. J. Blythe, F.C.M.A.

Non-Executive:

The Rt. Hon. The Lord Carrington, K.G; The Lord Rockley;

Sir Anthony Tennant; N. Clive Worms;

The Hon. Janet de Botton; The Baroness Dunn, D.B.E.

R. H. Aydon, *Secretary*

NORTH AMERICA AND SOUTH AMERICA

SALEROOMS

Christie's Inc.
502 Park Avenue
New York, New York 10022
Tel: (212) 546 1000   Fax: (212) 980 8163
Christopher J. Burge, *Chairman*
Stephen S. Lash, *Vice Chairman*
Patricia G. Hambrecht, *President*
Geoffrey Iddison, *Chief Operating Officer*

Christie's East
219 East 67th Street
New York, New York 10021
Tel: (212) 606 0400   Fax: (212) 737 6076
Catherine D. Elkies, *President*

Christie's Los Angeles
360 North Camden Drive
Beverly Hills, California 90210
Tel: (310) 385 2600   Fax: (310) 385 9292
Marcia Wilson Hobbs, *Chairman*
Jean-René Saillard, *Managing Director*
Andrea Fiuczynski, *Director of Specialist Departments*
Brooke Glassman Kanter, *Estates & Appraisals*

REPRESENTATIVES

Atlanta
Alison M. Thompson
P.O. Box 550652, Atlanta, Georgia 30355
Tel: (404) 846 0780   Fax: (404) 846 0790

Baltimore
Tel: (410) 832 7555

Boston
Elizabeth M. Chapin
Susan Florence, *Jewellery*
Brigitte Bradford
216 Newbury Street
Boston, Massachusetts 02116-2543
Tel: (617) 536 6000   Fax: (617) 536 0002

Chicago
Mary Ahern, Laura de Frise
Frances Blair, *Senior Director, Midwest*
Susan Florence, *Jewellery*
200 West Superior Street, Chicago, Illinois 60610
Tel: (312) 787 2765   Fax: (312) 951 7449

Dallas
Carolyn Foxworth
5500 Preston Road, Suite 210, Dallas, Texas 75205
Tel: (214) 521 1843   Fax: (214) 521 8265

Delaware
Andrew C. Rose
P.O. Box 4357, Greenville, Delaware 19807
Tel: (302) 421 5719   Fax: (302) 421 5719

Houston
Lisa Cavanaugh
5900 Memorial Drive, Suite 203, Houston, TX 77007
Tel: (713) 802 0191   Fax: (713) 802 0193

Miami
Vivian Pfeiffer, Caroline Waggoner, *Jewellery*
Alina Pedroso Arellano, Jean Kislak
110 Merrick Way, Suite 2A
Coral Gables, Florida 33134
Tel: (305) 445 1487   Fax: (305) 441 6561

Minneapolis
Carol V. Bemis, Kelly Perry
706 Second Avenue South, Suite 710
Minneapolis, Minnesota 55402
Tel: (612) 664 0478   Fax: (612) 644 0479

Montgomery (Southeast)
Carol W. Ballard
P.O. Box 231207, Montgomery, Alabama 36123
Tel: (334) 244 9688   Fax: (334) 244 9588

New Orleans
Susan Gore Brennan
240A Chartres Street
New Orleans, Louisiana 70130
Tel: (504) 522 0008   Fax: (504) 522 8005

Newport
Betsy D. Ray, Ralph Carpenter, *Consultant*
228 Spring St, Newport, Rhode Island 02840
Tel: (401) 849 9222   Fax: (401) 849 6322

Oklahoma City
Konrad Keesee
6421 Avondale Drive
Oklahoma City, Oklahoma 73116
Tel: (405) 843 9460   Fax: (405) 843 9460

Palm Beach
Meg Bowen, Caroline Waggoner, *Jewellery*
Helen Cluett
440 Royal Palm Way, Suite 103
Palm Beach, Florida 33480
Tel: (561) 833 6952   Fax: (561) 833 0007

Philadelphia
Susan Ravenscroft, Paul Ingersoll, *Consultant*
P.O. Box 1112, Bryn Mawr, Pennsylvania 19010
Tel: (610) 525 5493   Fax: (610) 525 0967

Puerto Rico
Carlos Condé III
P.O. Box 2254, San Juan, Puerto Rico 00902
Tel: (787) 725 1455   Fax: (787) 723 5787

St. Louis
Alden H. Pflager
P.O. Box 16805, St. Louis, MO 63105
Tel: (314) 994 1088   Fax: (314) 994 0348

San Francisco/Pacific Northwest
Laura Knoop King
3516 Sacramento Street
San Francisco, California 94118
Tel: (415) 346 6633   Fax: (415) 346 8084
For residents of Washington and Oregon
Tel: (800) 625 2373

Santa Barbara
Carlyle C. Eubank
P.O. Box 1598, Santa Ynez, CA 93460
Tel: (805) 688 2728   Fax: (805) 686 4548

Seattle
Tel: (206) 323 2264

Washington, D.C.
Cathy Sledz
Brittain Cudlip, Nuala Pell, Joan Gardner
Hamilton Court, 1228 31st Street N.W.
Washington, D.C. 20007
Tel: (202) 333 7459   Fax: (202) 342 0537

Canada
Montreal
Brenda Norris
Tel: (514) 932 5134   Fax: (514) 932 5134
Toronto
Suzanne E. Davis
170 Bloor Street West, Suite 210
Toronto, Ontario M5S IT9
Tel: (416) 960 2063   Fax: (416) 960 8815
Tel: (800) 960 2063 *(Canada)*
Vancouver
Jodi M. Norrison
555 West Hastings Street, Suite 700
Vancouver, British Columbia V6B 4N5
Tel: (604) 893 7017   Fax: (604) 893 7018
Tel: (800) 893 7017 *(Canada)*

Argentina
Cristina Erhart del Campo
Arroyo 850, 1007 Capital, Buenos Aires
Tel: (541) 393 4222   Fax: (541) 394 9578

Brazil
Rio de Janeiro
Candida Sodré
Marie Teresa Sodré
Rua Icatu 39, Apt. 203
Botafogo, Rio de Janeiro 22260-190
Tel: (5521) 539 9583   Fax: (5521) 286 8237
São Paulo
Paulo Figueiredo
Maria Teresa Sozio
Christina Paranos do Rio Branco
Alameda Casa Branca
851 conj. 121, 01408-001 São Paulo
Tel: (5511) 881 0435   Fax: (5511) 852 7244

Chile
Denise Ratinoff de Lira
Martin de Zamora 3611
Los Condes, Santiago de Chile
Tel: (562) 231 7349   Fax: (562) 232 2671

Mexico
Patricia Hernández
Miguel Cervantes, *Consultant*
Galileo 54, piso 2, Col. Polanco, Mexico D.F. 11560
Tel: (525) 281 5503, (525) 281 5463
Fax: (525) 281 5454

Uruguay
Cristina de Berenbau
Gral. French 1767, Montevideo 11500, Uruguay
Tel: (598) 260 2941   Fax: (598) 260 7723

Venezuela
Alain Jathière
Quinta las Magnolias, Calle Los Olivos
Los Chorros, Caracas
Tel: (582) 238 0355   Fax: (582) 235 7613

UNITED KINGDOM

SALEROOMS

Head Office
Christie, Manson & Woods Ltd.
8 King Street, St. James's, London SW1Y 6QT
Tel: (0171) 839 9060   Fax: (0171) 839 1611
Christopher Balfour, *Chairman*
François Curiel, *Vice Chairman*
John Lumley, *Vice Chairman*
Maria Reinshagen, *Vice Chairman*
The Earl of Halifax, *Vice Chairman*
Charles Cator, *Deputy Chairman*
D.A. Streatfeild, *Managing Director*

South Kensington
Christie's South Kensington Ltd.
85 Old Brompton Road, London SW7 3LD
Tel: (0171) 581 7611   Fax: (0171) 321 3321
W.A. Coleridge, F.R.I.C.S., *President*
Dermot Chichester, *Chairman*
P.A. Barthaud, *Managing Director*

Scotland
Christie's Scotland Ltd.
164-166 Bath Street, Glasgow G2 4TB
Tel: (0141) 332 8134   Fax. (0141) 332 5759
Dermot Chichester, *Chairman*
P. Arbuthnot, *Managing Director*

ENGLAND AND WALES

REPRESENTATIVES

Northumbria
Aidan Cuthbert
Eastfield House, Main Street
Corbridge, Northumberland NE45 5LA
Tel: (01434) 633181   Fax: (01434) 633891

North West
Victor Gubbins, F.R.I.C.S.
Eden Lacy
Lazonby, Penrith, Cumbria CA10 1BZ
Tel: (01768) 898 800   Fax: (01768) 898 020

Yorkshire
Thomas Scott F.S.A. (Scot)
Stephanie Bilton
Sir Nicholas Brooksbank, Bt.
192 Huntington Road, York YO3 9BN
Tel: (01904) 630911   Fax: (01904) 644448
Richard Compton, *Non-executive*

North-West Midlands & North Wales
Richard Roundell, F.R.I.C.S.
Dorfold Hall, Nantwich, Cheshire CW5 8LD
Tel: (01270) 627024   Fax: (01270) 628723

Nottinghamshire & Derbyshire
David Coke-Steel
Trusley Old Hall, Sutton-on-the-Hill
Ashbourne, Derbyshire DE6 5JG
Tel: (01283) 733783   Fax: (01283) 733076

South Midlands & South Wales
The Earl Fortescue
Simon Reynolds
111 The Promenade, Cheltenham, Glos. GL50 1PS
Tel: (01242) 518999   Fax: (01242) 576240
Rupert de Zoete, *Consultant*

East Midlands
Rupert Hanbury
The Old Dairy, Elton, Nr. Peterborough PE8 6SQ
Tel: (01832) 280 876   Fax: (01832) 280 877
Mrs. William Proby, *Non-executive*

East Anglia
Charles Bingham-Newland
Sackville Place, 44-48 Magdalen Street
Norwich NR3 1JU
Tel: (01603) 614546   Fax: (01603) 618176
Thomas Fellowes, *Non-executive*

Devon and Cornwall
The Hon. George Lopes, A.R.I.C.S.
Gnaton Estate Office, Yealmpton,
Plymouth, Devon PL8 2HU
Tel: (01752) 880636   Fax: (01752) 880968

West Country and Wiltshire
Richard de Pelet
Huntsman's Lodge, Inwood
Templecombe, Somerset BA8 0PF
Tel: (01963) 370518   Fax: (01963) 370605

South Dorset & Hampshire
Nigel Thimbleby
Wolfeton House, Nr. Dorchester
Dorset DT2 9QN
Tel: (01305) 268748   Fax: (01305) 265090

Essex & Hertfordshire
James Service
Hawkins Harvest, Great Bardfield
Essex CM7 4QW
Tel: (01371) 810189   Fax: (01371) 810028

Hampshire & Berkshire
Richard Wills
Middleton Estate Office
Longparish, Andover, Hampshire SP11 6PL
Tel: (01264) 720211   Fax: (01264) 720271

Sussex & Surrey
Mark Wrey
North Street, Petworth, West Sussex GU28 0DD
Tel: (01798) 344440   Fax: (01798) 344442

Kent
Gail Jessel
Ladham House, Goudhurst, Kent TN17 1DB
Tel: (01580) 212595   Fax: (01580) 212596

Christopher Proudfoot
The Old Rectory, Fawkham
Longfield, Kent DA3 8LX
Tel: (01474) 702 854   Fax: (01474) 702 854

SCOTLAND

North of Scotland
Lady Eliza Leslie Melville
Lochluichart, By Garve, Ross-shire IV23 2PZ
Tel: (01997) 414 370   Fax: (01997) 414 340

Tayside, Fife & Grampian
Roy Miller, F.R.I.C.S.
3/5 Mill Street, Perth PH1 5JB
Tel: (01738) 643088   Fax: (01738) 635227

Edinburgh & the Borders
Roy Miller, F.R.I.C.S.
Robert Lagneau
5 Wemyss Place, Edinburgh EH3 6DH
Tel: (0131) 225 4756/7   Fax: (0131) 225 1723

South West Scotland
Victor Gubbins F.R.I.C.S.
Eden Lacy, Penrith, Cumbria CA10 1BZ
Tel: (01768) 898 800   Fax: (01768) 898 020

Isle of Man
The Marchioness Conyngham
Myrtle Hill, Andreas Road
Ramsey, Isle of Man IM8 3UA
Tel: (01624) 814502   Fax: (01624) 814502

Channel Islands
Melissa Bonn
Richard de la Hey, *Consultant*
58 David Place, St. Helier, Jersey
Tel: (01534) 877582   Fax: (01534) 877540

REPUBLIC OF IRELAND
Desmond Fitz-Gerald, Knight of Glin
Glin Castle, Glin, Co. Limerick
Fax: (35368) 34 364
Private Residence
52 Waterloo Road, Dublin 4
Tel: (3531) 668 05 85   Fax: (3531) 668 02 71

NORTHERN IRELAND
Danny Kinahan
Castle Upton, Templepatrick
Co. Antrim BT39 0AH
Tel: (018494) 33480   Fax: (018494) 33410

WORLDWIDE SALEROOMS

Australia

Melbourne
The Lord Poltimore, *Chairman*
Roger McIlroy, *Managing Director*
Christie's Australia Pty. Ltd.
1 Darling Street, South Yarra, Melbourne
Victoria 3141
Tel: (613) 9820 4311   Fax: (613) 9820 4876

Greece

Athens
Elisavet Logotheti-Lyra, *Managing Director*
Christie's Hellas Ltd
26 Philellinon Street, 10558 Athens
Tel: (301) 324 6900   Fax: (301) 324 6925

Hong Kong

Anthony Lin, *Deputy Chairman*
Bonnie Lau, *General Manager*
Ellanor Notides, *Western Paintings, Asia*
Kwan S. Wong, *Chinese Paintings International*
Edmond Chin, *Western & Jadeite Jewellery*
Christie's Hong Kong Ltd.
2203-5 Alexandra House
16-20 Chater Road, Central, Hong Kong
Tel: (852) 2521 5396   Fax: (852) 2845 2646

Israel

Mary Gilben
Christie's (Israel) Ltd
Asia House, 4 Weizmann St, Tel Aviv 64239
Tel: (9723) 695 0695   Fax: (9723) 695 2751

Italy

Rome
Franz Ziegler, *Managing Director*
Francesco Alverà
Christie's (Int.) S.A., Palazzo Massimo Lancellotti,
Piazza Navona 114, Rome 00186
Tel: (396) 687 2787   Fax: (396) 686 9902

Monaco

Pascal Bégo
Christie's Monaco S.A.M.
Park Palace, 98000 Monte-Carlo
Tel: (377) 97 97 11 00   Fax: (377) 97 97 11 01

The Netherlands

Bernard Steyaert, *Managing Director*
Christie's Amsterdam B.V.
Cornelis Schuytstraat 57, 1071 JG Amsterdam
Tel: (3120) 57 55 255   Fax: (3120) 66 40 899

Singapore

Irene Lee
Cecilia Ong, *Consultant*
Christie's International Singapore Pte Ltd.
Unit 3, Parklane, Goodwood Park Hotel,
22 Scotts Road, Singapore 228221
Tel: (65) 235 3828   Fax: (65) 235 8128

Switzerland

Geneva
François Curiel, *President*
Guy Jennings, *Vice President*
Elisabeth Storm Nagy, *Vice President*
Franz Ziegler, *Managing Director*
Christie's (Int.) S.A.
8 Place de la Taconnerie, 1204 Geneva
Tel: (4122) 319 1766   Fax: (4122) 319 1767
Zürich
Maria Reinshagen, *Vice Chairman, Europe*
Dr. Brigit Bernegger, *Vice President*
Claudia Steinfels, *Administration Manager*
Christie's (Int.) A.G., Steinwiesplatz, 8032 Zürich
Tel: (411) 268 1010   Fax: (411) 268 1011

REPRESENTATIVES

Christie's Asia Region Office

Philip Ng, *Managing Director, Asia*
501 Orchard Road
15-02 Wheelock Place, Singapore 238880
Tel: (65) 737 3884   Fax: (65) 733 7975

Australia

Sydney
Nellie Dawes
180 Jersey Road, Woollahra, Sydney, NSW 2025
Tel: (612) 9326 1422   Fax: (612) 9327 8439
Adelaide
James and Ian Bruce
446 Pulteney Street, Adelaide S.A. 5000
Tel: (618) 8232 2860   Fax: (618) 8232 6506
Brisbane
Nicole Roberts
1st Floor, 482 Brunswick Street, Fortitude Valley
Brisbane 4006, Queensland
Tel: (617) 3254 1499   Fax: (617) 3254 1566
Perth
Cherry Lewis
68 Mount Street, Perth W.A.
Tel: (619) 321 5764   Fax: (619) 322 1387

Austria

Dr. Johanna Schönburg-Hartenstein, *Chairman*
Cornelia Pallavicini, *Managing Director*
Christie's Kunstauktionen GmbH
Kohlmarkt 4, 1010 Vienna
Tel: (431) 533 88 12   Fax: (431) 533 71 66

Belgium

Bernard Steyaert, *Chairman*
Bernard de Launoit, *General Manager*
Sabine Taevernier, *Contemporary Art*
Roland de Lathuy, *Old Master Pictures*
Christie's Belgium S.A.
33 Boulevard de Waterloo, 1000 Brussels
Tel: (322) 512 8830   Fax: (322) 513 3279

Czech Republic

Prague
H.S.H. The Princess Elisabeth Lobkowicz
Snemovni Ulice II, Mala Strana, 11800 Praha – 1
Tel: (4202) 5709 6127   Fax: (4202) 5709 6128

People's Republic of China

Shanghai
Lillian Chu
Christie's Shanghai Ltd
Suite 404, American International Centre
1376 Nanjing Road West, Shanghai 200040
Tel: (8621) 6279 8773   Fax: (8621) 6279 8771
Beijing
Ben Kong
Christie, Manson & Woods Ltd.
16b Citic Building, 19 Jianguomenwai Dajie
Beijing 100004, China
Tel: (8610) 6500 6517   Fax: (8610) 6500 6034

Denmark

Birgitta Hillingsø
Dronningens Tværgade 10, 1302 Copenhagen K
Tel: (45) 33 32 70 75   Fax: (45) 33 13 00 75

Finland

Barbro Schauman
VuorimiehenKatu 5A, 00140 Helsinki
Tel: (3589) 60 82 12   Fax: (3589) 66 06 87

France

Hubert de Givenchy, *President*
Hugues Joffre, *President du Directoire*
Bertrand du Vignaud
Franck Prazan
Christie's France S.A.
6 rue Paul Baudry, 75008 Paris
Tel: (331) 40 76 8585   Fax: (331) 42 56 2601
Aix-en-Provence
Fabienne Albertini-Cohen
28 rue Lieutaud, 13100 Aix en Provence
Tel: (33) 4 92 72 43 31   Fax: (33) 4 92 72 53 65
Bordeaux
Marie-Cecile Moueix
49 Cours Xavier Arnozan, 33000 Bordeaux
Tel: (33) 5 56 81 65 47   Fax: (33) 5 56 51 15 71
Centre et Val de Loire
Nicole de Yturbe
Château de Montgraham, 28400 Souance au Perche
Tel: (33) 2 37 29 13 66
Lyon
Vicomte Thierry de Lachaise
36 Place Bellecour, 69002 Lyon
Tel: (33) 4 78 42 83 82   Fax: (33) 4 78 42 83 84

Germany

Christopher Balfour, *Chairman*
Jörg-Michael Bertz, *Deputy Chairman*
Stefan Prinz von Ratibor, *General Manager*
Birgid Seynsche-Vautz, *Administrative Manager*
Berlin
Stefan Prinz von Ratibor, *General Manager*
Marianne Kewenig, *Senior Representative*
Frederik Schwarz, *Jewellery*
Viktoria von Specht
Fasanenstrasse 72, 10719 Berlin
Tel: (4930) 885 6950   Fax: (4930) 885 69595
Düsseldorf
Jörg-Michael Bertz, *Senior Specialist*
(19th & 20th Century Pictures)
Birgid Seynsche-Vautz, *Administration Manager*
Maike Borgwardt, *Valuation Manager*
Christie's (Deutschland) GmbH
P.O. Box 101810 Inselstrasse 15, 40479 Düsseldorf
Tel: (49211) 491 5930   Fax: (49211) 492 0339
Frankfurt
Charlotte Prinzessin von Croÿ
Gérard Goodrow, Nina von Ondarza
Arndtstrasse 18, 60325 Frankfurt am Main
Tel: (4969) 74 50 21   Fax: (4969) 75 20 79
Hamburg
Christiane Gräfin zu Rantzau
Wentzelstrasse 21, 22301 Hamburg
Tel: (4940) 279 4073   Fax: (4940) 270 4497

Munich
Marie Christine Gräfin Huyn
Residenzstrasse 27, 80333 Munich
Tel: (4989) 22 95 39   Fax: (4989) 29 63 02
Stuttgart
Claudia Freiin von Saint-André
Relenbergstrasse 69, 70174 Stuttgart
Tel: (49711) 226 9699   Fax: (49711) 226 0607

Greece

Christie's Thessaloniki
Aristotelous 8, 546 23 Thessaloniki
Tel: (3031) 244 607   Fax: (3031) 242 931

India

Bombay
Amrita Jhaveri
3, Shelleys Estate, 30, P. J. Ramchandani Marg
Mumbai 400 039, India
Tel: (9122) 285 5649   Fax: (9122) 288 1387
New Delhi
Rohini Khosla, *Consultant*
Tel/Fax: (9111) 687 4316

Indonesia

Jakarta
Mrs Deborah C. Iskandar
Christie, Manson & Woods Ltd
The Regent Jakarta
Jl Rasuna Said, Jakarta 12920, Indonesia
Tel: (6221) 527 2606   Fax: (6221) 527 2605

Italy

Milan
Clarice Pecori Giraldi, Franz Ziegler
Domenico Filipponi
Christie's (Int.) S.A.
Piazza Santa Maria delle Grazie 1, 20123 Milan
Tel: (392) 46 70 141   Fax: (392) 46 70 14 29
Turin
Sandro Perrone di San Martino
Palazzo Carpano
Via Maria Vittoria 4, 10123 Turin
Tel: (39) 11561 9453   Fax: (39) 11542 710
Florence
Alessandra Niccolini di Camugliano
Casella Postale 62, 56038 Ponsacco (PI)
Tel/Fax: (39587) 735487
Genoa
Rachele Guicciardi
Via Belvedere Montaldo 5, 16124 Genoa
Tel: (3910) 247 1204   Fax: (3910) 246 5351
Venice
Bianca Arrivabene Valenti Gonzaga
Casella Postale 602, 30125 Venezia Centrale
Tel/Fax: (3941) 277 0086

Japan

Sachiko Hibiya, *President & Vice-Chairman*
Roddy Ropner, *Managing Director & Vice-President*
Christie's Japan Ltd., Sankyo Ginza Blg. 4/F
6-5-13 Ginza, Chuo-ku, Tokyo 104
Tel: (813) 3571 0668   Fax: (813) 3571 5853

Lebanon

Beirut
P.O. Box 11-3252, Beirut
Tel: (96) 11 737 859   Fax: (96) 11 737 860

Luxembourg

Countess Marina von Kamarowsky
rue 16 Wurth-Paquet, 2737 Luxembourg
Tel: (352) 44 04 95   Fax: (352) 44 04 92

Malaysia

Kuala Lumpur
Miss Lim Meng Hong
Tunku Zahia Sulong, *Consultant*
c/o Medan Setia Satu
Plaza Damansara, 50490 Kuala Lumpur
Tel: (603) 252 5001   Fax: (603) 252 2001

The Netherlands

P.O. Box 4019, 3006 AA Rotterdam
Tel/Fax: (3110) 212 0553

Norway

Benedicte Løvenskiold Dyvik
Christie's, Colbjornsensgt, 1, N-0256 Oslo 2
Tel: (4722) 44 12 42   Fax: (4722) 55 92 36

Portugal

Mafalda Pereira Coutinho
Rua da Lapa 67, 1200 Lisbon
Tel: (3511) 396 9700   Fax: (3511) 396 9732

South Africa

Cape Town
Juliet Lomberg
14 Hillwood Road, Claremont, Cape Town 7700
Tel: (2721) 761 2676   Fax: (2721) 762 7129
Johannesburg
Harriet Hedley
P.O. Box 72126, Parkview, Johannesburg 2122
Tel: (2711) 486 0967   Fax: (2711) 646 0390

South Korea

Mrs Shin Duk-Young
Christie's Korea, Hotel Shilla, 5F
202, 2-Ga, Jangchung-Dong, Chung-ku
Seoul, 100 392, Korea
Tel: (82 2) 230 3139   Fax: (82 2) 230 3138

Spain

Madrid
Casilda Fz-Villaverde y Silva, Pablo Melendo
Christie's Iberica S.L.
Antonio Maura 10, 28014 Madrid
Tel: (341) 532 66 26/7   Fax: (341) 523 12 40
Barcelona
Piru Cantarell de Andreu
Mallorca, 235, 08008 Barcelona
Tel: (343) 487 8259   Fax: (343) 487 8504

Sweden

Stockholm
Lillemor Malmström
Sturegatan 26, 11436 Stockholm
Tel: (468) 662 0131   Fax: (468) 660 0725
South of Sweden
Baroness Irma Silfverschiold
230 41 Klagerup
Tel: (4640) 44 03 60   Fax: (4640) 44 03 71

Switzerland

Lugano
Manoli Traxler
Christie's (Int.) S.A., Via Soave, 9, 6900 Lugano
Tel: (4191) 922 2031   Fax: (4191) 922 2032

Taiwan

Anthony Lin, *Deputy Chairman*
Carol Huang
Christie's Hong Kong Ltd, Taiwan Branch
13/F Suite 1302, 207 Tun Hua South Road
Section 2, Taipei, Taiwan
Tel: (8862) 736 3356   Fax: (8862) 736 4856

OTHER SERVICES

Christie's Education

Robert Cumming, *Chairman*
London
63 Old Brompton Road, London SW7 3JS
Tel: (0171) 581 3933   Fax: (0171) 589 0383
Deborah Lambert, Dr. Michael Michael
Caroline de Lane Lea, Janet Martin
Course Directors
Modern Art Studies (London)
Tel: (0171) 436 3630   Fax: (0171) 436 3631
Jean Hodgins, *Course Director*
New York
502 Park Avenue, New York, NY 10022
Tel: (212) 546 1092   Fax: (212) 446 9566
Sandra Joys, *Director*
Paris
Hôtel Salomon de Rothschild
11 rue Berryer, 75008 Paris
Tel: (331) 42 25 1090   Fax: (331) 42 25 1091
Marie-Laure de Cazotte, *Course Director*

Christie's Fine Art Security Service Ltd

42 Ponton Road
Nine Elms, London SW8 5BA
Tel: (0171) 622 0609   Fax: (0171) 978 2073

Christie's Great Estates

1850 Old Pecos Trail, Suite D
Santa Fe, New Mexico 87505
Tel: (505) 983 8733   Fax: (505) 982 0348
Kay Coughlin, *President*

Christie's International Motor Cars

360 North Camden Drive
Beverly Hills, California 90210
Tel: (310) 385 2699   Fax: (310) 385 0246

The Jack Barclay Showroom
2-4 Ponton Road, London SW8 5BA
Tel: (0171) 389 2851   Fax: (0171) 627 8917
David Gooding, *Managing Director*

Spink and Son Ltd

5 King Street, St. James's, London SW1Y 6QS
Tel: (0171) 930 7888   Fax: (0171) 839 4853

Spink Singapore pte Ltd

No. 1 Parklane, Goodwood Park Hotel
22 Scotts Road, Singapore 228221
Tel: (65) 738 4919   Fax: (65) 738 2404

Spink America

4th Floor, 55 East 59th Street
New York, NY 10022
Tel: (212) 546 1056   Fax: (212) 750 5874
James Lamb, *President*

INDEX